F6

Paper F6 Taxation
(UK)
Study Manual
Finance Act 2011
June 2012
and December
2012 exams

ACCA

British Library Cataloguing-in-Publication Data
A catalogue record for this book is available from the British Library

Published by InterActive World Wide Limited
Westgate House, 8-9 Holborn
London ECIN 2LL

www.iaww.com/publishing

ISBN 978-1-908888-04-4

Fifth Edition 2012
Printed in Romania

We are grateful to [the Chartered Institute of Management Accountants] (*only where applicable*) [and] [the Institute of Chartered Accountants in England and Wales] (*only where applicable*) for permission to reproduce past exam questions. The answers have been prepared by InterActive World Wide.

London
School of Business
& Finance

shaping success in business and finance

Foreword

Thank you for choosing to study with the London School of Business and Finance.

A dynamic, quality-oriented and innovative educational institution, the London School of Business and Finance offers specialised programmes, designed with students and employers in mind. We are always at the frontline, driving the latest professional developments and trends.

LSBF attracts the highest-quality candidates from over 140 countries worldwide. We work in partnership with leading accountancy firms, banks and best-practice organisations – enabling thousands of students to realise their full potential in accountancy, finance and the business world.

With an international perspective, LSBF has developed a rich portfolio of professional qualifications and executive education programmes. To complement our face-to-face and cutting-edge online learning products, LSBF is now pleased to offer tailored study materials to support students in their preparation for exams.

The exam-focused content in this manual will provide you with a comprehensive and up-to-date understanding of the ACCA syllabus. We have an award-winning team of tutors, who are highly experienced in helping students through their professional exams and have received consistently excellent feedback.

I hope that you will find this manual helpful and wish you the best of luck in your studies.

Aaron Etingen

ACCA, MSI, Founder and CEO

Contents

London
School of Business
& Finance

shaping success in business and finance

F6

About ACCA
Paper F6
Taxation (UK)

Aim of the Paper

To develop knowledge and skills relating to the tax system as applicable to individuals, single companies, and groups of companies.

Outline of the Syllabus

1. Trading Profits
2. Capital Allowances
3. Employment Income
4. Rental Income
5. Investment Income
6. Personal Tax Computations
7. National Insurance
8. Inheritance Tax
9. Corporation Tax
10. Capital Gains Tax Computations
11. Value Added Tax

Format of the Exam Paper

The syllabus is assessed by a three-hour paper based examination.

The paper will be predominantly computational and will have five questions, all of which will be compulsory.

Question one will focus on income tax and question two will focus on corporation tax. The two questions will be for a total of 55 marks, with one of the questions being for 30 marks and the other being for 25 marks.

Question three will focus on chargeable gains (either personal or corporate) and will be for 15 marks.

Questions four and five will be on any area of the syllabus, can cover more than one topic and will be for 15 marks. Question four or five could be on inheritance tax or corporation tax including groups and overseas aspects of corporation tax

There will always be at a minimum of 10 marks on value added tax. These marks will normally be included within question one or question two, although there might be a separate question on value added tax.

National insurance contributions will not be examined as a separate question, but may be examined in any question involving income tax or corporation tax.

Groups and overseas aspects of corporation tax will only be examined in either question two or question five.

Questions one or two might include a small element of chargeable gains.

Any of the five questions might include the consideration of issues relating to the minimisation or deferral of tax liabilities.

The examination assumes basic knowledge from ACCA paper F3 – (basic format of profit & loss account/ Income Statement, the straight line and reducing balance method of depreciation etc).

The examiner is David Harrowven – he has been a very long standing examiner with the ACCA. He was the examiner for ACCA Paper 2.3 from December 2001 to June 2007.

Tax rates and allowances

The following tax rates and allowances are to be used in answering the questions

INCOME TAX

2011/12		**Normal rates** %	**Dividend rates** %
Basic rate	£1 to £35,000	20	10
Higher rate	£35,001 to £150,000	40	32.5
Additional rate	£150,001 and above	50	42.5

A starting rate of 10% applies to savings income where it falls within the first £2,560 of taxable income.

Personal allowances	**£**
Personal allowance	7,475
Personal allowance for those aged 65 to 74	9,940
Personal allowance for those aged 75 and over	10,090
Income limit for age-related allowances	24,000
Income limit for standard allowances	100,000

Cars Benefit Percentage

The base level of CO_2 emissions is 125 grams per kilometre.

	%
Petrol cars with CO_2 emissions of 75 grams per kilometre or less	5
Petrol cars with Co_2 emissions between 76 and 120 grams per kilometre	10

Car Fuel Benefit

The base level figure for calculating the car fuel benefit is £18,800.

Authorised Mileage Allowance Payments (AMAP): Cars

First 10,000 business miles is 45p per mile.

Any miles in excess of 10,000 is 25p per mile.

Pension Scheme Limits

Annual allowance	£50,000
Lifetime allowance	£1,800,000

The maximum contribution that can qualify for tax relief without any earnings is £3,600.

Individual Savings Accounts (ISA) Limits

	£
Cash ISA	5,340
Stocks & Shares ISA	10,680
Overall Limit	10,680

CAPITAL ALLOWANCES

Plant and Machinery

Main pool – writing down allowance	20%
Special rate pool – writing down allowance	10%
Annual investment allowance – First £100,000 of expenditure	100%

Motor cars: purchases since 6 April 2009 (1 April 2009 for limited companies)

– CO_2 emissions up to 110g/km	100%
– CO_2 emissions of between 111g/km and 160g/km	20%
– CO_2 emissions over 160g/km	10%

Corporation Tax

Financial year	2009	2010	2011
Small profits rate	21%	21%	20%
Main rate	28%	28%	26%
Lower limit (£)	300,000	300,000	300,000
Upper limit (£)	1,500,000	1,500,000	1,500,000
Marginal relief fraction	7/400	7/400	3/200

Marginal relief Standard fraction x (U-A) x N/A

VALUE ADDED TAX

Standard rate	20%
Registration limit	£73,000
Deregistration limit	£71,000

RATES OF INTEREST

Official rate of interest:	4%
Interest on underpaid tax:	3% (assumed)
Interest on overpaid tax;	0.5% (assumed)

CAPITAL GAINS TAX

Rates of tax	– Lower rate	18%
	– Higher rate	28%
Annual exemption		£10,600
Entrepreneurs' relief		
	– Lifetime limit	£10,000,000
	– Rate of tax	10%

NATIONAL INSURANCE CONTRIBUTIONS (NOT CONTRACTED OUT RATES)

Class 1 Employee

£1 to £7,225 per year	Nil
£7,226 to £42,475 per year	12%
£42,476 and above per year	2%

Class 1 Employer

£1 to £7,072 per year	Nil
£7,073 and above per year	13.8%
Class 1A	13.8%
Class 2	£2.50 per week

Class 4

£1 to £7,225 per year	Nil
£7,226 to £42,475 per year	9%
£42,476 and above per year	2%

INHERITANCE TAX

Rates

£1 to £325,000	Nil
Excess – Death rate	40%
– Lifetime rate	20%

Taper relief

Years before death	Percentage reduction %
Over 3 but less than 4 years	20
Over 4 but less than 5 years	40
Over 5 but less than 6 years	60
Over 6 but less than 7 years	80

F6

Syllabus and Study Guide

Taxation (UK) (F6)
June & December 2012

This syllabus and study guide is designed to help with planning study and to provide detailed information on what could be assessed in any examination session.

THE STRUCTURE OF THE SYLLABUS AND STUDY GUIDE

Relational diagram of paper with other papers

This diagram shows direct and indirect links between this paper and other papers preceding or following it. Some papers are directly underpinned by other papers such as Advanced Performance Management by Performance Management. These links are shown as solid line arrows. Other papers only have indirect relationships with each other such as links existing between the accounting and auditing papers. The links between these are shown as dotted line arrows. This diagram indicates where you are expected to have underpinning knowledge and where it would be useful to review previous learning before undertaking study.

Overall aim of the syllabus

This explains briefly the overall objective of the paper and indicates in the broadest sense the capabilities to be developed within the paper.

Main capabilities

This paper's aim is broken down into several main capabilities which divide the syllabus and study guide into discrete sections.

Relational diagram of the main capabilities

This diagram illustrates the flows and links between the main capabilities (sections) of the syllabus and should be used as an aid to planning teaching and learning in a structured way.

Syllabus rationale

This is a narrative explaining how the syllabus is structured and how the main capabilities are linked. The rationale also explains in further detail what the examination intends to assess and why.

Detailed syllabus

This shows the breakdown of the main capabilities (sections) of the syllabus into subject areas. This is the blueprint for the detailed study guide.

Approach to examining the syllabus

This section briefly explains the structure of the examination and how it is assessed.

Study Guide

This is the main document that students, tuition providers and publishers should use as the basis of their studies, instruction and materials. Examinations will be based on the detail of the study guide which comprehensively identifies what could be assessed in any examination session. The study guide is a precise reflection and breakdown of the syllabus. It is divided into sections based on the main capabilities identified in the syllabus. These sections are divided into subject areas which relate to the sub-capabilities included in the detailed syllabus. Subject areas are broken down into sub-headings which describe the detailed outcomes that could be assessed in examinations. These outcomes are described using verbs indicating what exams may require students to demonstrate, and the broad intellectual level at which these may need to be demonstrated (*see intellectual levels below).

Learning Materials

ACCA's approved learning partner - content (ALP-c) is the programme through which ACCA approves learning materials from high quality content providers designed to support study towards ACCA's qualifications.

ACCA has one approved Platinum Approved Learning Partner content which is BPP Learning Media. In addition, there are a number of Gold Approved Learning Partners - content.

For information about ACCA's Approved Learning Partners - content, please go to ACCA's Content Provider Directory.

The Directory also lists materials by Subscribers. These materials have not been quality assured by ACCA but may be helpful if used in conjunction with approved learning materials. You will also find details of Examiner suggested Additional Reading which may be a useful supplement to approved learning materials.

ACCA's Content Provider Directory can be found here:

http://www.accaglobal.com/learningproviders/ alpc/content_provider_directory/search/.

INTELLECTUAL LEVELS

The syllabus is designed to progressively broaden and deepen the knowledge, skills and professional values demonstrated by the student on their way through the qualification.

The specific capabilities within the detailed syllabuses and study guides are assessed at one of three intellectual or cognitive levels:

Level 1: Knowledge and comprehension
Level 2: Application and analysis
Level 3: Synthesis and evaluation

Very broadly, these intellectual levels relate to the three cognitive levels at which the Knowledge module, the Skills module and the Professional level are assessed.

Each subject area in the detailed study guide included in this document is given a 1, 2, or 3 superscript, denoting intellectual level, marked at the end of each relevant line. This gives an indication of the intellectual depth at which an area could be assessed within the examination. However, while level 1 broadly equates with the Knowledge module, level 2 equates to the Skills module and level 3 to the Professional level, some lower level skills can continue to be assessed as the student progresses through each module and level. This reflects that at each stage of study there will be a requirement to broaden, as well as deepen capabilities. It is also possible that occasionally some higher level capabilities may be assessed at lower levels.

LEARNING HOURS

The ACCA qualification does not prescribe or recommend any particular number of learning hours for examinations because study and learning patterns and styles vary greatly between people and organisations. This also recognises the wide diversity of personal, professional and educational circumstances in which ACCA students find themselves.

Each syllabus contains between 23 and 35 main subject area headings depending on the nature of the subject and how these areas have been broken down.

GUIDE TO EXAM STRUCTURE

The structure of examinations varies within and between modules and levels.

The Fundamentals level examinations contain 100% compulsory questions to encourage candidates to study across the breadth of each syllabus.

The Knowledge module is assessed by equivalent two-hour paper based and computer based examinations.

The Skills module examinations are all paper based three-hour papers. The structure of papers varies from ten questions in the *Corporate and Business Law* (F4) paper to four 25 mark questions in *Financial Management* (F9). Individual questions within all Skills module papers will attract between 10 and 30 marks.

The Professional level papers are all three-hour paper based examinations, all containing two sections. Section A is compulsory, but there will be some choice offered in Section B.

For all three hour examination papers, ACCA has introduced 15 minutes reading and planning time.

This additional time is allowed at the beginning of each three-hour examination to allow candidates to read the questions and to begin planning their answers before they start writing in their answer books. This time should be used to ensure that all the information and exam requirements are properly read and understood.

During reading and planning time candidates may only annotate their question paper. They may not write anything in their answer booklets until told to do so by the invigilator.

The Essentials module papers all have a Section A containing a major case study question with all requirements totalling 50 marks relating to this case. Section B gives students a choice of two from three 25 mark questions.

Section A of each of the Options papers contains 50-70 compulsory marks from two questions, each attracting between 25 and 40 marks. Section B will offer a choice of two from three questions totalling 30-50 marks, with each question attracting between 15 and 25 marks.

The pass mark for all ACCA Qualification examination papers is 50%.

GUIDE TO EXAMINATION ASSESSMENT

ACCA reserves the right to examine anything contained within the study guide at any examination session. This includes knowledge, techniques, principles, theories, and concepts as specified.

For the financial accounting, audit and assurance, law and tax papers except where indicated otherwise, ACCA will publish *examinable documents* once a year to indicate exactly what regulations and legislation could potentially be assessed within identified examination sessions.

For paper based examinations regulation issued or legislation **passed** on or before 30th September annually, will be assessed from June 1st of the following year to May 31st of the year after. Please refer to the examinable documents for the paper for more information.

Regulation issued or legislation passed in accordance with the above dates may be examinable even if the **effective** date is in the future.

The term issued or passed relates to when regulation or legislation has been formally approved.

The term effective relates to when regulation or legislation must be applied to an entity transactions and business practices.

The study guide offers more detailed guidance on the depth and level at which the examinable documents will be examined. The study guide should therefore be read in conjunction with the examinable documents list.

Syllabus

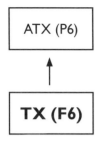

AIM

To develop knowledge and skills relating to the tax system as applicable to individuals, single companies, and groups of companies.

MAIN CAPABILITIES

On successful completion of this paper candidates should be able to:

A   Explain the operation and scope of the tax system

B   Explain and compute the income tax liabilities of individuals

C   Explain and compute the corporation tax liabilities of individual companies and groups of companies

D   Explain and compute the chargeable gains arising on companies and individuals

E   Explain and compute the inheritance tax liabilities of individuals

F   Explain and compute the effect of national insurance contributions on employees, employers and the self employed

G   Explain and compute the effects of value added tax on incorporated and unincorporated businesses

H   Identify and explain the obligations of tax payers and/or their agents and the implications of non-compliance

RELATIONAL DIAGRAM OF MAIN CAPABILITIES

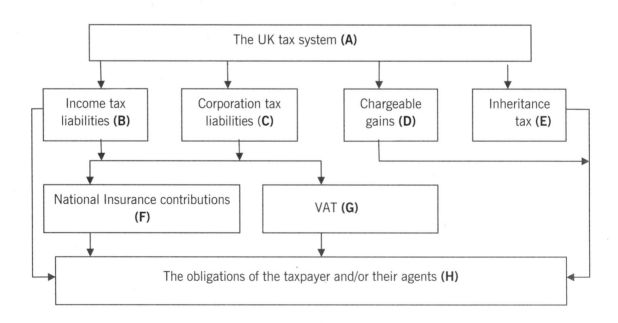

RATIONALE

The syllabus for Paper F6, Taxation, introduces candidates to the subject of taxation and provides the core knowledge of the underlying principles and major technical areas of taxation as they affect the activities of individuals and businesses.

Candidates are introduced to the rationale behind – and the functions of – the tax system. The syllabus then considers the separate taxes that an accountant would need to have a detailed knowledge of, such as income tax from self-employment, employment and investments, the corporation tax liability of individual companies and groups of companies, the national insurance contribution liabilities of both employed and self employed persons, the value added tax liability of businesses, and the chargeable gains arising on disposals of investments by both individuals and companies.

Having covered the core areas of the basic taxes, candidates should be able to compute tax liabilities, explain the basis of their calculations, apply tax planning techniques for individuals and companies and identify the compliance issues for each major tax through a variety of business and personal scenarios and situations.

DETAILED SYLLABUS

A   The UK tax system

1   The overall function and purpose of taxation in a modern economy

2   Different types of taxes

3   Principal sources of revenue law and practice

4   Tax avoidance and tax evasion

B   Income tax liabilities

1   The scope of income tax

2   Income from employment

3   Income from self-employment

4   Property and investment income

5   The comprehensive computation of taxable income and income tax liability

6   The use of exemptions and reliefs in deferring and minimising income tax liabilities

C   Corporation tax liabilities

1   The scope of corporation tax

2   Taxable total profits

3   The comprehensive computation of corporation tax liability

4   The effect of a group corporate structure for corporation tax purposes

5   The use of exemptions and reliefs in deferring and minimising corporation tax liabilities

D   Chargeable gains

1   The scope of the taxation of capital gains

2   The basic principles of computing gains and losses

3   Gains and losses on the disposal of movable and immovable property

4   Gains and losses on the disposal of shares and securities

5   The computation of capital gains tax payable by individuals

6   The use of exemptions and reliefs in deferring and minimising tax liabilities arising on the disposal of capital assets

E   Inheritance tax

1   The scope of inheritance tax

2   The basic principles of computing transfers of value

3   The liabilities arising on chargeable lifetime transfers and on the death of an individual

4   The use of exemptions in deferring and minimising inheritance tax liabilities

5   Payment of inheritance tax

F National insurance contributions

1 The scope of national insurance

2 Class 1 and Class 1A contributions for employed persons

3 Class 2 and Class 4 contributions for self-employed persons

G Value added tax

1 The scope of value added tax (VAT)

2 The VAT registration requirements

3 The computation of VAT liabilities

4 The effect of special schemes

H The obligations of taxpayers and/or their agents

1 The systems for self-assessment and the making of returns

2 The time limits for the submission of information, claims and payment of tax, including payments on account

3 The procedures relating to enquiries, appeals and disputes

4 Penalties for non-compliance

APPROACH TO EXAMINING THE SYLLABUS

The syllabus is assessed by a three-hour paper-based examination.

Assessment: Taxation (UK)

The paper will be predominantly computational and will have five questions, all of which will be compulsory.

- Question one will focus on income tax and question two will focus on corporation tax. The two questions will be for a total of 55 marks, with one of the questions being for 30 marks and the other being for 25 marks.

- Question three will focus on chargeable gains (either personal or corporate) and will be for 15 marks.

- Questions four and five will be on any area of the syllabus, can cover more than one topic, and will be for 15 marks.

There will always be a minimum of 10 marks on value added tax. These marks will normally be included within question one or question two, although there might be a separate question on value added tax.

There will always be between 5 and 15 marks on inheritance tax. Inheritance tax can be included within questions three, four or five.

National insurance contributions will not be examined as a separate question, but may be examined in any question involving income tax or corporation tax.

Groups and overseas aspects of corporation tax maybe examined in either question two, question four or question five.

A small element of chargeable gains could be included in questions other than question three.

Any of the five questions might include the consideration of issues relating to the minimisation or deferral of tax liabilities.

Study Guide

A   THE UK TAX SYSTEM

I.   The overall function and purpose of taxation in a modern economy

a)   Describe the purpose (economic, social etc.) of taxation in a modern economy.[2]

2.   Different types of taxes

a)   Identify the different types of capital and revenue tax.[1]

b)   Explain the difference between direct and indirect taxation.[2]

3.   Principal sources of revenue law and practice

a)   Describe the overall structure of the UK tax system.[1]

b)   State the different sources of revenue law.[1]

c)   Appreciate the interaction of the UK tax system with that of other tax jurisdictions.[2]

4.   Tax avoidance and tax evasion

a)   Explain the difference between tax avoidance and tax evasion.[1]

b)   Explain the need for an ethical and professional approach.[2]

Excluded topics

- *Anti-avoidance legislation.*

B   INCOME TAX LIABILITIES

I.   The scope of income tax

a)   Explain how the residence of an individual is determined.[1]

Excluded topics

- *The treatment of a person who comes to the UK to work or a person who leaves the UK to take up employment overseas.*

- *Foreign income, non-residents and double taxation relief.*

- *Income from trusts and settlements.*

2.   Income from employment

a)   Recognise the factors that determine whether an engagement is treated as employment or self-employment.[2]

b)   Recognise the basis of assessment for employment income.[2]

c)   Compute the income assessable.[2]

d)   Recognise the allowable deductions, including travelling expenses.[2]

e)   Discuss the use of the statutory approved mileage allowances.[2]

f)   Explain the PAYE system.[1]

g)   Identify P11D employees.[1]

h)   Compute the amount of benefits assessable.[2]

i)   Explain the purpose of a dispensation from HM Revenue & Customs.[2]

k)   Explain how charitable giving can be made through a payroll deduction scheme.[1]

Excluded topics

- *The calculation of a car benefit where emission figures are not available.*

- *The exemption for zero emission company motor cars.*

- *Share and share option incentive schemes for employees.*

- *Payments on the termination of employment, and other lump sums received by employees.*

3   Income from self-employment

a)   Recognise the basis of assessment for self-employment income.[2]

b)   Describe and apply the badges of trade.[2]

c)   Recognise the expenditure that is allowable in calculating the tax-adjusted trading profit.[2]

d)   Recognise the relief that can be obtained for pre-trading expenditure.[2]

e) Compute the assessable profits on commencement and on cessation.[2]

f) Change of accounting date

i) Recognise the factors that will influence the choice of accounting date.[2]
ii) State the conditions that must be met for a change of accounting date to be valid.[1]
iii) Compute the assessable profits on a change of accounting date.[2]

g) Capital allowances

i) Define plant and machinery for capital allowances purposes.[1]
ii) Compute writing down allowances, first-year allowances and the annual investment allowance.[2]
iii) Compute capital allowances for motor cars, including motor cars already owned at 6 April 2009 (1 April 2009 for companies).[2]
iv) Compute balancing allowances and balancing charges.[2]
v) Recognise the treatment of short life assets[2]
vi) Explain the treatment of assets included in the special rate pool.[2]

h) Relief for trading losses

i) Understand how trading losses can be carried forward.[2]
ii) Explain how trading losses can be carried forward following the incorporation of a business.[2]
iii) Understand how trading losses can be claimed against total income and chargeable gains.[2]
iv) Explain and compute the relief for trading losses in the early years of a trade.[1]
v) Explain and compute terminal loss relief.[1]

i) Partnerships and limited liability partnerships

i) Explain how a partnership is assessed to tax.[2]
ii) Compute the assessable profits for each partner following a change in the profit sharing ratio.[2]
iii) Compute the assessable profits for each partner following a change in the membership of the partnership.[2]
iv) Describe the alternative loss relief claims that are available to partners.[1]

v) Explain the loss relief restriction that applies to the partners of a limited liability partnership.[1]

Excluded topics

- *The 100% allowance for expenditure on renovating business premises in disadvantaged areas, flats above shops and water technologies.*

- *Capital allowances for industrial buildings, agricultural buildings, patents, scientific research and know how.*

- *Enterprise zones.*

- *Investment income of a partnership.*

- *The allocation of national profits and losses for a partnership.*

- *Farmers averaging of profits.*

- *The averaging of profits for authors and creative artists.*

- *Loss relief for shares in unquoted trading companies.*

4 Property and investment income

a) Compute property business profits.[2]

b) Explain the treatment of furnished holiday lettings.[1]

c) Describe rent-a-room relief.[1]

d) Compute the amount assessable when a premium is received for the grant of a short lease.[2]

e) Understand how relief for a property business loss is given.[2]

f) Compute the tax payable on savings income.[2]

g) Compute the tax payable on dividend income.[2]

h) Explain the treatment of individual savings accounts (ISAs) and other tax exempt investments.[1]

Excluded topics

- *The deduction for expenditure by landlords on energy-saving items.*

- *Junior ISAs.*

London
School of Business
& Finance
shaping success in business and finance

5 The comprehensive computation of taxable income and income tax liability

a) Prepare a basic income tax computation involving different types of income.[2]

b) Calculate the amount of personal allowance available generally, and for people aged 65 and above.[2]

c) Compute the amount of income tax payable.[2]

d) Explain the treatment of interest paid for a qualifying purpose.[2]

e) Explain the treatment of gift aid donations.[1]

f) Explain the treatment of property owned jointly by a married couple, or by a couple in a civil partnership.[1]

Excluded topics

- *The blind person's allowance and the married couple's allowance.*
- *Tax credits.*
- *Maintenance payments.*
- *The income of minor children.*

6 The use of exemptions and reliefs in deferring and minimising income tax liabilities

a) Explain and compute the relief given for contributions to personal pension schemes, using the rules applicable from 6 April 2011.[2]

b) Describe the relief given for contributions to occupational pension schemes, using the rules applicable from 6 April 2011.[1]

c) Explain how a married couple or a couple in a civil partnership can minimise their tax liabilities.[2]

Excluded topics

- *The conditions that must be met in order for a pension scheme to obtain approval from HM Revenue & Customs.*
- *The enterprise investment scheme.*
- *Venture capital trusts.*

C CORPORATION TAX LIABILITIES

1. The scope of corporation tax

a) Define the terms 'period of account', 'accounting period', and 'financial year'.[1]

b) Recognise when an accounting period starts and when an accounting period finishes.[1]

c) Explain how the residence of a company is determined.[2]

Excluded topics

- *Investment companies.*
- *Close companies.*
- *Companies in receivership or liquidation.*
- *Reorganisations.*
- *The purchase by a company of its own shares.*
- *Personal service companies.*

2 Taxable total profits

a) Recognise the expenditure that is allowable in calculating the tax-adjusted trading profit.[2]

b) Explain how relief can be obtained for pre-trading expenditure.[1]

c) Compute capital allowances (as for income tax).[2]

d) Compute property business profits.[2]

e) Explain the treatment of interest paid and received under the loan relationship rules.[1]

f) Explain the treatment of gift aid donations.[2]

g) Understand how trading losses can be carried forward.[2]

h) Understand how trading losses can be claimed against income of the current or previous accounting periods.[2]

i) Recognise the factors that will influence the choice of loss relief claim.[2]

j) Explain how relief for a property business loss is given.[1]

k) Compute taxable total profits.[2]

Excluded topics

- *Research and development expenditure.*
- *Non-trading deficits on loan relationships.*
- *Relief for intangible assets.*

London
School of Business
& Finance

shaping success in business and finance

3 The comprehensive computation of corporation tax liability

a) Compute the corporation tax liability and apply marginal relief.[2]

b) Explain the implications of receiving franked investment income.[2]

4 The effect of a group corporate structure for corporation tax purposes

a) Define an associated company and recognise the effect of being an associated company for corporation tax purposes.[2]

b) Define a 75% group, and recognise the reliefs that are available to members of such a group.[2]

c) Define a 75% capital gains group, and recognise the reliefs that are available to members of such a group.[2]

d) Compare the UK tax treatment of an overseas branch to an overseas subsidiary.[2]

e) Calculate double taxation relief.[2]

f) Explain the basic principles of the transfer pricing rules.[2]

Excluded topics

- *Relief for trading losses incurred by an overseas subsidiary.*

- *Consortia.*

- *Pre-entry gains and losses.*

- *The anti-avoidance provisions where arrangements exist for a company to leave a group within six years of receiving an asset by way of a no gain/no loss transfer.*

- *Controlled foreign companies.*

- *Foreign companies trading in the UK.*

- *Expense relief in respect of overseas tax.*

- *Election for the exemption of profits from an overseas branch.*

- *Transfer pricing transactions not involving an overseas company.*

5 The use of exemptions and reliefs in deferring and minimising corporation tax liabilities:

The use of such exemptions and reliefs is implicit within all of the above sections 1 to 4 of part C of the syllabus, concerning corporation tax.

D CHARGEABLE GAINS

1. The scope of the taxation of capital gains

a) Describe the scope of capital gains tax.[2]

b) Explain how the residence and ordinary residence of an individual is determined.[2]

c) List those assets which are exempt.[1]

Excluded topics

- *Assets situation overseas and double taxation relief.*

- *Partnership capital gains.*

2 The basic principles of computing gains and losses

a) Compute capital gains for both individuals and companies.[2]

b) Calculate the indexation allowance available to companies.[2]

c) Explain the treatment of capital losses for both individuals and companies.[1]

d) Explain the treatment of transfers between a husband and wife or between a couple in a civil partnership.[2]

e) Compute the amount of allowable expenditure for a part disposal.[2]

f) Explain the treatment where an asset is damaged , lost or destroyed, and the implications of receiving insurance proceeds and reinvesting such proceeds.[2]

Excluded topics

- *Small part disposals of land.*

- *Losses in the year of death.*

- *Relief for losses incurred on loans made to traders.*

- *Negligible value claims.*

3 Gains and losses on the disposal of movable and immovable property

a) Identify when chattels and wasting assets are exempt.[1]

b) Compute the chargeable gain when a chattel is disposed of.[2]

c) Calculate the chargeable gain when a wasting asset is disposed of.[2]

d) Compute the exemption when a principal private residence is disposed of.[2]

London
School of Business
& Finance
shaping success in business and finance

e) Calculate the chargeable gain when a principal private residence has been used for business purposes.[2]

f) Identify the amount of letting relief available when a principal private residence has been let out.[2]

Excluded topics

- *The disposal of leases and the creation of sub-leases.*

4 Gains and losses on the disposal of shares and securities

a) Calculate the value of quoted shares where they are disposed of by way of a gift.[2]

b) Explain and apply the identification rules as they apply to individuals and to companies, including the same day, nine day, and 30 day matching rules.[2]

c) Explain the pooling provisions.[2]

d) Explain the treatment of bonus issues, rights issues, takeovers and reorganisations.[2]

e) Explain the exemption available for gilt-edged securities and qualifying corporate bonds.[1]

Excluded topics

- *A detailed question on the pooling provisions for shares as they apply to limited companies.*

- *The small part disposal rules applicable to rights issues.*

- *Substantial shareholdings.*

- *Gilt-edged securities and qualifying corporate bonds other than the fact that they are exempt.*

5 The computation of capital gains tax payable by individuals

a) Compute the amount of capital gains tax payable.[2]

6 The use of exemptions and reliefs in deferring and minimising tax liabilities arising on the disposal of capital assets

a) Explain and apply entrepreneurs' relief as it applies to individuals.[2]

b) Explain and apply rollover relief as it applies to individuals and companies.[2]

c) Explain and apply holdover relief for the gift of business assets.[2]

d) Explain and apply the incorporation relief that is available upon the transfer of a business to a company.[2]

Excluded topics

- *Reinvestment relief.*

- *Entrepreneurs' relief for associated disposals.*

E INHERITANCE TAX

1 The scope of inheritance tax

a) Describe the scope of inheritance tax.[2]

b) Identify and explain the persons chargeable.[2]

Excluded topics

- *Pre 18 March 1986 lifetime transfers.*

- *Transfers of value by close companies.*

- *Domicile, deemed domicile, and non-UK domiciled individuals.*

- *Trusts.*

2 The basic principles of computing transfers of value

a) State, explain and apply the meaning of transfer of value, chargeable transfer and potentially exempt transfer.[2]

b) Demonstrate the diminution in value principle.[2]

c) Demonstrate the seven year accumulation principle taking into account changes in the level of the nil rate band.[2]

Excluded topics

- *Excluded property.*

- *Related property.*

- *The tax implications of the location of assets.*

- *Gifts with reservation of benefit.*

- *Associated operations.*

3 The liabilities arising on chargeable lifetime transfers and on the death of an individual

a) Understand the tax implications of chargeable lifetime transfers and compute the relevant liabilities.[2]

b) Understand the tax implications of transfers within seven years of death and compute the relevant liabilities.[2]

c) Compute the tax liability on a death estate.[2]

d) Understand and apply the transfer of any unused nil rate band between spouses.[2]

Exluded topics

- *Specific rules for the valuation of assets (values will be provided).*

- *Business property relief.*

- *Agricultural relief.*

- *Relief for the fall in value of lifetime gifts.*

- *Quick succession relief.*

- *Double tax relief.*

- *Variation of wills and disclaimers of legacies.*

- *Grossing up on death.*

- *Post mortem reliefs.*

- *Double charges legislation.*

4 The use of exemptions in deferring and minimising inheritance tax liabilities

a) Understand and apply the following exemptions:

   i) small gifts exemption[2]

   ii) annual exemption[2]

   iii) normal expenditure out of income[2]

   iv) gifts in consideration of marriage[2]

   v) gifts between spouses[2]

Excluded topics

- *Gifts to charities.*

- *Gifts to political parties.*

- *Gifts for national purposes.*

5 Payment of inheritance tax

a) Identify who is responsible for the payment of inheritance tax.[2]

b) Advise on the due date for payment of inheritance tax.[2]

Excluded topics

- *Administration of inheritance tax other than listed above.*

- *The instalment option for the payment of tax.*

- *Interest and penalties.*

F NATIONAL INSURANCE CONTRIBUTIONS

1 The scope of national insurance

a) Describe the scope of national insurance.[1]

2 Class 1 and Class 1A contributions for employed persons

a) Compute Class 1 NIC.[2]

b) Compute Class 1A NIC.[2]

Excluded topics

- *The calculation of directors' national insurance on a month by month basis.*

- *Contracted out contributions.*

3 Class 2 and Class 4 contributions for self-employed persons

a) Compute Class 2 NIC.[2]

b) Compute Class 4 NIC.[2]

Excluded topics

- *The offset of trading losses against non-trading income.*

G VALUE ADDED TAX

1. The scope of value added tax (VAT)

a) Describe the scope of VAT.[2]

b) List the principal zero-rated and exempt supplies.[1]

2 The VAT registration requirements

a) Recognise the circumstances in which a person must register for VAT.[2]

b) Explain the advantages of voluntary VAT registration.[2]

c) Explain the circumstances in which preregistration input VAT can be recovered.[2]

d) Explain how and when a person can deregister for VAT.[1]

e) Explain the conditions that must be met for two or more companies to be treated as a group for VAT purposes, and the consequences of being so treated.[1]

3 The computation of VAT liabilities

a) Explain how VAT is accounted for and administered.[2]

b) Recognise the tax point when goods or services are supplied.[2]

c)   List the information that must be given on a VAT invoice.[1]

d)   Explain and apply the principles regarding the valuation of supplies.[2]

e)   Recognise the circumstances in which input VAT is non-deductible.[2]

f)   Compute the relief that is available for impairment losses on trade debts.[2]

g)   Explain the circumstances in which the default surcharge, a serious misdeclaration penalty, and default interest will be applied.[1]

h)   Explain the treatment of imports, exports and trade within the European Union.

Excluded topics

- *VAT periods where there is a change of VAT rate.*

- *Partial exemption.*

- *In respect of property and land: leases, do-it-yourself builders, and a landlord's option to tax.*

- *Penalties apart from those listed in the study guide.*

4   The effect of special schemes

a)   Describe the cash accounting scheme , and recognise when it will be advantageous to use the scheme.[2]

b)   Describe the annual accounting scheme, and recognise when it will be advantageous to use the scheme.[2]

c)   Describe the flat rate scheme, and recognise when it will be advantageous to use the scheme.[2]

Excluded topics

- *The second-hand goods scheme.*

- *The capital goods scheme.*

- *The special schemes for retailers.*

H   THE OBLIGATIONS OF TAX PAYERS AND/OR THEIR AGENTS

1   The systems for self-assessment and the making of returns

a)   Explain and apply the features of the self-assessment system as it applies to individuals.[2]

b)   Explain and apply the features of the self-assessment system as it applies to companies.[2]

2   The time limits for the submission of information, claims and payment of tax, including payments on account

a)   Recognise the time limits that apply to the filing of returns and the making of claims.[2]

b)   Recognise the due dates for the payment of tax under the self-assessment system.[2]

c)   Compute payments on account and balancing payments/repayments for individuals.[2]

d)   Explain how large companies are required to account for corporation tax on a quarterly basis.[2]

e)   List the information and records that taxpayers need to retain for tax purposes.[1]

Excluded topics

- *The payment of CGT by annual instalments.*

3   The procedures relating to enquiries, appeals and disputes

a)   Explain the circumstances in which HM Revenue & Customs can enquire into a self-assessment tax return.[2]

b)   Explain the procedures for dealing with appeals and disputes.[1]

4   Penalties for non-compliance

a)   Calculate interest on overdue tax.[2]

b)   State the penalties that can be charged.[2]

London
School of Business
& Finance

shaping success in business and finance

SUMMARY OF CHANGES TO F6 (UK)

RATIONALE FOR CHANGES TO STUDY
GUIDE PAPER F6 (UK)

ACCA periodically reviews its qualification
syllabuses so that they fully meet the needs
of stakeholders such as employers, students,
regulatory and advisory bodies and learning
providers.

The main areas that have been added to the
syllabus are shown in Table I below:

Table I – Additions to F6 (UK)

Section and subject area	Syllabus content
B3 Income from self-employment – *Excluded topics*	Industrial buildings allowance (IBA)
B4 Property and investment income – *Excluded topics*	Junior ISAs
C4 Group Structure – *Excluded topics*	Profits from overseas branch

The main areas that have been added to the
syllabus are shown in Table 2 below:

Table 2 – Deletions from F6 (UK)

Section and subject area	Syllabus content
B3g)vii) Income from self-employment	Industrial buildings allowance (IBA)
B3g)viii) Income from self-employment	IBA
B3 Income from self-employment – *Excluded topics*	40% FYA
B3 Income from self-employment – *Excluded topics*	Apportionment of AIA
B3 Income from self-employment – *Excluded topics*	Calculation of IBA
B3 Income from self-employment – *Excluded topics*	Additional loss relief
B4 Property and Investment Income – *Excluded topics*	Pension additional tax charge
B4 Property and Investment Income – *Excluded topics*	Anti-forestalling provisions
C2 Taxable total profits – *Excluded topics*	Extended loss relief
C3c) The comprehensive computation of corporation tax liability	Exemptions and reliefs (as repetition of C5)
C3 The comprehensive computation of corporation tax liability – *Excluded topics*	The corporate venturing scheme
C4 Group Structure – *Excluded topics*	Overseas dividends
D2 Computing gains and losses – *Excluded topics*	Disposals prior to 23 June 2010
D6 Use of exemptions – *Excluded topics*	Entrepreneurs' relief qualifying limits prior to 22 June 2010

The main areas that have been amended or clarified in the syllabus are shown in Table 3 below:

Table 3 – Amendments to F6 (UK)

Section and subject area	Amendment
Approach to examining	Groups and overseas aspects can also be examined in question four
Approach to examining	A small element of chargeable gains could be included in questions other than question three
Approach to examining	Inheritance tax specified as between 5 and 15 marks on every paper, within questions three, four or five
B6a) Use of exemptions	Pensions rules will only be examined from 6 April 2011
E3 The liabilities arising on chargeable lifetime transfers and on the death of an individual – Excluded topics	Double grossing up on death amended to Grossing up on death
F3g) The computation of VAT liabilities	A serious misdeclaration penalty replaced with a penalty for an incorrect VAT return
H1b) Corporate self assessment	Use of iXBRL
H3a) Procedures relating to compliance checks	'Enquiry' changed to 'compliance check' to agree to HMRC terminology
H4a) Penalties for non-compliance	Interest on overdue tax replaced with late payment interest

London
School of Business
& Finance

shaping success in business and finance

F6

Pilot Paper

Please note that the Pilot Paper is the original **ACCA** document and is for guidance only. It has not been updated for any subsequent changes in laws and regulations, so some technical details may have changed since the original Pilot Paper was issued. For up-to-date exam questions and answers, please see the relevant Revision Kit.

Taxation
(United Kingdom)

Paper F6 (UK)

Time allowed

Reading and planning: 15 minutes
Writing: 3 hours

ALL FIVE questions are compulsory and MUST be attempted.
Rates of tax and tables are printed on pages 2–4.

Do NOT open this paper until instructed by the supervisor.

During reading and planning time only the question paper may be annotated. You must NOT write in your answer booklet until instructed by the supervisor.

This question paper must not be removed from the examination hall.

The Association of Chartered Certified Accountants

ALL FIVE questions are compulsory and MUST be attempted

1   On 31 December 2006 Mark Kett ceased trading as a marketing consultant. He had been self-employed since 6 April 2001, and had always made his accounts up to 5 April. On 1 January 2007 Mark commenced employment as the marketing manager of Sleep-Easy plc. The company runs a hotel. The following information is available for the tax year 2006–07:

Self-employment

(1)   Mark's tax adjusted trading profit for the nine-month period ended 31 December 2006 is £19,200. This figure is before taking account of capital allowances.

(2)   The tax written down values for capital allowances purposes at 6 April 2006 were as follows:

	£
General pool	13,800
Expensive motor car	14,600

The expensive motor car was used by Mark, and 40% of the mileage was for private purposes.

(3)   On 15 June 2006 Mark had purchased office furniture for £1,900. All of the items included in the general pool were sold for £18,800 on 31 December 2006. On the cessation of trading Mark personally retained the expensive motor car. Its value on 31 December 2006 was £11,800.

Employment

(1)   Mark is paid a salary of £3,250 (gross) per month by Sleep-Easy plc, from which income tax of £620 per month has been deducted under PAYE.

(2)   During the period from 1 January 2007 to 5 April 2007 Mark used his private motor car for business purposes. He drove 2,500 miles in the performance of his duties for Sleep-Easy plc, for which the company paid an allowance of 16 pence per mile. The relevant HM Revenue & Customs authorised mileage rate to be used as the basis of an expense claim is 40 pence per mile.

(3)   On 1 January 2007 Sleep-Easy plc provided Mark with an interest free loan of £80,000 so that he could purchase a new main residence.

(4)   During the period from 1 January 2007 to 5 April 2007 Mark was provided with free meals in Sleep-Easy plc's staff canteen. The total cost of these meals to the company was £400.

Property income

(1)   Mark let out a furnished property throughout the tax year 2006-07. He received gross rents of £8,600, 5% of which was paid to a letting agency. During December 2006 Mark spent £540 on replacing dilapidated furniture and furnishings.

(2)   From 6 April 2006 to 31 December 2006 Mark let out a spare room in his main residence, receiving rent of £350 per month.

Investment income

(1)   During the tax year 2006–07 Mark received dividends of £2,880, interest from government stocks (gilts) of £1,900, and interest of £430 from an individual savings account (ISA). These were the actual cash amounts received.

(2)   On 3 May 2006 Mark received a premium bond prize of £100.

Other information

(1)   On 15 December 2006 Mark made a gift aid donation of £780 (net) to a national charity.

(2)   Mark's payments on account of income tax in respect of the tax year 2006–07 totalled £11,381.

Required:

(a) Compute the income tax payable by Mark for the tax year 2006–07, and the balancing payment or repayment that will be due for the year. (22 marks)

(b) Advise Mark as to how long he must retain the records used in preparing his tax return for the tax year 2006–07, and the potential consequences of not retaining the records for the required period. (3 marks)

(25 marks)

2 (a) Scuba Ltd is a manufacturer of diving equipment. The following information is relevant for the year ended 31 December 2006:

Operating profit

The operating profit is £170,400. The expenses that have been deducted in calculating this figure include the following:

	£
Depreciation and amortisation of lease	45,200
Entertaining customers	7,050
Entertaining employees	2,470
Gifts to customers (diaries costing £25 each displaying Scuba Ltd's name)	1,350
Gifts to customers (food hampers costing £80 each)	1,600

Leasehold property

On 1 April 2006 Scuba Ltd acquired a leasehold office building that is used for business purposes. The company paid a premium of £80,000 for the grant of a twenty-year lease.

Purchase of industrial building

Scuba Ltd purchased a new factory from a builder on 1 July 2006 for £240,000, and this was immediately brought into use. The cost was made up as follows:

	£
Drawing office serving the factory	34,000
General offices	40,000
Factory	98,000
Land	68,000
	240,000

Plant and machinery

On 1 January 2006 the tax written down values of plant and machinery were as follows:

	£
General pool	47,200
Expensive motor car	22,400

The following transactions took place during the year ended 31 December 2006:

		Cost/ (Proceeds) £
3 January 2006	Purchased machinery	22,800
29 February 2006	Purchased a computer	1,100
4 May 2006	Purchased a motor car	10,400
18 August 2006	Purchased machinery	7,300
15 November 2006	Sold a lorry	(12,400)

The motor car purchased on 4 May 2006 for £10,400 is used by the factory manager, and 40% of the mileage is for private journeys. The lorry sold on 15 November 2006 for £12,400 originally cost £19,800.

Scuba Ltd is a small company as defined by the Companies Acts.

Property income

Scuba Ltd lets a retail shop that is surplus to requirements. The shop was let until 31 December 2005 but was then empty from 1 January 2006 to 30 April 2006. During this period Scuba Ltd spent £6,200 on decorating the shop, and £1,430 on advertising for new tenants. The shop was let from 1 May 2006 to 31 December 2006 at a quarterly rent of £7,200, payable in advance.

Interest received

Interest of £430 was received from HM Revenue & Customs on 31 October 2006 in respect of the overpayment of corporation tax for the year ended 31 December 2005.

Other information

Scuba Ltd has no associated companies, and the company has always had an accounting date of 31 December.

Required:

(i) Compute Scuba Ltd's tax adjusted trading profit for the year ended 31 December 2006. You should ignore value added tax (VAT); (15 Marks)

(ii) Compute Scuba Ltd's corporation tax liability for the year ended 31 December 2006. (4 marks)

(b) Scuba Ltd registered for value added tax (VAT) on 1 April 2004. The company's VAT returns have been submitted as follows:

Quarter ended	VAT paid/ (refunded) £	Submitted
30 June 2004	18,600	One month late
30 September 2004	32,200	One month late
31 December 2004	8,800	On time
31 March 2005	3,400	Two months late
30 June 2005	(6,500)	One month late
30 September 2005	42,100	On time
31 December 2005	(2,900)	On time
31 March 2006	3,900	On time
30 June 2006	18,800	On time
30 September 2006	57,300	Two months late
31 December 2006	9,600	On time

Scuba Ltd always pays any VAT that is due at the same time that the related return is submitted.

During February 2007 Scuba Ltd discovered that a number of errors had been made when completing its VAT return for the quarter ended 31 December 2006. As a result of these errors the company will have to make an additional payment of VAT to HM Revenue & Customs.

Required:

(i) State, giving appropriate reasons, the default surcharge consequences arising from Scuba Ltd's submission of its VAT returns for the quarter ended 30 June 2004 to the quarter ended 30 September 2006 inclusive. (8 marks)

(ii) Explain how Scuba Ltd can voluntarily disclose the errors relating to the VAT return for the quarter ended 31 December 2006, and state whether default interest will be due, if (1) the net errors in total are less than £2,000, and (2) the net errors in total are more than £2,000. (3 marks)

(30 marks)

3   Paul Opus disposed of the following assets during the tax year 2006–07:

(1) On 10 April 2006 Paul sold 5,000 £1 ordinary shares in Symphony Ltd, an unquoted trading company, for £23,600. He had originally purchased 40,000 shares in the company on 23 June 2004 for £110,400.

(2) On 15 June 2006 Paul made a gift of his entire shareholding of 10,000 £1 ordinary shares in Concerto plc to his daughter. On that date the shares were quoted on the Stock Exchange at £5.10–£5.18, with recorded bargains of £5.00, £5.15 and £5.22. Paul's shareholding had been purchased on 29 April 1992 for £14,000. The shareholding is less than 1% of Concerto plc's issued share capital, and Paul has never been employed by Concerto plc. The indexation factor from April 1992 to April 1998 is 0.170, and from April 1992 to June 2006 it is 0.297.

(3) On 9 August 2006 Paul sold a motor car for £16,400. The motor car had been purchased on 21 January 2003 for £12,800.

(4) On 4 October 2006 Paul sold an antique vase for £8,400. The antique vase had been purchased on 19 January 2006 for £4,150.

(5) On 31 December 2006 Paul sold a house for £220,000. The house had been purchased on 1 April 2000 for £114,700. Paul occupied the house as his main residence from the date of purchase until 30 June 2003. The house was then unoccupied until it was sold on 31 December 2006.

(6) On 16 February 2007 Paul sold three acres of land for £285,000. He had originally purchased four acres of land on 17 July 2005 for £220,000. The market value of the unsold acre of land as at 16 February 2007 was £90,000. The land has never been used for business purposes.

(7) On 5 March 2007 Paul sold a freehold holiday cottage for £125,000. The cottage had originally been purchased on 28 July 2005 for £101,600 by Paul's wife. She transferred the cottage to Paul on 16 November 2006 when it was valued at £114,800. The cottage is not a business asset for taper relief purposes.

Paul's taxable income for the tax year 2006–07 is £15,800.

Required:

Compute Paul's capital gains tax liability for the tax year 2006–07, and advise him by when this should be paid.

(20 marks)

4   Li Fung commenced in self-employment on 1 October 2002. She initially prepared accounts to 30 June, but changed her accounting date to 31 March by preparing accounts for the nine-month period to 31 March 2006. Li's trading profits since she commenced self-employment have been as follows:

	£
Nine-month period ended 30 June 2003	18,600
Year ended 30 June 2004	24,900
Year ended 30 June 2005	22,200
Nine-month period ended 31 March 2006	16,800
Year ended 31 March 2007	26,400

Required:

(a) **State the qualifying conditions that must be met for a change of accounting date to be valid.**   (3 marks)

(b) **Compute Li's trading income assessments for each of the five tax years 2002–03, 2003–04, 2004–05, 2005–06 and 2006–07.**   (9 marks)

(c) **Advise Li of the advantages and disadvantages for tax purposes of changing her accounting date from 30 June to 31 March.**   (3 marks)

(15 marks)

5   Loser Ltd's results for the year ended 30 June 2004, the nine month period ended 31 March 2005, the year ended 31 March 2006 and the year ended 31 March 2007 are as follows:

	Year ended 30 June 2004 £	Period ended 31 March 2005 £	Year ended 31 March 2006 £	Year ended 31 March 2007 £
Trading profit/(loss)	86,600	(25,700)	27,300	(78,300)
Property business profit	–	4,500	8,100	5,600
Charges on income	(1,400)	(800)	(1,200)	(1,100)

The charges on income are all donations to a national charity paid under the gift aid scheme.

Loser Ltd does not have any associated companies.

Required:

(a) **State the factors that will influence a company's choice of loss relief claims. You are not expected to consider group relief.**
(3 marks)

(b) **Assuming that Loser Ltd claims relief for its losses as early as possible, compute the company's profits chargeable to corporation tax for the year ended 30 June 2004, the nine month period ended 31 March 2005, the year ended 31 March 2006 and the year ended 31 March 2007. Your answer should clearly identify the amount of any losses that are unrelieved.**
(5 marks)

(c) **Explain how your answer to (b) above would have differed if Loser Ltd had ceased trading on 31 March 2007.**
(2 marks)

(10 marks)

End of Question Paper

London School of Business & Finance
shaping success in business and finance

Introduction to UK Tax

Context

This section gives an introduction to the UK tax system, how it works and some of the terminology involved. It also explains the rationale as to why certain taxes are imposed.

Exam hints

This section is unlikely to form a question in its own right. You may however be asked to discuss parts of the chapter in a question.

Key learning points

- The government's tax policy takes into consideration the amount of revenue that needs to be generated to cover public spending. It also acts as a tool to encourage people to behave in a certain way. For example, there are tax incentives to encourage people to save.

- The government can also use taxation as a method of addressing environmental concerns. For example, there are tax incentives to encourage business to purchase low emission cars.

- Each year the Chancellor introduces his budget (Finance Bill). Once this Bill has been passed by Parliament it becomes a Finance Act. This course covers the Finance Act 2011.

- The administration of taxes in the UK is done by Her Majesty's Revenue and Customs (HMRC).

- There is a difference between tax evasion, which is illegal and tax avoidance, which is legal. In the exam, you may be required to distinguish between the two.

The overall function and purpose of taxation in a modern economy

The government must impose taxes on the population to ensure they can raise revenue for public spending, such as the health service and schools.

The government can also use taxation as a method of encouraging people to behave in a certain way. For example, taxation policy encourages people to do the following:

*   Investing money into a pension scheme for the future

*   Donations to charity through the gift aid scheme

*   Investing money into an Individual Savings Account (ISA)

It also uses taxation as a method of discouraging the following:

*   Spending on cigarettes and alcoholic drinks by imposing heavy taxes on them

*   Ownership of motor vehicles by imposing fuel and road taxes

SOCIAL ISSUES

The government can also use taxation as a method of attempting social justice and the redistribution of wealth amongst the population.

For example, income tax rates are higher for those individuals that earn more and inheritance tax only taxes wealth over a certain threshold.

Each tax has a different social impact on the population:

Direct and indirect taxes

Direct taxes such as income tax and capital gains tax only tax those that directly have income or gains arising.

Indirect taxes such as value added tax, tax the final consumer regardless of who they are.

Progressive taxes

Progressive taxes such as income tax mean that only those people with income over a certain level will be subject to the tax. Under income tax, as the level of income increases, so does the rate of income tax. This ensures that those that earn more are taxed more too. This helps the government with the redistribution of wealth between the population.

ENVIRONMENTAL ISSUES

The government also use the UK tax system as a method of encouraging the population to consider their impact on the environment. For example, fuel duties and road taxes are imposed to discourage motoring. There are also tax incentives for business to buy environmentally beneficial plant and machinery or low emission cars.

Different types of taxes

The government has a number of taxes that it can impose. These are:

Income tax (IT) – Tax payable by individuals on their regular income

National Insurance Contributions (NICs) – Tax payable by individuals who are employed or self employed on their earnings

Capital gains tax (CGT) – Tax payable by individuals on their capital gains on the disposal of assets

Inheritance tax (IHT) – Tax payable on death and certain transfers of value during a person's lifetime

Corporation tax (CT) – Tax payable by companies on their income and their gains

Value Added Tax (VAT) – Tax payable on the supply of goods and services by companies and businesses

During the F6 course, we will look at each of these taxes in greater depth, starting with income tax

Principal sources of revenue law and practice

Tax law is made via statute. Each year the Chancellor introduces his budget (Finance Bill). Once this Bill has been passed by Parliament it becomes a Finance Act. Tax law is also clarified through case law over the years.

The budget given in March 2011 became the Finance Act 2011.

Each Finance Act is normally the current tax legislation for 12 months – the financial year for companies and the tax year for individuals.

The financial year for a company runs from 1 April to 31 March. In the exam you will be studying the financial year 2011 (FY 2011 = 1 April 2011 – 31 March 2012).

The tax year for an individual runs from 6 April to the following 5 April. In the exam, you will be studying the tax year 2011/2012, which runs from 6 April 2011 – 5 April 2012.

The administration of taxes in the UK is done by Her Majesty's Revenue and Customs (HMRC). HMRC are responsible for the administration and collection of income tax, capital gains tax, corporation tax and VAT. The staff that work for HMRC are known as 'Officers of Revenue and Customs'.

Interaction with other tax Jurisdictions

Although the UK has its own tax legislation, as a member of the European Union it has certain responsibilities. There must be free movement of capital and workers between European Union countries, legislation must not be discriminatory.

There is also free exchange of information between European Union revenue authorities.

The UK has negotiated tax treaties with many non-EU countries. These provide rules to determine where income and gains may be taxed, and often contain anti-discrimination rules.

Even where no tax treaty exists relief is normally given if income or gains are taxed in more than one country.

Tax avoidance and evasion

In the exam, you may need to distinguish between tax avoidance and tax evasion:

TAX EVASION

Tax evasion is deliberately misleading HMRC about your tax liability. This could be done in a number of ways including:

- Not declaring information to HMRC – for example, not declaring a source of income on which tax should be payable

- Giving false information to HMRC – for example overstating your expenses to be deducted from trading income

Tax evasion is illegal and as such can be a criminal offence. Penalties can include imprisonment and fines.

TAX AVOIDANCE

Tax avoidance is tax planning to reduce your tax liability. It includes things such as putting money into a tax free individual savings account (ISA) rather than into a normal bank account, where income tax would be payable on the interest.

Tax avoidance is legal but any tax avoidance schemes must be disclosed to HMRC.

Ethics

Principles and framework

As a professional tax adviser or accountant it is absolutely essential that you conduct your affairs at all times following the professional code of ethics. ACCA publish a Code of Ethics and Conduct which covers the standards and ethical requirements expected of its members. The Code of Ethics and Conduct sets out the principles and framework for applying those principles. It is important that members are familiar with the principles and how they are expected to be applied in the real world.

Where a member has any doubts about their course of actions, they are required to assess how the actions fit in with the principles. The ACCA has a helpline which is available to members for guidance.

The fundamental principles are:

a) Objectivity - Avoid conflicts of interest; do not act for two companies one buying shares and the other selling shares if objectivity will be compromised.

b) Professional – Behave professionally at all times, comply with relevant laws and avoid any action that discredits the profession. Members should also be truthful and honest at all times and never make overstated claims or try to discredit the work of others.

c) Technical competence – Keep up to date with new tax rules and legislation. Never take on work which you are not able to complete and make the limits of your technical abilities clear to avoid misrepresentation.

d) Integrity – Be honest and do not assist clients in committing an offence.

e) Confidentiality – Client information should not be disclosed to other parties without the client's permission including HMRC. The exception to this rule applies if an accountant has knowledge or suspicion that a person has committed a money laundering offence.

The ACCA provides a framework for applying the principles as set out above.

Various threats to the principles exist and it is the member's responsibility to identify, assess and take action to minimise or avoid the threats. Where a member cannot take the necessary action to minimise or eliminate the threat, he should decline the appointment or resign from acting from the client.

Examples of threats are:

- Self-interest threat – family members' interests impact on the member

- Self-review threat – having the ability to review previous work with an aim of highlighting potential risks and mitigating actions

- Advocacy threat – an opinion or position is enhanced by the member to a point where future objectivity is affected

- Familiarity threat – a member has acted for an individual for a long time and takes at face value what he is told without looking further into the impact

- Intimidation threats – after acting for a client, threats of a physical or mental (perceived or otherwise) are made against the member

Conflict of interest

A conflict of interest will arise where the member is asked to act for a husband and wife in a divorce or where the firm audits two companies who have legal action outstanding between them. A member should take reasonable steps to identify circumstances that could pose a conflict of interest. Any communications with clients should be in writing.

Once a conflict of interest is recognised, the member should put into place safeguards. The main safeguard is to communicate with both parties to inform them of the conflict of interest and seek the consent of the parties to act for them. If the consent is refused, the member should not continue to act.

Where a member cannot take the necessary action to minimise or eliminate the conflict of interest, he should decline the appointment or resign from acting from the client.

New clients

Before taking on new clients – a member of the ACCA must assess

- Risk to the integrity of the practice on accepting the work. For any tax planning work, the planning must be within the current legal framework (tax avoidance) rather than outside the legal framework (tax evasion).

- Whether the practice has adequate skills and competence to carry out the work.

On accepting new clients, a member of the ACCA must ask permission from the client to contact the old advisers to request information. If the client refuses then the ACCA member should consider not acting for them.

The existing advisers should be asked if there is any reason, professional or otherwise, for not accepting the engagement. Speaking with the current advisers is of the upmost importance as it may highlight an area which prevents the appointment being accepted. It is still up to the member to decide, after discussions with the current advisers, whether or not to accept the appointment.

Once the new appointment has been agreed the tax adviser should issue a letter of engagement setting out terms and conditions and expected fee levels.

Client error

Information provided to HMRC must be accurate and complete. A member must not assist a client to plan or commit an offence.

If client has made an error the ACCA member must decide whether the error is genuine or deliberate/ fraudulent. Where the error is a deliberate evasion of tax, criminal proceedings may be bought under tax law and money laundering legislation.

The member should explain to the client the need to notify HMRC and make a full disclosure. If the client refuses, the member must explain the potential consequences of their actions in writing. If the client still refuses, the member should cease to act and write to HMRC stating that the firm no longer acts for the client but not stating the reason why.

Money laundering regulations

Money laundering is defined as benefiting from or concealing the proceeds of a crime, and this includes the proceeds of tax evasion.

Prior to accepting a new client, a member should verify his identity by reliable and independent means. If the client is an individual this would be a passport, proof of address, driving licence, correspondence with HMRC. If the client is a company, this would be Companies House searches and then obtaining individual proofs of identity on each of the directors.

Records should be kept for at least 5 years after the end of the client relationship.

Members are required to implement measures and to report suspicions to the appropriate authority. Failure to allow these legislative requirements will often be a criminal offence. Where a member has suspicions that a client's activities are not legal it should be reported to a money laundering reporting officer (MLRO). A MLRO should be appointed by the firm and it is their duty to decide whether to report a transaction to the Serious Organised Crime Agency (SOCA).

If a report is made, the client should not be informed as this is an offence – tipping off.

2

Introduction
to
Income Tax

Context

Income tax computations are used to compute the total income tax payable by a person each tax year and are a very important area of the syllabus. It is highly likely that you will have to produce an income tax computation and calculate the income tax payable by an individual.

Income tax is a tax on the regular income earned by an individual during the tax year.

Exam hints

This is examined very frequently in the F6 exam, so it is very important that you are fully aware of the standard tests in this area and how to apply them to the scenarios.

This area has featured regularly as question 1 on the F6 paper.

Key learning points

- Income tax is paid by individuals on taxable income earned in the tax year.

- Some income received during the year is exempt income, which means there is no income tax payable on it. Taxable income does have income tax payable on it and is included in the income tax computation for the tax year.

- Taxable income must be included in the income tax computation GROSS. Therefore you must "gross up" any taxable income that has been received net.

- The personal allowance is a tax free amount that all individuals are entitled to each tax year to reduce down their taxable income. The personal allowance for 2011/12 is £7,475.

- The personal allowance is gradually reduced to nil where a person's adjusted net income exceeds £100,000.

- Older taxpayers may be entitled to higher personal allowance, known as the personal age allowance. The amount of personal age allowance depends upon the taxpayer's age at the end of the tax year.

- The rate of income tax payable depends on the type of income it is classified as. Income can be classified as non savings income, savings income or dividend income and the income is taxed in that order.

- For 2011/12, an additional rate of 50% applies where taxable income exceeds £150,000.

- If an individual makes a gift aid donation to charity during the year or pays interest on a qualifying loan, this can have an impact on the amount of income tax payable.

Proforma income tax computation 2010/11

	£
Trading income	x
Employment income	x
Rental income	x
Savings income (most received net x 100/80)	x
Dividend income (received net x 100/90)	x̲
Total income	x
Less: interest on qualifying loans (paid gross)	(x̲)
Net income	X
Less: PA/PAA	(x̲)
Taxable income	X̲

Calculation of income tax:

	£
Non savings income x 20%/40%/50%	X
Savings income x 10%/20%/40%/50%	X
Dividend income x 10%/32.5%/42.5%	X̲
Income tax liability	X
Less: tax deducted at source	
10% tax credits on dividends	(x)
20% x Interest	(x)
PAYE on salary	(x̲)
Tax payable/repayable under self assessment	X̲/(X̲)

Scope of Income Tax

Income tax is paid by individuals on **taxable income** earned in the **tax year** (also known as "fiscal year").

The tax year for your exam is the tax year 2011/12. The tax year 2011/12 runs from 6 April 11-5 April 12.

In this text we are concerned only with UK income received by UK resident individuals. An individual is resident in the UK for a tax year if:

a)   he is present for 183 days or more in the UK; or

b)   substantial visits are made to the UK. This is defined as averaging 91 days a year over four or more consecutive years.

Types of income

An income tax computation may contain the following types of income:

Trading income – income from self-employed business

Employment income – income from your employment such as salary or bonus

Rental income – income from renting out a property

Savings income – income from bank or building society

Dividend income – income received from shares

EXEMPT INCOME

You pay income tax on your taxable income that you have earned during the tax year. In the exam, you will need to be able to identify which income is **exempt** from income tax (i.e. you pay no income tax on it) and which income is taxable.

In the exam, if you see exempt income in a question, you should leave it out of your income tax computation and state it is exempt in your answer, so the examiner knows the reason for its omission.

Examples of exempt income include the following:
- Interest on National Savings and Investment Certificates
- Income from Individual Savings Account (ISA)
- Winnings from Premium Bonds

TAXABLE INCOME

Taxable income can either be received gross by the individual (i.e. you receive the whole amount) or net of income tax. Where income is received net of income tax, part of the income has been withheld and paid over to HMRC on your behalf. For example, you may be paid a gross salary by your employer, yet when your wages are paid into your bank account, you do not receive your full gross salary. This is because your employer has deducted taxes on your behalf and paid them directly to HMRC. You only receive the NET figure in your bank account.

In the exam, you will need to be able to identify if the taxable income you have received is gross or net and then deal with it accordingly.

Taxable income

RECEIVED GROSS
"By Assessment"

RECEIVED NET
"By deduction at source"

Some income is received gross (i.e. no tax has been deducted at source). The tax on this income is collected by HMRC under the self-assessment rules.

Some income is received net of income tax. This tax is deducted at source and paid directly to HMRC. The individual receives the net amount.

Examples include:

Property income

Trading income

National Savings & Investment Bank account interest

Interest on government securities and gilts

Interest from quoted companies

Examples include:

Building society interest (net of 20%)

Bank interest (net of 20%)

Dividends from UK companies (net of 10%)

Employment income (net of PAYE)

Interest from unquoted companies (net of 20%)

Savings income

All savings income is assessable in the tax year in which it is received or credited to the taxpayer. The gross amount must be included.

(a)   Interest which is received gross

- National Savings and Investment Bank Accounts (NS&IB) – Investment accounts and Easy Access Savings Accounts (EASAs)

- UK government stock (e.g. Treasury Stock)

(b)   Interest received net

This income is received net of 20 per cent tax and must be grossed up by 100/80.

- Building society interest

- Bank deposit interest

- Interest from corporate bonds (e.g. debenture and loan stock) issued by unquoted companies

London
School of Business
& Finance

shaping success in business and finance

Dividend income

UK dividends are received net of a 10% tax 'credit' and so must be grossed up by 100/90. The tax credit arising can be deducted in calculating tax payable but is not repayable.

The additional rate for dividends is 42.5%. Dividends are therefore, taxed as follows:

- at 10% if they fall below the higher rate threshold of £35,000,
- at 32.5% if they fall between the higher rate of £35,000 and the additional rate threshold of £150,000
- at 42.5% if they exceed the additional rate threshold of £150,000

Foreign Dividends

The tax credit operates as it does in relation to dividends from a UK resident company; foreign dividend income is grossed up at 100/90, the gross income is taxed at 10%, 32.5% or 42.5% and there is a 10% notional tax credit. The tax credit is not repayable.

Learning example 2.1

Charlie has received the following income during the tax year 2011/12:

	£
• Bank interest	800
• Premium bond winnings	1,000
• Gross salary	23,000
• Dividend income	90

Required

Calculate Charlie's net income figure that would appear in his income tax computation for 2011/12.

Personal allowance (PA)

The personal allowance is a tax free amount that all individuals are entitled to each tax year to reduce their taxable income. The personal allowance for 2011/12 remains at £7,475.

The personal allowance is given in full in the year in which a taxpayer dies and is not transferable to another individual.

The personal allowance is used against taxable income in the following order: non-savings income, then savings income and finally against dividend income.

Learning example 2.2

Sally has received the following income during the tax year:

	£
Trading income	17,500
Bank interest	600
Rental income	2,500
Dividend income	4,500

Required

Calculate Sally's taxable income for the tax year 2011/12.

Reduction in personal allowance

For the tax year 2011/12, the standard personal allowance is reduced gradually to nil where a person's adjusted net income exceeds £100,000. Adjusted net income is defined as net income less gross personal pension contributions and gift aid donations.

The personal allowance is reduced by £1 for every £2 that a person's adjusted net income exceeds £100,000.

Effectively, an individual will not have a personal allowance where their adjusted net income is in excess of £114,950. The effective marginal rate of income tax between £100,000 and £114,950 is 60%.

Learning example 2.3

James has received the following income during the tax year:

	£
Trading income	152,000
Bank interest	600
Dividend income	4,500

Required

Calculate James's income tax liability for the tax year 2011/12.

Personal age allowance (PAA)

Older taxpayers may be entitled to a more generous personal allowance, known as the personal age allowance. The amount of personal age allowance depends upon the taxpayer's age at the end of the tax year:

	£
Age (65 – 74)	9,940
Age 75 and over	10,090

These higher personal allowances are granted instead of the usual personal allowance, not in addition to it. You will be given the rates of PAA in the exam.

RESTRICTION OF THE PERSONAL AGE ALLOWANCE

Where the adjusted net income, defined as net income less any gift aid donations and pension contributions made during the year, of the taxpayer is greater than £24,000, the PAA is cut by £1 for every £2 of income over £24,000. The maximum reduction brings the PAA back to that of a taxpayer under the age of 65 i.e. £7,475.

CALCULATION OF PAA:

	£
Maximum PAA	9,940/10,090
Less restriction	
½ (adjusted net income – 24,000)	(X)
Revised PAA (never below £7,475)	X

London
School of Business
& Finance
shaping success in business and finance

Learning example 2.4

Dylan is 71 years of age and has net income of:

(a)   £25,000
(b)   £35,000

Required

Compute Dylan's taxable income in 2011/12.

Calculation of income tax

Once taxable income has been calculated, the amount of income tax payable must now be worked out.

An individual taxpayer is allocated one set of tax bands. The tax bands for 2011/12 will be given in the exam and are as follows:

Savings starting rate	£1 - £2,560	10%
Basic rate	£1 - £35,000	20%
Higher rate	£35,001 - £150,000	40%
Additional rate	£150,000 and above	50%

The application of the tax bands depends upon the type of income included in the computation and are applied on a cumulative basis. The order of application is non-savings, then savings, then, finally, dividend income.

Non-savings

Non-savings income (including earned income) less interest paid on a qualifying loan and personal allowance is taxable at 20%/40%/50%.

Savings

A savings starting rate of 10% applies to the first £2,560 of savings income.

If non-savings income exceeds £2,560, the starting rate of 10% does not apply. In these cases, savings income is taxed at 20% if it falls below the higher rate threshold of £35,000, at the higher rate of 40% if it falls between the higher rate threshold of £35,000 and the additional rate threshold of £150,000, and at the additional rate of 50% if it exceeds the additional rate threshold of £150,000.

Dividend

Dividends are taxed as follows:
*   at 10% if they fall below the higher rate threshold of £35,000 (if basic rate band is available);

*   at 32.5% if they fall between the higher rate of £35,000 and the additional rate threshold of £150,000 (if higher rate band is available);

*   at 42.5% if they exceed the additional rate threshold of £150,000

Rates of income tax

The rate of income tax suffered depends on which tax band the income falls into. There are three tax bands:

	Taxable income £	Non savings income	Savings income	Dividend income
Starting rate band	0-2,560	20%	10% (note 1)	10%
Basic rate band	2,561-35,000	20%	20%	10%
Higher rate band	35,001-150,000	40%	40%	32.5%
Additional rate band	£150,001 and over	50%	50%	42.5%

Note 1: Will not apply if non-savings income is > £2,560.

Learning example 2.5

Ebenezer has the following information for 2011/12:

	£
Gross salary (PAYE = £313)	9,000
Bank interest (received)	1,000
ISA interest	300
National Savings Bank interest	165
British Telecom dividends (received)	3,600

Required

Calculate Ebenezer's tax payable for 2011/12.

Learning example 2.6

Edith has the following income during the tax year 2011/12:

	£
Trading income	155,000
Bank interest	8,000 (net)
Rental income	500
Dividend income	12,000 (net)

Required

Calculate Edith's income tax liability for 2011/12.

Gift aid donations

The Gift Aid scheme was established several years ago as a means of providing a tax incentive for individuals and companies to make charitable donations.

The gift is treated as if it were made net of 20% income tax and the charity can then recover the amount of tax which is deemed to have been deducted at source. The gift is not shown in the donor's tax computation, but the following provisions apply:

The donor's basic rate band is extended by the gross amount of the gift (amount paid x 100/80). This extension ensures that relief at the higher rate or additional rate is automatically given to higher rate or additional rate taxpayers.

Impact of gift aid donation on income tax computation

If the tax payer is a basic rate tax payer: the gift aid donation has no impact on the income tax computation

If the tax payer is a higher rate or additional rate tax payer: the basic rate band of £35,000 is extended by the GROSS donation. This means that more income is taxed at 20% and less is taxed at 40% or 50%.

Extension of basic rate band: 35,000 + (donation x 100/80)

If the tax payer is an additional rate tax payer: the higher rate band limit of £150,000 is extended by the GROSS donation. This means that more income is taxed at 40% and less at 50%.

Extention of additional rate band: £150,000 + (donation x 100/80)

Interest payable on qualifying loans

Interest paid on certain loans is deductible from a taxpayer's total income. This interest is generally paid gross. The main types of eligible loans are as follows:

*   A loan to purchase plant and machinery which is necessarily acquired for use in the taxpayer's employment

*   A loan to purchase plant and machinery for use in the business of a partnership in which the taxpayer is a partner.

*   A loan to purchase an interest in a partnership.

The interest is deducted against income in the following order: non-savings income, savings income, dividend income.

Learning example 2.7

Bob is a single man and has the following information for 2011/12:

	£
Share of trading profits from partnership	160,000
Barclays bank interest received	1,920
Interest from National Savings Certificates	800
British Gas dividends (received)	2,700

Bob pays £2,400(net) as a gift aid donation during the year 2011/12. Personal pension contributions amounting to £50,000 (net) were also made.

Required

Calculate Bob's tax liability for 2011/12.

Learning example 2.8

Katie is a single woman and received dividends of £2,250(net) and bank interest of £720 net in 2011/12. Her non-savings income in 2011/12 is:

		£	
Part a	48,245	(assume that Katie pays £2,000 of interest on a qualifying loan)
Part b	48,245	(assume that Katie pays £1,600 of donation under gift aid scheme)

Required

Show the income tax payable for each situation in 2010/11.

Spouses and Civil Partners

Spouses and civil partners are taxed as separate individuals, each with their own personal allowances and reliefs.

Joint property

Where property is owned jointly, any income generated from the property is split equally. If the property is not owned equally, a joint declaration can be made to HMRC before the start of the tax year to specify the actual proportion of income to be taxed on each individual.

For example if Chris owns 10% of a rental property and his wife Alice owns 90% then if no declaration is made each will be taxed on one half of the income. If a declaration is made, Chris will be taxed on 10% of the income and Alice on 90% of the income.

Tax planning

The total income tax liability of a married couple or civil partners can be minimized if they each take full advantage of their available reliefs, personal allowances and basic rate and higher rate tax bands.

If one member of the couple has a higher income than the other transferring assets from that member to the other results in the income from that asset arising to the other member.

Alternatively a share of an asset can be passed to the member with the lower income:

- If the share transferred is less than 50% no declaration should be made so that 50% of the income is taxed on the member with the lower income.

- If the share transferred is more than 50% a declaration should be made so that actual share of the income is taxed on the member with the lower income.

Learning example 2.9

Jack and Craig are civil partners. Jack has investment income of £200,000 and Craig has no income.

Required

Calculate the couple's total income tax liability if:

1. no action is taken

2. Jack transfers 25% of the assets to Craig and a declaration is made, and

3. Jack transfers 25% of the assets to Craig and no declaration is made.

Learning summary

- Individuals are liable for income tax on their worldwide income where they are resident, ordinarily resident and domiciled in the UK.

- Individuals are taxed according to tax years, which cover a period 6 April-5 April.

- An individual's income is classified as earned, savings or dividend income for a particular tax year.

- Earned income includes income from employment and self-employment.

- Savings income can be received gross or net of basic rate income tax. Where it is received net, it should be grossed up to be included in the income tax computation.

- Dividend income is deemed to be received net. It should be grossed up by 100/90.

- Gift aid payments and personal pension contributions extend the basic rate band to give relief to higher rate taxpayers.

- All taxpayers are entitled to a personal allowance of £7,475. Individuals over the age of 65 have an additional age allowance, which is reduced by £1 for every £2 of income over £24,000. The age allowance can never be reduced to less than £7,475.

- The personal allowance is reduced once the income levels exceed £100,000.

Learning solution 2.1

Charlie 2011/12

		£
Employment income		23,000
Savings income	(800 x 100/80)	1,000
Dividend income	(90 x 100/90)	100
Net income		24,100

Premium bond winnings are exempt from income tax

Learning solution 2.2

Sally 2011/12

		£
Trading income		17,500
Bank interest	(600 x 100/80)	750
Rental income		2,500
Dividend income	(4500 x 100/90)	5,000
Net income		25,750
Less PA		(7,475)
Taxable income		18,275

Learning solution 2.3

James 2011/12

		£
Trading income		152,000
Bank interest	(600 x 100/80)	750
Dividend income	(4500 x 100/90)	5,000
Net income		157,750
Less PA		-
Taxable income		157,750

Splits into:

	£
Non savings income	152,000
Savings income	750
Dividend income	5,000
	157,750

Tax:

	£	£
Non savings:		
	35,000 x 20%	7,000
	115,000 x 40%	46,000
	2,000 x 50%	1,000
Savings:	750 x 50%	375
Dividends	5,000 x 42.5%	2,125
Income tax liability		**56,500**

No personal allowance is available as James's adjusted net income of £157,750 exceeds £114,950.

Learning solution 2.4

Dylan 2011/12

		(a)	(b)
	£	£	£
Net income		25,000	35,000
Less: PAA	9,940		
½ x (25,000 – 24,000)	(500)		
	9,440	(9,440)	
PAA	9,940		
Less: ½ x (35,000 – 24,000)	(5,500)		
	4,440		
Restricted to £7,475			(7,475)
Taxable income		15,560	27,525

Learning solution 2.5

Ebenezer – 2011/12 tax computation

	£
Employment income	9,000
Bank interest (1,000 x 100/80)	1,250
NSB interest	165
Dividend income (3,600 x 100/90)	4,000
Net income	14,415
Less: PA	(7,475)
Taxable income	6,940

ISA interest is exempt from income tax

Income tax calculation:

You now need to identify what type of taxable income you are left with. Remember that the personal allowance is used up in the same order that you tax in: non savings, savings, and dividends.

Taxable income of £6,940 splits into:

	£
Non savings:	1,525
Savings	1,415
Dividend	4,000
	6,940

Tax:

		£
Non savings:	1,525 x 20%	305
Savings	1,035 x 10%	103
Up to starting rate	2,560	
Savings (1,415 – 1,035)	380 x 20%	76
Dividend	4,000 x 10%	400
	6,940	

	£
Income tax liability	884
Less: Tax deducted at source:	
Dividends	(400)
Savings income	(250)
PAYE	(313)
Income tax repayable	(79)

Learning solution 2.6

Edith 2011/12

	£
Trading income	155,000
Savings income (8,000 x 100/80)	10,000
Rental income	500
Dividend income (12,000 x 100/90)	13,333
Net income	178,833
Less PA	-
Taxable income	178,833

Splits into:

	£	
Non savings income	155,500	(155,000 + 500)
Savings income	10,000	
Dividend income	13,333	
	178,833	

Tax:

		£	£
Non savings:			
	35,000 x 20%		7,000
	115,000 x 40%		46,000
	5,500 x 50%		2,750
Savings:	10,000 x 50%		5,000
Dividends	13,333 x 42.5%		5,666
Income tax liability			66,416

The requirement has only asked for income tax liability and as such, you do not need to deduct tax suffered at source

Learning solution 2.7

Bob 2011/12

	£
Trading profits	160,000
Savings income (1,920 x 100/80)	2,400
Dividend income (2,700 x 100/90)	3,000
Total income	165,400
Less: PA (W)	(7,475)
Taxable income	157,925

Interest from National Savings Certificates is exempt from income tax

Splits into:

		£
Non savings income	152,525 (160,000 –7,475)	
Savings income		2,400
Dividend income		3,000
		157,925

Tax:

		£	£
Non savings:			
Basic rate band extension (W1)	100,500 x 20%		20,100
	52,025 x 40%		20,810
Savings:	2,400 x 40%		960
Dividends	3,000 x 32.5%		975
Income tax liability			**42,845**

W1 Basic rate band extension
Pension: £50,000 x 100/80 = 62,500
Gift Aid: £2,400 x 100/80 = 3,000

Adjusted net income is £ 165,400 – 65,500 = 99,900.

Therefore, a full personal allowance is available, with the basic rate band extended to £100,500 (35,000 + 62,500 + 3,000) and the higher rate band to £215,500 (150,000 + 62,500+ 3,000)

Learning solution 2.8

Katie 2011/12

	Part A	Part B
Non savings	48,245	48,245
Dividend income (2,250 x 100/90)	2,500	2,500
Savings income (720 x 100/80)	900	900
Total income	51,645	51,645
Less: Interest paid on a qualifying loan	(2,000)	-
Net income	49,645	51,645
Less: PA	(7,475)	(7,475)
Taxable income	42,170	44,170

Part A: income tax

Splits into:

		£
Non savings income	38,770 (48,245 − 2,000 − 7,475)	
Savings income	900	
Dividend income	2,500	
	42,170	

Tax:

	£	£
Non savings:	35,000 x 20%	7,000
	3,770 x 40%	1,508
	38,770	
Savings:	900 x 40%	360
Dividends	2,500 x 32.5%	812
Income tax liability		9,680
Less tax suffered at source:		
Dividends		(250)
Savings		(180)
Income tax payable		9,250

Part B: income tax

Splits into:

		£
Non savings income	40,770 (48,245 − 7,475)	
Savings income	900	
Dividend income	2,500	
	44,170	

Tax:

	£	£
Non savings: basic rate band extension (W1)	37,000 x 20%	7,400
	3,770 x 40%	1,508
	40,770	
Savings:	900 x 40%	360
Dividends	2,500 x 32.5%	812
Income tax liability		10,080
Less tax suffered at source:		
Dividends		(250)
Savings		(180)
Income tax payable		9,650

W1 extension of basic rate band due to gift aid donation

£1,600 x 100/80 = £2,000
£35,000 + 2,000 = £37,000

Learning solution 2.9

	Jack	Craig	Total tax
	£	£	£
1. Taxable income	200,000	Nil	
Tax payable			
£35,000 @ 20%	7,000		
£115,000 @ 40%	46,000		
50,000 @ 50%	25,000		
	78,000		78,000

No advantage is taken of Craig's personal allowance and basic and higher rate bands.

	Jack	Craig	Total tax
2. Total income	150,000	50,000	
Less Personal allowance	-	(7,475)	
Taxable income	150,000	42,525	
Tax payable			
£35,000/35,000 @ 20%	7,000	7,000	
£115,000/7,525 @ 40%	46,000	3,010	
	53,000	10,010	63,010

Although both Jack and Craig are higher rate taxpayers Jack is not entitled to a personal allowance.

	Jack	Craig	Total tax
3. Total income	100,000	100,000	
Less Personal allowance	(7,475)	(7,475)	
Taxable income	92,525	92,525	
Tax payable			
£35,000 @ 20%	7,000	7,000	
£57,525 @ 40%	23,010	23,010	
	30,010	30,010	60,020

3

Employment
Income

Context

This chapter is focusing on the rules for determining a person's employment income. Employment income is received net of tax. The employer acts as a tax collector and deducts the tax at source. This is called the PAYE system of collecting tax.

Employment income is assessable based on the employee's earnings during the tax year. A person who has employment income will pay income tax on it.

Exam hints

Employment income is a very important topic for your exam and is likely to be tested in question one of the paper.

Key learning points

- Salary and bonus form part of an individual's employment income and are taxed on a receipts basis.
- Benefits in kind are also taxed as part of employment income.
- Some benefits are taxed on higher paid employees only. Others are taxable on both higher and lower paid employees.
- There are special rules for the calculation of benefits in kind, such as company cars. You must learn these rules for your exam.

Proforma employment income

	£
Salary/bonus	X
Benefits	X
Reimbursed expenses	X̲
	X
Less allowable expenses:	
• Donation to charity under a payroll deduction scheme	(X)
• Contributions to an occupational pension plan	(X)
• Travel, subsistence and entertaining incurred wholly, exclusively and necessarily in the performance of the office or employment	(X)
• Subscription to a professional body	(X)
• Deficit on a mileage allowance	(X̲)
Employment income	X

Employment income – basis of assessment

Employment income is based on the emoluments received in the tax year of assessment irrespective of when the emoluments were earned.

Emoluments are treated as being received on the earliest of the following:

- When the emoluments are received.

- When the person was entitled to receive the emoluments.

Where the employee is a director, earnings are received at the earliest of:

1. Earlier of the two dates above

2. The date the earnings are credited to directors loan account or similar account in the company's accounting records

3. The end of the company's period of account if the amount has been determined by then, or the date of determination if this is after the end of the period of account.

Salary/Bonus/Commission

The amount of salary assessable in a particular tax year is the actual amount earned in the tax year.

The bonus/commission is normally assessable in the tax year in which the bonus is received.

The rule to determine when a bonus is treated as being received, is the earliest of the following:

- When the bonus is actually received.

- When the person was entitled to receive the bonus.

Learning example 3.1

Dick is employed by ABC plc and his salary was £30,000. On 1 February 2012 his salary was increased to £36,000.

Additionally Dick receives a bonus each March based on the companies results:

	Bonus
	£
Y/e 31 December 2010	3,000
Y/e 31 December 2011	10,000

Required

Compute Dick's employment income for 2011/12

Benefit valuations

Employment income not only includes the salary and bonus that you receive as part of your job. It also includes any perks of the job you may receive as well, such as medical insurance, a company car, membership of a gym. These perks are known as 'benefits in kind'.

In the exam, you will have to know the rules about how to calculate the value of a benefit.

There are two main categories of benefits: exempt benefits and taxable benefits.

Exempt benefits

Certain benefits are exempt from income tax irrespective of earnings levels. The more common examples include:

(1)   Relocation – first £8,000 of removal expenses provided employee does not already live within reasonable daily travelling distance of his new employer, and these are incurred by the end of the tax year in which employment was commenced.

(2)   Entertainment provided by third parties (corporate Hospitality)

(3)   Long-service awards (20 years or more, no similar award made in past 10 years and valued at < £50 per year of service)

(4)   Parking at the workplace

(5)   Staff canteen provided available for all employees

(6)   Private use of a mobile phone. The mobile phone contract must be in the name of the company and not the employee, otherwise the employee must claim for the deduction of business calls themselves

(7)   Job-related accommodation

(8)   Cheap loans that do not exceed £5,000 at any point during the tax year

(9)   Private medical insurance premiums paid to cover treatment when employee is outside the UK in performance of duties. Where the duties are conducted in the UK, the premiums are taxable and are extended to cover premiums paid for family members.

(10)   Eye tests and glasses for employees using VDUs

(11)   Workplace nursery or play scheme. Where the employer does not provide its own nursery, but contracts with an approved childcare provider, the first £55 per week is exempt for basic rate taxpayers, but is reduced to £28 per week for higher rate taxpayers and £22 per week for additional rate taxpayers. Childcare must be available to all employees

(12)   Staff suggestion schemes unless the award exceeds £5,000 (anything over £5,000 is taxable)

(13)   Gifts of goods or vouchers if the total cost is < £250 per annum. If > £250, full amount is taxable, not just the excess.

(14)   Authorised mileage allowance paid by employer for an employee using their own car for business purposes

(15)   Occupational pension contributions

(16)   The first 15p per day of luncheon vouchers

(17) Staff parties provided cost per staff member per year (incl. VAT) is £150 or less. Where the £150 limit is exceeded, the whole amount is taxable, not just the excess. The limit can be split over several parties

(18) Death in service benefit contributions

(19) Overnight personal expenses paid by employer (telephone calls home, laundry, newspapers etc) up to £5 per night for UK stays and up to £10 per night for overseas stays

(20) Work related training and related costs, including the cost of training materials and use of assets made available during training

(21) Indemnity insurance premiums paid by employer

These benefits are exempt and so can be left out of your employment income working. However, if a question includes these benefits, the workings should show why you have excluded them i.e. state they are exempt.

Taxable benefits

Whether a benefit is taxable on an individual depends on whether the individual is a higher or lower paid employee.

- Lower paid employee: individual earning < £8,500 per annum

- Higher paid employee (also known as P11D): individual earning > £8,500 per annum

To determine whether an individual earns > £8,500 per annum, add:

- salary, bonus, commission etc

- the taxable value of benefits calculated as if the employee earned > £8,500 per annum,

then deduct:

- pension contributions and

- charitable donations made under the payroll giving scheme.

Benefits taxable on higher paid (P11D) employees only

The following benefits are taxable on higher paid employees only:

1. Medical insurance

2. Company cars

3. Fuel for private motoring

4. Van benefit

5. Accommodation benefit

6. Council tax benefit

7. Living expenses benefit

8. Use benefit

9. Transfer benefit

10. Beneficial loans

11. Gift benefit

London School of Business & Finance

shaping success in business and finance

Reporting of taxable benefits

Taxable benefits are reported on form PIID. These must be completed for all employees, except excluded employees, and filed with HMRC by 6 July following the end of the tax year to which they relate.

If the employer holds a dispensation against reporting certain benefits (usually travel expenses), these expenses do not have to be reported on the PIID. Where the employer provides no other taxable benefits and a dispensation is in place, HMRC will generally allow the employer to cease filing PIID forms. It is the employer's responsibility to notify HMRC of any change in circumstances.

A dispensation will only be given for benefits and expenses for which the employee could claim full tax relief.

Class Ia NIC

Most taxable benefits are subject to class IA National Insurance at 13.8%. This must be paid over by 19 July following the end of the tax year to which the liability relates. The taxable benefit will be exempt from class IA NIC if:

* Within class I

* Covered by a PIID dispensation

* Provided to employees earning < £8,500 per annum

Let's look at each of these benefits in more detail and see how they are calculated:

I   MEDICAL INSURANCE

Medical insurance benefit arises when an employer pays medical insurance premiums for the benefit of an employee.

Medical insurance Benefit:

Medical insurance Benefit = the medical insurance premiums paid

For example, if the employer pays a premium for medical insurance for an employee of £600, the cost of this is the benefit to the employee i.e. the employee will have a benefit of £600

2   COMPANY CARS

Calculation of benefit

The car benefit is assessable on an employee where an employer provides an employee with the private use of a motor car. The car benefit is calculated using the list price of the vehicle and depends upon the car's CO_2 emissions. For 2011/12, the base level of CO_2 emissions used to calculate company car benefits is reduced from 130g per kilometre to 125g per kilometre.

The benefit is reduced for periods of non-availability i.e. repairs covering a continuous period of less than 30 days, or is made available or ceases to be available. This is generally done via a pro-rating of the benefit using actual days.

Where an employee makes a personal contribution to the running costs of the car, this reduces the overall benefit assessed on the employee.

Where the car qualifies as a pool car (available for use by more than one employee, not usually kept overnight near the residence of an employee and private use is merely incidental), then no benefit will arise on the employee for use of the pool car.

Car benefit = [% x list price(Xa) x X/12] −amount employee pays employer towards the running cost

Calculation of list price of car (Xa)

This is the price of the car given upon first registration. It includes charges for delivery and standard accessories. Where the purchase price of the car included optional extras, excluding equipment required for disable drivers, these must be added to the list price. Where optional extras are added after the car has been first made available to the employee, these must also be added, unless they are required for disabled drivers, or cost less than £100 each.

List price of car when first registered	X
Plus: Cost of extras paid for by employer	X
Less: Contribution employee gives employer towards the capital cost of the car (UL = £5,000)	(X)
	Xa

Capital contributions in excess of the £5,000 are ignored.

Formula to determine the percentage

The CO_2 baseline figure required for calculating the percentage will be given in the examination.

Diesel cars have a supplement of 3% of the cars list price added to the taxable benefit.

OPTION 1	OPTION 2	OPTION 3	OPTION 4
CO_2 EMISSION	CO_2 EMISSION	CO_2 EMISSION	CO_2 EMISSION
≤ 75 grams/km	76-120 grams/km	121-125 grams/km	125 (given) + grams/km
PETROL 5% (given)	PETROL 10% (given)	PETROL 15%	15%/18% + $(CO_2 - 130) \div 5$
DIESEL 8%	DIESEL 13%	DIESEL 18%	UPPER LIMIT = 35%

Where a company car has a zero CO_2 emissions figure, there is no benefit in kind arising. The provision of a zero emission company car is not examinable

Learning example 3.2

Phil is provided with a company car by his employer on 1 July 2011. The petrol car has CO_2 emissions of 191g/km and a list price of £17,000. Phil has made a capital contribution of £6,000 towards the purchase of the car. He also pays £100 per month towards the running costs of the car.

Required

Calculate Phil's car benefit in kind for 2011/12

London
School of Business
& Finance
shaping success in business and finance

3   FUEL BENEFIT

The fuel benefit applies when the employer pays for all or some fuel for private mileage for the car provided to the employee.

The taxable benefit is calculated as a percentage of a base figure. For 2011/12 the base figure is £18,800, which is given in the exam.

£

Fuel benefit =   % x 18,800

=   X ◄──────── (time apportion if not had fuel benefit for full tax year)

The percentage used in the calculation of the fuel benefit is exactly the same as the percentage used in the calculation of the car benefit.

If an employee gives the employer a contribution towards the cost of the private fuel this does not reduce the fuel benefit.

If the employee reimburses the employer for the full cost of the private fuel then the fuel benefit is nil.

Learning example 3.3

Using the previous example (3.2), Phil is also provided with fuel for his company car by his employer. The total cost of the fuel is £3,500 and Phil uses the company car for 80% business purposes and 20% private purposes.

Phil is required to pay £5 per month to his employer for the private fuel

Required

What is Phil's fuel benefit in kind for 2011/12?

Learning example 3.4

Tom has an annual salary of £47,000 and is supplied with a Ford Focus on 1 October 2011 which has a list price of £17,000. Tom contributed £7,000 towards the cost of the car.

The company paid £1,700 for his road tax, insurance and other running costs. His total mileage during 2011/12 amounted to 15,000 and he estimated that 75% is related to business use. Tom is required to pay £75 per month towards the car (£25 is for private fuel). All diesel is paid by the company. The CO_2 emission is 182 grams per kilometre.

Required

Compute Tom's employment income for 2011/12.

4   VAN BENEFIT

The annual scale charge used to calculate the van benefit when an employee is provided with a company van for private use is £3,000.

The van benefit is proportionately reduced if the van is only available for part of the fiscal year. The van benefit is also reduced if the employee gives the employer a contribution toward the running costs of the van.

A further taxable benefit arises if the employer provides fuel for private use, with no reduction for any partial contribution made by the employee towards the cost of such fuel. The amount of this taxable benefit for 2011/12 is £550. This figure is reduced if the fuel is only available for part of the fiscal year.

Van benefit = £3,000 x X/12 – contribution employee makes to the employer
towards the van's running costs.

Van fuel benefit = £550 x X/12

Learning example 3.5

Charlie's employer provides him with a van that he can use privately on 6 April 2011. The van has 80% business use and 20% private use. Charlie's employer also pays for:

	£
Road tax	175
Insurance	800
Repairs	1,100
Total running costs	2,075

Charlie pays £20 per month towards the running costs of the van

Required

What is Charlie's van benefit for 2011/12?

5   ACCOMMODATION BENEFIT

Job related accommodation

If accommodation provided by the employer is "job related" then no taxable benefit arises.

Accommodation is job-related if:

- it is necessary for the employee to reside in the accommodation for the proper performance of his job (e.g. a nanny who is required to live in the employer's accommodation in order to look after the children);

- the accommodation is provided for the better performance of the employee's duties and it is customary for such accommodation to be provided (e.g. soldiers living in army barracks provided by the employer);

- there is a special threat to the employee's security and the accommodation is provided as part of the security arrangements.

Non job related accommodation

If accommodation provided by the employer is "not job related" then a taxable benefit arises. The benefit is calculated as follows:

Living accommodation benefit:

- **If the employer RENTS the property:**

    Benefit is HIGHER of:

	£		£
Rateable (or annual) value x X/12	X	Rent paid by employer	X
Less employee contributions	(X)	Less employee contributions	(X)
Accommodation benefit:	X	Accommodation benefit:	X

- **If the employer OWNS the property:**

	£
Rateable value x X/12	X
Plus: additional charge (only applies the property cost the employer > £75,000)	
("cost"– 75,000) x 4.00% (official rate of interest) x X/12	X
Less: any employee contributions	(X)
Accommodation benefit	X

NB the benefit will be time apportioned if the employee has not lived in the property for the full tax year. (X/12: X is the number of months available during the fiscal year.)

To calculate "cost" for the additional charge:

	£
Original cost or MV of the property when first occupied by the employee	X
Add: cost of capital improvements paid by employer before the start of the current tax year	X
	X

NB: Use market value if the property was acquired by the employer more than six years before it was made available to the employee.

Learning example 3.6

Susie was provided with the use of a company flat on 6 April 2007. The flat cost her employer £140,000 on 1 March 1998. The annual value of the flat is £2,500.

The market value of the flat on 6 April 2007 was £170,000 and on 6 April 2011 was £190,000. The employer built on a sun room in April 2010 which cost £15,000.

Susie pays her employer £200 per month in rent to live in the flat.

Required

Calculate Susie's taxable benefit in 2011/12. The official rate of interest is 4.00%.

6   COUNCIL TAX BENEFIT

If an employer provides living accommodation to an employee, the employee is taxed not only on the accommodation but also on the cost to the employer of paying for the council tax in connection with the accommodation.

Council tax benefit:

amount employer has paid for the council tax – any contributions from employee = X

So for example, the employer paid council tax of £2,000 for the property lived in by the employee.

The employee will have a taxable benefit of £2,000

7   LIVING EXPENSES BENEFIT

If an employer provides living accommodation for an employee, the employee is taxed not only on the accommodation benefit but also on the cost to the employer of providing ancillary services in connection with that accommodation.

Ancillary services include such items as heating and lighting, repairs and maintenance and cleaning.

The provision of furniture for the employee's use is also included under the heading of ancillary services and is assessed in the same way as assets with private use.

If the accommodation is job related then the benefit attributable to ancillary services cannot exceed 10% of the net earnings (excluding ancillary services).

Net earnings is made up of: total employment income less expenses and pension contributions

Learning example 3.7

Roger's employer provides him with a company flat on 30 June 2011 and pays the following expenses in relation to the flat from 1 July 2011 to 5 April 2012:

	£
Electricity	840
Gas bill	1,100
Cleaning costs	900
Total costs	2,840

Required

Calculate the living expenses benefit that arises on Roger for 2011/12.

8   USE OF ASSET BENEFIT

If an employee is lent an asset by their employer that they can use privately, a benefit arises. Common examples are computers, furniture and TV sets.

The benefit is determined as follows:

	£
20% x Open market value when first provided x X/12	X
Less: any employee contributions	(X)
Use benefit	X

NB the benefit will be time apportioned if the employee has not had use of the asset for the full tax year. (X/12: X is number of months available during fiscal year.)

Learning example 3.8

John is provided with living accommodation and his employer pays for living expenses of £2,260 and lends him furniture to use in the accommodation which cost his employer £8,400.

Assume John has a salary of £25,000.

Assume the taxable accommodation benefit is £5,000.

Required

(a)   Compute John's employment income in 2011/12 if the accommodation is not job related.

(b)   Compute John's employment income in 2011/12 if the accommodation is job related.

9   TRANSFER OF ASSET BENEFIT

If the asset loaned to an employee is subsequently sold or given to an employee, then the employee is additionally assessed on the transfer benefit.

The transfer benefit is the HIGHER of:

	£			£
MV of the asset when first provided	X	MV at time of gift		X
Less use benefits already assessed	(X)	Less contribution paid to employer	(X)	
Less contributions paid to the employer for gift	(X)	for the gift		
	X			X

Learning example 3.9

Hillary has been given a camera by her employer on 1 September 2011, which cost £560. She made a contribution of £100 towards the camera.

Required

Calculate the table benefit arising on Hillary for 2011/12.

10   BENEFICIAL LOAN BENEFIT

This occurs where an employer makes a loan to an employee and the rate of interest paid on this loan is less than the official rate.

The interest saved on this loan is a tax free benefit to the employee provided the total amount of

loans provided to that employee are ≤ £5,000.

If the loans provided to the employee are > £5,000 then the employee must pay income tax on the interest they have saved.

Method of computing the loan benefit

Method 1 - The average method

The amount of loan outstanding at the start and end of the tax year are averaged and then multiplied by the official rate (4.00%). The interest actually paid by the employee is then subtracted, giving the assessable loan benefit.

Method 2 - The accurate method

The amount of interest at the official rate is computed precisely. Interest actually paid is then subtracted, giving the assessable loan benefit.

The first method is quicker and easier and is generally used. However, either the employee or HMRC may insist that the accurate method should be used. The employee will do so if this if it results in a lower assessment and HMRC may do so if it appears that the "average" method is being used to deliberately exploit tax avoidance.

Learning example 3.10

Sonia took out a loan from her employer. At the start of the tax year 2011/12, the loan outstanding totalled £25,000. Sonia made a repayment on 7 July 2011 of £10,000. During the year, Sonia paid interest to her employer of £75.

Required

What is the beneficial loan benefit using both the average and accurate method in 2011/12? Assume the official rate of interest is 4%

11   GIFT BENEFIT

The taxable benefit is the market value of the asset at the time of the gift.

The employee is then treated as if that asset cost market value.

The most common type of gift made by an employer is shares in the company the employee is working for.

Learning example 3.11

Maxwell is finance director of Mount plc.

The company's accounts show the following information:

Years ended 31 May:	2010	2011	2012
	£	£	£
Salary, as finance director	42,000	45,000	48,000
Performance bonus	9,000	12,000	16,000

The performance bonus is determined and paid in the August following the accounting year end.

In 2010 Maxwell was provided with a motor car with a list price of £27,000. The CO_2 emissions were 113 g/km. All diesel and expenses were paid by the company. Maxwell drove a total of 15,000 miles in 2011/12, of which 10,000 were for private purposes. He reimbursed the company £500 in respect of private diesel.

Maxwell also has had the use of a company house since 6 April 2011, whose annual value is £5,000 and which is provided rent free. The house had cost £90,000 in 1988 and its market value in April 2011 was £180,000.

Maxwell was provided with home cinema equipment for his personal use since 6 April 2008 when it cost £1,500. On 6 April 2011 the equipment was sold to Maxwell for £300 when its market value was £425.

The company pays private medical insurance for all its employees. Maxwell's share of the group premium was £600 for 2011/12. In July 2011 he needed to have minor surgery and the cost to the insurance company was £3,500.

Required

Calculate Maxwell's employment income for 2011/12.

Benefits taxable on all employees (both lower and higher paid)

VOUCHERS

If an employee is given vouchers by their employer, a benefit arises. The benefit is calculated as the cost to employer, less any contribution made by the employee.

LIVING ACCOMMODATION

The living accommodation benefit that we met earlier arises on both higher AND lower paid employees.

Learning summary

- Benefits apply to all employees and directors earning over £8,500 per annum. Certain benefits are exempt on all employees.

Exam standard question

James is a married man and he has a daughter, Vespa aged 2.

The following information is available for James for 2011/12:

(1)   James is employed by Security Squadron Ltd and is paid a salary of £100,700 per year. In addition to his salary, James was paid a bonus of £90,000 on 21 April 2012. He had become entitled to this bonus on 19 March 2012.

(2)   James contributed 10% of his salary of £100,700 into the employer's occupational pension scheme, which is registered with HMRC.

(3)   The employer, Security Squadron Ltd, also pays into the pension scheme for James, and during 2011/12, they made a gross payment of £15,000 into the pension scheme.

(4)   On 6 August 2011 Security Squadron Ltd provided James with an interest free loan of £70,000 so that he could purchase a yacht. James repaid £10,000 of the loan on 5 December 2011, and the balance of the loan remains outstanding.

(5)   During the tax year 2011/12, Vespa attended Security Squadron Ltd's workplace nursery. The cost to the company of providing this nursery place was £9,100.

(6)   James was provided with two mobile phones. They both cost the employer £400.

(7)   James was also provided with a diesel powered motor car. The car has a list price of £89,000 and James made a capital contribution of £4,000 towards the car, when it was first provided. The official CO_2 emissions rate for the car is 190 gm per kilometre. Private fuel is also provided. The car was available to James throughout 2011/12.

(8)   James received dividends of £8,007 during 2011/12 from his shares in Security Squadron Ltd.

Required

Calculate James's income tax liability for 2011/12

Learning solution 3.1

	£
Salary (10/12 x 30,000 + 2/12 x 36,000)	31,000
Bonus (March 2012)	10,000
Employment income	41,000

London
School of Business
& Finance

shaping success in business and finance

Learning solution 3.2

List price: £17,000 – 5,000 = 12,000

NB the capital contribution to the list price of the car is capped at £5,000

CO_2 %:   15% + ((190 -125) ÷ 5) = 28%

NB The CO_2 emission figure is rounded down to 190

Car Benefit:

		£
Car Benefit:	12,000 x 28% x 9/12	2,520
Less: employee contribution	100 x 9	(900)
		1,620

NB the car benefit has been time apportioned as it was first provided in July 2011 (9 months)

Learning solution 3.3

		£
Fuel BIK:	28% x 18,800 =	5,264
		X 9/12 (as only available from July 2011)
	=	3,948

NB: There is no deduction for the £5 per month contribution made by Phil.

If Phil did reimburse the full cost of the private fuel, there would be no fuel benefit arising

Learning solution 3.4

	£	£
Salary		47,000
Benefits:		
Car benefit 15% + (180 – 125)/5 + 3% = 29%		
29% x (17,000 – 5,000) x 6/12	1,740	
Less: Contributions towards the running costs of the car (50 x 6)	(300)	
		1,440
Fuel benefit 29% x 18,800 x 6/12		2,726
Employment income		51,166

Learning solution 3.5

Van Benefit:

	£
Van benefit	3,000
Less employee contribution	(240)
	2,760

NB if the employer also paid for private fuel for the van, there would be an additional fuel benefit of £550

Learning solution 3.6

2011/12 Accommodation Benefit

	£
Basic Charge: annual value	2,500
Additional charge	
4% x (170,000 + 15,000 – 75,000)	4,400
Less:	
Rent Susie pays her employer for the use of the accommodation (12 x 200)	(2,400)
Accommodation benefit	4,500

Learning solution 3.7

The living expenses benefit is the cost to the employer, less any employee contributions:

	£
Electricity	840
Gas bill	1,100
Cleaning costs	900
Total costs	2,840

Learning solution 3.8

(a) Not job related accommodation

	£
Salary	25,000
Benefits	
Accommodation benefit	5,000
Living expenses benefit	2,260
Use benefit (20% x 8,400)	1,680
Employment income	33,940

(b) Job related accommodation

	£
Salary	25,000
Benefits	
Accommodation benefit	-
Living expenses benefit, lower of:	
- 10% x 25,000 = £2,500	
- Cost of ancillary services (2,260 + 1,680) = £3,940	2,500
Employment income	27,500

Learning solution 3.9

	£
MV at time of gift	560
Less contribution	(100)
Benefit	460

London
School of Business
& Finance

shaping success in business and finance

Learning solution 3.10

Average method:

		£
$\dfrac{25,000 + 15,000}{2} \times 4\%$	=	800
Less actual interest paid		(75)
Beneficial loan benefit		725

Accurate method:

		£
6 April – 6 July (3 months)	$3/12 \times 25,000 \times 4\%$	250
7 July – 5 April (9 months)	$9/12 \times 15,000 \times 4\%$	450
		700
Less actual interest paid		(75)
Beneficial loan benefit:		625

Learning solution 3.11

Employment income 2011/12

	£
Salary (2/12 x £45,000 + 10/12 x £48,000)	47,500
Performance bonus (received in August 2011)	12,000

Benefits:

Car benefit (10 + 3% x £27,000) — 3,510

The CO_2 emissions are ≤ 120g/km but above 75g/km. The 'relevant percentage' is restricted to a maximum of 10% + 3% (diesel) = 13%.

Fuel (13% x £18,800)
There is no deduction for the reimbursement of part of the deisel provided — 2,440

Living accommodation:

	£
Annual value	5,000
Additional value benefit (£180,000* - £75,000) x 4.00%	4,200

Transfer benefit: greater of:

a)	MV when first provided	1,500	
	Use benefits		
	08/09, 09/10, 10/11	(900)	
	(20% X 1,500) X 3		
	Less: price paid	(300)	
	Transfer benefit	300	300
b)	MV when transferred	425	
	Price paid by employee	(300)	
	Transfer benefit	125	

	£
Private medical insurance	600
Employment income	75,554

Note: * The house was acquired by the employer more than six years before it was made available to the employee, therefore MV is used instead of the cost.

Solution to exam standard question

James – Income tax liability 2011/12

	£	£
Employment income		
Salary		100,700
Pension contributions (107,000 x 10%)		(10,070)
		90,630
Bonus		90,000
Pension payment by employer (exempt)		-
Beneficial loan (W1)		1,733
Workplace nursery (exempt)		-
Mobile phone – one is exempt		-
Mobile phone – one is chargeable £400 x 20%		80
Company car benefit (W2)		26,350
Fuel benefit		5,828
Dividend income £8,007 x 100/90		8,897
Net income		223,518
Personal allowance (net income exceeds the maximum - £114,950)		(0)
Taxable income		223,518

Tax liability:
Non-savings

	£	
35,000 at 20%	7,000	
115,000 at 40%	46,000	
64,621 at 50%	32,310	
214,621		
Dividends		
8,897 at 42.5%	3,781	
223,518		
IT Liability	89,091	

(1) Beneficial loan

 The benefit of the beneficial loan using the average method is £1,733
 ((70,000 + 60,000)/2 = 65,000 at 4% x 8/12).

 Using the strict method the benefit is £1,733
 ((70,000 at 4% x 4/12= £933) + (60,000 at 4% x 4/12= 800)).

 Therefore, either method will produce the same result.

(2) Company car benefit

 List price is £89,000 less the capital contributions of £4,000 = £85,000
 CO_2 % = [18% + (190 – 125)/5] = 31%

 Benefit = £85,000 x 31% = £26,350

(3) Fuel benefit is £18,800 x 31% = £5,828

Tutorial notes:

The bonus will have been treated as being received during 2011/12 as James became entitled to it during that tax year (earlier than receipt).

London
School of Business
& Finance

shaping success in business and finance

4

Employment
Income
Deductions and
PAYE

Context

In the previous chapter, we looked at the calculation of employment income including salary, bonus and benefits in kind. To complete our employment income, there are also certain allowable expenses that can be deducted, which we will study in this chapter.

Also, it is important to be able to identify whether an individual is employed or self employed (i.e. a sole trader). This is because there are important differences between the calculation of employment income and trading income, as well as differences as to how the income tax is collected.

There are also different types of National Insurance Contributions payable, depending on whether you are employed or self employed. We will learn more about this in a later chapter.

The examiner expects students to be aware of the factors that determine when a person should be treated as employed or self employed.

Finally, we will look at the administrative aspects of having employees, known as the PAYE system.

Exam hints

Employment income is a very important topic for your exam and is likely to be tested in question one of the paper.

Employed versus self employed is the type of discussion topic that could come up on one of the smaller questions on the paper, such as question 4 or 5.

Key learning points

- There are a number of deductible expenses that reduce down employment income. These include contributions to an occupational pension scheme, donations via payroll giving scheme and certain travel expenses.

- If an employee uses their own car for business purposes then they are entitled to a mileage allowance. This may lead to a deduction from employment income.

- There are criteria that HMRC will use to determine if an individual is employed or self employed.

- The PAYE system is used to collect the income tax and national insurance contributions from employed individuals on a regular basis, and pay them over to HMRC.

Employment income recap

In the previous chapter we looked at the first part of the employment income working. That included the calculation of salary, bonus and benefits in kind.

In this chapter, we are going to look at the deductions that can be made from employment income:

Employment income

	£
Salary/bonus	X
Benefits	X
Reimbursed expenses	X̲
	X

Less allowable expenses:

•	Donation to charity under a payroll deduction scheme	(X)
•	Contributions to an occupational pension plan	(X)
•	Travel, subsistence and entertaining incurred wholly, exclusively and necessarily in the performance of the office or employment	(X)
•	Subscription to a professional body	(X)
•	Deficit on a mileage allowance	(X̲)
	Employment income	X̲

General rule for deducting expenses

The rules governing the amounts that may be deducted for tax purposes from remuneration subject to tax as employment income are extremely strict. To qualify for deduction, expenses must be incurred wholly, exclusively and necessarily by the employee for the performance of their duties of employment.

Considering each part of the statement...

Wholly, exclusively

The following are examples were expenses have not been deductible because they are not deemed to have been incurred wholly and exclusively

- Meal expenses paid out of meal allowances

- Cost of ordinary clothing

- Telephone rental installed for business reasons but in the employee's private residence

Necessarily

This situation arises most often where an employer reimburses an employee for certain costs. Once the employee is reimbursed, the expense should be reported on a PIId and the employee makes a claim for tax relief for the expense.

HMRC may seek to disallow the expense on the basis it was not necessary. The two main cases involve journalists and the claiming of expenses relating to newspapers and magazines. The journalists argued that the expenses were incurred as a necessary part of enabling them to perform their duties. HMRC argued that the reading of other newspapers and magazines was not necessary to perform the duties of a journalist.

The fact that the expenses had been reimbursed by the employer was of no relevance as to whether or not HMRC would argue that the expense was necessary.

In the performance of duties

The expense has to be incurred in the performance of the duties of the relevant employment. Examples where the courts have found against the taxpayer are:

* Expenditure by a Rugby league player on diet supplements in order to improve and maintain fitness

* Expenses incurred by a teacher at her home for preparation of lessons, marking, etc

* A headmaster's course to improve background knowledge

Expenses which are allowable

Certain expenditure is specifically deductible in the computation of taxable earnings i.e subscriptions to professional bodies, mileage allowance, contributions to occupational pension schemes and donations under a payroll giving scheme. These are covered in more detail below.

Donation to charity under payroll giving scheme

If an employee makes a donation to charity through the payroll giving scheme, the donation is deducted directly from employment income. This makes it a tax efficient way for an employee to donate to charity. For example, if an employee donates £100 to charity via the payroll giving scheme, then their employment income is reduced down by £100.

Contribution to an occupational pension scheme

If a person pays into an occupational pension plan, the employee's contribution is deducted from their employment income (see chapter 5 for more details)

Travel expenses

Where an employee commutes to work, the cost of this commuting, from home to their normal place of work, is not available for tax relief.

Tax relief is available where the employee has to travel further to a temporary place of work (a workplace which is not their normal workplace for a period up to 24 months in duration), than their normal place of work, in order to perform their duties of employment e.g. audit staff visiting client premises are allowed to claim the additional miles, over and above those in travelling to their office.

If the employee is a site–based employee, with no fixed normal place of work, the travel costs of all journeys made from home to work are available for tax relief, provided the assignment or place of work, does not last more than 24 months.

HOME

NOT ALLOWABLE   ALLOWABLE DEDUCTION

NORMAL PLACE OF WORK   SPECIAL PLACE OF WORK

ALLOWABLE DEDUCTION   Special place of work:
                                           Temporary work place
                                                (< 2years)
                                          Not normal work place e.g.
                                                  client

Subscriptions

If an employee pays a subscription to an approved professional body, then the subscription may be deducted from employment income, provided it is relevant to their employment.

Mileage allowance

Where an employee uses their own car to carry on their employer's business, then the employee is entitled to receive a mileage allowance from the employer to compensate him for the additional costs incurred in running the car.

The amount which can be received tax free is the amount set by HMRC and the amount is called the Authorised Mileage Allowance Payment (AMAP).

First 10,000 business miles   45p per mile
Excess over 10,000   25p per mile

Where the employer pays an amount less than the AMAP limits, the employee is entitled to claim tax relief (from HMRC) on the difference.

Conversely, where an employer pays more than the AMAP limits, the excess is subject to income tax on the employee.

The employer may also pay a tax free mileage allowance of up to 5p per mile for each passenger carried on the employer's business. If less than this amount is paid the employee may not claim tax relief for the shortfall.

The tax free mileage allowance for motor bikes is 24p per mile, and for bicycles 20p per mile.

NIC will also be due on any taxable element for payment in excess of AMAP limits. The NICs due are both employees and employers class 1.

Learning example 4.1

Katya has a salary of £30,000 and uses her own car for her employer's business and receives a mileage allowance of 50p per business mile.

Katya drives 13,000 business miles during the year 2011/12.

Required

(a)   Compute Katya's employment income for 2011/12.

(b)   Compute the employment income for 2011/12 if instead Katya received 30p per business mile.

Employed v self-employed

A worker's status affects both income tax and national insurance.

A worker who is considered to be employed will pay income tax on their receipts as earnings and is subject to class 1 national insurance contributions. Their employer is also expected to pay class 1 national insurance at 13.8% of earnings above an earnings limit. The income tax is paid under Pay As You Earn (PAYE) and is paid earlier than under self-employment.

A worker who is considered self-employed is taxed on their receipts as trading income and is subject to class 4 national insurance and voluntary class 2 national insurance payments. No employer's class 1 national insurance is due. Deductions for tax purposes for self employed worker's are more generous than for employed workers (wholly and exclusively rather than wholly, exclusively and necessarily in the course of duties). Income Tax and class 4 National Insurance payments are made under self-assessment and after the profits have been earned.

Employment is a contract of service while self employment is a contract for services.

Factors affecting employment or self-employment

It is not possible to elect to be self-employed. Whether a person is self-employed or employed is a matter of fact. Unfortunately, legislation does not define 'self-employment' and so the rules and their interpretation have evolved through the courts.

The distinction between employment and self-employment can be a fine one. Factors which may be of importance in deciding are:

(1) **Contract** – if there is a contract of services, this tends to suggest employment, whereas a contract for services suggests self employment.

(2) **Integral position** – if the individual holds an integral position within the organisation, e.g. chairman, he must be employed.

(3) **Risk** – Employees usually receive a regular wage or salary; they are paid whether or not their employer is making a profit and do not risk their own capital in the business. Self employed people are normally paid a separate fee for each job they do; they may make losses as well as profits and may lose their capital if the business fails.

(4) **Control** – can the individual choose place of work, hours of work and method? If so he is likely to be self employed. Is he subject to direction of another person? Does a master/servant relationship exist? If so he is likely to be employed.

(5) **Legal rights** – liable to class 1 national insurance contributions or has the right to receive regular remuneration, holiday pay, redundancy pay or benefits, this can indicate employment rather than self employment.

(6) **Equipment/ Exclusivity** – In general, employees do not provide their own equipment but self employed do.

In general, an employee is employed by just one employer and is an integral part of that employer's business. Self-employed people normally have a number of clients and are not integral to any of their clients' businesses.

(7) **Substitute** – an employed person cannot provide a substitute worker to do the job.

Where a person works almost entirely for one organisation, there is a very strong argument for treating this person as employed.

HMRC will not consider only one factor in making an assessment of whether an individual is employed or self employed.

This can be remembered by the mnemonic: CIRCLES

Summary of implications

	Employed	**Self-employed**
Type of income	Employment income	Trading income
Basis of assessment	Receipts basis	Current year basis, with special rules in opening and closing years
Income assessed	Earnings received from the employment including taxable benefits	All trading profits including adjustments for private use
Allowable expenses	Wholly, exclusively and necessarily incurred in the performance of the duties of the employment	Wholly and exclusively incurred for the purposes of the trade
NIC	Class 1 primary	Class 2 and Class 4
Payment of IT and NIC	Monthly via PAYE system	Self assessment for IT and Class 4 NICs-payments on account and balancing payment Class 2 NICs – by two equal instalments payable by 31 January during the tax year and 31 July following the tax year

The PAYE system

Sugar   Hi! Branson why are you looking so sad?

Branson   I've started a business recently and I don't understand the PAYE system!

Sugar   Don't be upset! I'll explain it to you. It's really quite simple. Employers are actually unpaid tax collectors of HMRC. Before paying their employees' salaries they have to deduct tax and National Insurance and then pay the net salaries to the employees.

Branson   But how much tax and National Insurance will I have to deduct?

Sugar   PAYE works on a cumulative basis. HMRC gives employers tax and national insurance tables (Tables A-D) which allow you to work out the relevant calculations based on the salaries. You record your calculations on deduction working sheets called P11s.

    The tables also enable you to work out your employer's national insurance that you have to pay over to HMRC. Don't forget the total tax and National Insurance must be paid over to HMRC 14 days after the end of the tax month, i.e. the 19th.

Branson   I'm also confused about these tax-free allowances that employees are entitled to.

Sugar   Well, every tax year HMRC will send you a code for each employee on a form called a P9. The most common coding is L – which indicates the employee is entitled to the basic personal allowance of £7,475.

    Codings are also used cumulatively so every month the employee gets 1/12 of his allowances, which reduces his taxable income. In certain cases where the employee receives large benefits in kind he could have a K code which is a negative allowance and will increase his taxable income.

Branson   I think I'm beginning to understand the system. So as long as I carry out the monthly procedures I should be okay!

Sugar   Not so fast! During the year one of your employees could decide to leave. You would then have to fill in a P45 showing the total tax and pay to date and the code number used. Three copies of the P45 are given to the employee: two parts pass on to his new employer and one copy for himself. The old

London
School of Business
& Finance

shaping success in business and finance

employer sends a copy to HMRC. If a new employee does not have a P45 you have to make sure he fills in a P46 which will enable you to deduct tax on a cumulative basis right away.

Branson   That sounds quite straightforward! I hope that's all there is as I'm beginning to get hungry!

Sugar   All you think of is food, my friend! Finally, you have to do your year end returns. You have to fill in a P60 for each employee showing his total pay, tax and National Insurance for the tax year. A copy of this form, a P60, is given to each employee by 31 May following the end of the fiscal year. These details are then further summarised on a P35 which shows the total tax and National Insurance for your business. You have to send these forms to HMRC by the 19th May following the end of the fiscal year. Don't forget to submit your PIIDs showing any benefits in kind for directors and employees earning more than £8,500 pa a bit later on the 6th July. Class IA NIC on all taxable benefits is payable on the 19th July following the tax year.

Branson   My tummy is rumbling now, Sugar! You've been so helpful, why don't you join me for something sweet.

Sugar   Sounds irresistible! Let's go!

Important dates for PAYE system

All employers are required to operate PAYE and NIC and make deductions for these from employees' pay.

Whilst the basic operation of this system is for you to self-study, please ensure you are aware of the following forms:

P35   Employers' end of year summary.

P14/P60   Given to each employee listing gross pay, tax deducted and NIC for the year. The P60 must be given to the employee by **31 May 2012 for 2011/12**.

P9D   Return of taxable benefits for employees earning below £8,500.

PIID   Return of taxable benefits for directors and higher paid employees. The PIID must be given to the employee by **6 July 2012 for 2011/12**.

P45   Given to employee on leaving employment.

Learning summary

- Employment involves a contract of services, whereas self-employment is a contract for services.

- Many factors influence whether an individual is deemed employed or self-employed. The strength of each factor depends on upon the case.

• Income tax from employment is collected under the PAYE system.

Exam standard question

George is employed by Loggia Ltd. The company pays George a salary of £50,000 for the tax year ended 5 April 2012.

In addition to this, the company also provides George with the benefit of living in the company's house and George has lived there since 6 September 2011. The property was purchased on 1 January 2007 for £350,000 and the company has spent £40,000 on an extension and conservatory during April 2009. A further £4,000 was spent on building a garage at the property in October 2011 after George had moved in.

The value of the property on 6 September 2011 was £400,000 and it has an annual value of £8,000 per annum. George pays Loggia Ltd £500 per month in rent for the property.

Furniture in the property cost £5,600 during August 2011 and the company has also agreed to pay £400 towards the utility bills for the period 6 September to 5 April 2012.

Required

(a) Calculate the benefits that will be taxable on George for the year ended 5 April 2012.

(b) State the date by which George should receive the form P11D, detailing the benefits.

(c) State the criteria that must be met for the provision of accommodation to be defined as job related accommodation and state the tax effect, should this provision be deemed to be job related accommodation.

George has indicated to you that although he will be including his salary details on his self assessment tax return, he will not be declaring his benefits.

(d) Briefly explain from an ethical viewpoint how you, as a trainee Chartered Certified Accountant, should deal with this suggestion from George that no disclosure is made to HMRC of his benefits.

Learning solution 4.1

(a)

	£	£
(1) Salary		30,000
(2) Bonus		Nil
(3) Benefits		
Mileage allowance received (50p x 13,000)	6,500	
Less: AMAP (10,000 x 45p)	(4,500)	
(3,000 x 25p)	(750)	
Mileage allowance benefit		1,250
		31,250

(b)

	£	£
(1) Salary		30,000
(2) Bonus		Nil
(3) Benefits		
Mileage allowance received (30p x 13,000)	3,900	
Less: AMAP (10,000 x 45p)	(4,500)	
(3,000 x 25p)	(750)	

Mileage allowance deficit		(1,350)
Employment income		28,650

Solution to exam standard question

(a) Benefits:	£	£
Accommodation		
Annual value of the property	8,000	
Additional cost:		
£[(350,000 + 40,000) − 75,000] × 4%	12,600	
	20,600	
Pro rate for the time lived there		
X 7/12 =		12,017
Less rent paid by George (£500 × 7)		(3,500)
Taxable benefit		8,517
Use of furniture £5,600 × 20% × 7/12		653
Running costs paid by Loggia Ltd		400

(b)   The PII D should be provided to George by the employer by 6 July 2012.

(c)   Job related accommodation must be provided for one of the following reasons:

- Where it is necessary for the proper performance of the employee's duties.

- Where is will enable the better performance of the employee's duties.

- Where there is a special threat to the employee's security.

The impact of the accommodation being JRA, is the benefit of the accommodation is not taxable. The use of the assets and the running costs, however, are still assessable although the benefit valuation for this will be limited to 10% of the net remuneration of the employee.

(d)   The matter is one of professional judgement, and a trainee Chartered Certified Accountant would be expected to act honestly and with integrity.

George should therefore be advised to disclose details of the benefits to HMRC.

If such disclosure is not made the Certified Accountant would be obliged to report under the money laundering regulations, and also consider ceasing to act for George.

In these circumstances the Certified Accountant would be advised to notify HMRC that he no longer acts for George although the Accountant would not need to provide any reason for this.

5

Pensions

Context

If a person pays into a registered pension plan, this will reduce their income tax payable. It is a tax efficient way of saving for the future.

For the purposes of the exam, you will need to be able to compute the tax relief that is given when an individual pays into a pension, as well as the implications when the pension is used to provide income in the future.

Exam hints

Pensions could be included in the exam in one of two ways. Most likely, you will be dealing with the computational aspect, giving the individual tax relief in the income tax computation. You may find however, that the examiner could ask you to give written tax advice to an individual who is thinking of making payments into a pension scheme, explaining the tax implications of such a payment

Key learning points

- There are two types of pension schemes: personal pension schemes (PPS) and occupational pension schemes (OPS).

- The maximum gross contribution eligible for tax relief is the higher of 100% x UK relevant earnings and the basic amount of £3,600.

- The method of giving tax relief depends of the type of pension that you are paying into. For a PPS, tax relief is given through the extension of the basic rate band. For OPS, tax relief is given by making a deduction from employment income.

- There is a maximum input into a pension in the tax year. This is known as the annual allowance. There are tax consequences if this is exceeded.

- There is also a maximum input into a pension over the individual's lifetime. This is known as the lifetime allowance and there are tax consequences if it is exceeded.

Types of pensions

There are two types of pensions that an individual may decide to pay into. These are:

Personal Pension Scheme (PPS)

Anyone can have a personal pension scheme e.g. sole trader, employee, non-worker. Contributions to the PPS can be made by the individual and any other third party.

Occupation Pension Scheme (OPS)

Occupational pensions are only available to employees, as they are set up by their employer. Contributions to the OPS can be made by both the employee and the employer.

Contribution to pension schemes

An individual can make contributions of up to the higher of £3,600 and his relevant earnings (employment income, trading income and income from furnished holiday accommodation) for the tax year. Any contributions to a personal pension plan are made net of basic rate tax (20%). To qualify for tax relief, the individual must be under the age of 75.

Non-taxpayers can contribute £2,880 in any one year and receive tax relief of £720, giving a total pension saving with tax relief of £3,600 gross per annum.

Therefore, the maximum gross contribution eligible for tax relief is the HIGHER of:

100% x UK relevant earnings   The basic amount £3,600

UK relevant earnings:

	£
Trading income	x
Employment income	x
Income from furnished holiday lettings	x
	x

Learning example 5.1

Humera has made a gross contribution to her pension scheme during the year of £15,000. She has UK relevant earnings of £45,000 and joined the pension scheme on 6 April 2011.

Sid has made a gross contribution to his pension scheme during the year of £20,000. He has UK relevant earnings of £10,000 and joined the pension scheme on 6 April 2011.

Required

What is the maximum amount of tax relief available for the pension contributions made by Humera and Sid?

Giving tax relief on contributions

Personal pension scheme (PPS)

If a person pays into a personal pension plan the payment is treated as if it were made net of 20% income tax and the pension plan can then recover the amount of tax which is deemed to have been deducted at source from HMRC.

HMRC will then top up the PPS, by paying the 20% directly to the pension provider.

This is also known as "relief given at source"

Impact on IT computation of individual:

Basic rate tax payer: There is no impact on the IT computation

Higher or additional rate tax payer: The donor's basic rate and higher rate band is extended by the gross contribution (amount paid x 100/80) of the contribution. (i.e. the same way as gift aid donations)

This extension ensures that relief at the higher or additional rate is automatically given to higher or additional rate taxpayers.

Learning example 5.2

Harpal has employment income of £65,000 and makes a contribution to his personal pension scheme of £9,800 (net).

He has no other income in the tax year.

Required

How much does the pension fund receive? Calculate his income tax liability for 2011/12.

Occupation pension plan (OPS)

If a person pays into an occupational pension plan, the employee's contribution is deducted from their employment income. These payments are deemed to be the gross payment.

There is no further top up from HMRC

This is also known as "net pay arrangements"

Learning example 5.3

Terry has employment income of £34,500 and makes a contribution to his occupational pension scheme of £5,600

He has no other income in the tax year.

Required

How much does the pension fund receive? Calculate his income tax liability for 2011/12.

Employer's contributions

If the employer contributes to a pension scheme, the employer contributions are an exempt benefit for the employee. The contribution is also an allowable deduction for the employer

Annual Allowance

The total contributions into a pension scheme for a tax year are limited to the annual allowance. For 2011/12, the annual allowance is £50,000.

If the annual allowance is not fully used in any tax year it is now possible to carry forward any unused allowance for up to three tax years. However, a carry forward is only possible if a person is a member of a pension scheme for a particular year. Therefore, in any tax year, when a person is not a member of a pension scheme, the annual allowance will be lost. The new rules apply from 6 April 2011, however a notional £50,000 limit is used for three years prior to the 2011/12 tax year to ascertain any brought forward figure.

Learning example 5.4

Basil and Cybil have made the following gross personal pension contributions during the tax years 2008/09, 2009/10 and 2010/11:

	Basil	Cybil
	£	£
2008/09	56,000	42,000
2009/10	31,000	Nil
2010/11	Nil	38,000

Basil was not a member of a pension scheme for the tax year 2010/11 and Cybil was not a member of a pension scheme for the tax year 2009/10.

Required

What are the unused allowances brought forward for each of them into the tax year 2011/12?

Where contributions into the pension scheme exceed the annual allowance, there is an income tax charge on the individual at the individual's marginal rate.

Learning example 5.5

For the tax year 2011/12 Mary has trading profit of £240,000, and made gross personal pension contributions of £75,000. She does not have any brought forward unused annual allowances.

Required

What is Mary's income tax liability for 2011/12?

Lifetime Allowance

An individual can accrue a maximum tax free pension fund value during their lifetime. This is known as the lifetime allowance and for 2011/12, this is £1,800,000.

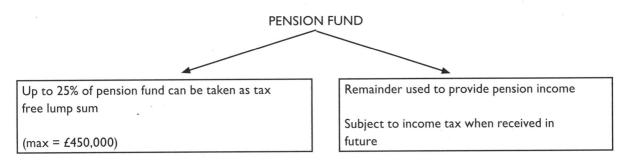

The lifetime allowance is only relevant when the individual takes either a lump sum or becomes entitled to a pension scheme.

The lifetime allowance applies to everyone irrespective of the type of scheme to which they belong. For a defined benefit scheme, a calculation factor of 20:1 is required to establish an individual's entitlement. This means that a final salary pension which pays £75,000 per annum is deemed to have a value of £1,500,000.

A pension payment can only be made to a person under the age of 55 if the member is incapacitated by ill health. Up until the age of 75, an individual can take either a lump sum and regular payments, regular payments, or no pension at all.

Up to 25% of the pension fund can be taken as a tax-free lump sum, subject to the lifetime allowance. The remainder is used to fund a regular pension income.

If the lifetime allowance is exceeded on the value of the pension fund to vest in a lump sum, a tax charge of 55% is levied on the value of the pension fund vested in excess of the lifetime allowance.

Where excess funds are used to vest to provide a pension income, the rate of income tax is 25%.

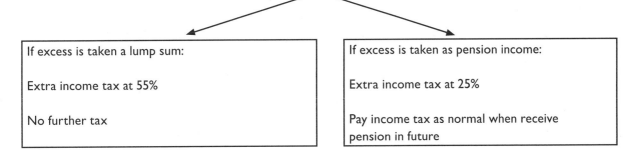

Learning summary

- Payments into a personal pension scheme attract tax relief at the basic rate. Where the individual is a higher or additional rate taxpayer, the basic rate band is extended by the level of pension contributions.

- Individuals can pay the lower of £3,600 and their relevant earnings up to a maximum of £50,000 into their pension each tax year. This is known as the annual allowance.

- Non-taxpayers are entitled to pay £2,880 into a pension scheme in any tax year.

- The maximum value of a pension before it becomes taxable is £1,800,000.

Exam standard question

You are a trainee accountant and your manager has asked for your help regarding two taxpayers who have all made personal pension contributions during the tax year 2011/12.

Merry

Merry, aged 30, is self employed as an estate agent. Her trading profits and pension contributions are as follows:

	Trading profit	Pension contributions (gross)
	£	£
2008/09	60,000	25,000
2009/10	62,000	25,000
2010/11	80,000	50,000
2011/12	105,000	80,000

Pippa

Pippa, aged 54, is self employed as a dentist. Her trading profit and pension contributions are as follows:

	Trading profit	Pension contributions (gross)
	£	£
2008/09	110,000	45,000
2009/10	150,000	45,000
2010/11	160,000	50,000
2011/12	190,000	70,000

Required

For each of the two taxpayers, calculate their income tax liabilities for 2011/12.

Learning solution 5.1

Humera

The maximum gross contribution eligible for tax relief is the HIGHER of:

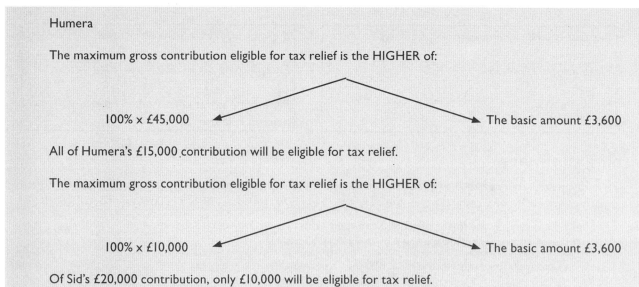

100% x £45,000   The basic amount £3,600

All of Humera's £15,000 contribution will be eligible for tax relief.

The maximum gross contribution eligible for tax relief is the HIGHER of:

100% x £10,000   The basic amount £3,600

Of Sid's £20,000 contribution, only £10,000 will be eligible for tax relief.

London
School of Business
& Finance

shaping success in business and finance

Learning solution 5.2

The pension fund will receive:

	£
From Harpal:	9,800 (net of 20%)
From HMRC:	2,450 (top up with 20%)
	12,250

Harpal 2011/12

	£	£
Employment income		65,000
Less PA		(7,475)
Taxable income		57,525 (all non savings income)
Income tax:		
Basic rate band (W)	47,250 x 20% = 9,450	
Higher rate band	10,275 x 40% = 4,110	
	57,525	
IT liability		13,560

(W) Basic rate band extension

35,000 + (100/80 x 9,800) = £47,250

Learning solution 5.3

The pension fund will receive:

From Terry:	5,600 (gross)

Terry 2011/12

	£
Employment income (W)	28,900
Less PA	(7,475)
Taxable income	21,425 (all non savings income)
Income tax:	
Basic rate band £21,425 x 20% =	4,285
IT liability	4,285

(W) Employment income

	£
Salary	34,500
Less contribution to OPS	(5,600)
Employment income	28,900

Learning solution 5.4

Unused allowances brought forward are as follows:

Basil	Contribution	Allowance	Unused to carry forward
	£	£	£
2008/09	56,000	50,000	Nil
2009/10	31,000	50,000	19,000
2010/11	Nil	Nil (not a member)	Nil
Unused c/f			19,000

Cybil	Contribution	Allowance	Unused to carry forward
	£	£	£
2008/09	42,000	50,000	8,000
2009/10	Nil	Nil (not a member)	Nil
2010/11	38,000	50,000	12,000
Unused c/f			21,000

Learning solution 5.5

Mary 2011/12

	£
Trading profit	240,000
Annual allowance charge (W1)	25,000
Less PA (W2)	(Nil)
Taxable income	265,000 (all non savings income)

Income Tax		£
Basic rate (W3)	110,000 x 20%	22,000
Higher rate (W4)	115,000 x 40%	46,000
	225,000	
Additional rate	40,000 x 50%	20,000
	265,000	
IT Liability		88,000

(W1) Annual allowance charge

	£
Contribution	75,000
Annual allowance	(50,000)
Annual allowance charge	25,000

(W2) There is no personal allowance as adjusted net income = £190,000 (265,000 - 75,000) which exceeds £114,950.

(W3) Basic rate band

The basic rate band will be extended by the gross personal pension contributions to £110,000 (35,000 + 75,000)

(W4) Higher rate band

The higher rate band is extended to £225,000 (150,000 + 75,000).

London
School of Business
& Finance

shaping success in business and finance

Solution to exam standard question

Merry – Income tax computation 2011/12

		£
Trading profit		105,000
Annual allowance charge (W1)		Nil
		105,000
Less PA (W2)		(7,475)
Taxable income		97,525
Income tax:		
Basic rate (W3)	£97,525 x 20%	19,505

(W1) Annual allowance charge	£	£
Unused allowance b/f		
2008/09	50,000-25,000	25,000
2009/10	50,000-25,000	25,000
2010/11	50,000-50,000	Nil
B/f		50,000
Add allowance for 2011/12		50,000
Total allowance for 2011/12		100,000

Contributions < £100,000 so no allowance charge

(W2) PA
Adjusted net income = £25,000 (105,000 – 80,000) so PA in full

(W3) Basic rate band
Extended Basic rate band = £115,000 (35,000 + 80,000)

Pippa – Income tax computation 2011/12

		£
Trading profit		190,000
Annual allowance charge (W1)		10,000
		200,000
Less PA (W2)		(Nil)
Taxable income		200,000
Income tax:		
Basic rate (W3)	£105,000 x 20%	21,000
Higher rate (W4)	£95,000 x 40%	38,000
Income tax liability		59,000

(W1) Annual allowance charge	£	£
Unused allowance b/f		
2008/09	50,000-45,000	5,000
2009/10	50,000-45,000	5,000
2010/11	50,000-50,000	Nil
B/f		10,000
Add allowance for 2011/12		50,000
Total allowance for 2011/12		60,000

Contributions £70,000
Annual allowance charge = £10,000 (70,000 – 60,000)

(W2) PA
Adjusted net income = £130,000 (200,000 – 70,000)
  ➤ £114,950 so no PA

(W3) Basic rate band
Extended Basic rate band = £105,000 (35,000 + 70,000)

(W4) Higher rate band
Extended higher rate band = £220,000 (150,000 + 70,000)

6

Property Income

Context

This chapter deals with rental income from land or property in the United Kingdom or technically, property business profits. This chapter should highlight the differences between rental profits for companies and for individuals.

One of the main areas where they differ is in connection with losses. Companies can relieve property business losses against total profits of the loss making CAP and then against total profits of future CAPs but normally individuals carry forward these losses and offset them against the first available future property business profits or profits on furnished holiday letting properties.

The chapter covers the basic computational issues and assessment of such income, including the treatment of premiums granted or received on short leases, and the special rules for furnished holiday lettings and rent-a-room relief.

Exam hints

The property income calculation will form part of the income tax question on the paper. You may be asked to calculate the property income for an individual for the tax year, which will then feed through into the main income tax computation.

Property income is classified as non savings income in the income tax computation.

Key learning points

- Property income is calculated on an accruals basis. It is calculated by taking the accrued rental income for the tax year and deducting accrued allowable expenses for the tax year.

- If an individual has a property income loss for the tax year, this is carried forward against property income in future tax years.

- If an individual rents out a furnished room in their own home, they are eligible for rent a room relief of £4,250.

- Special rules apply to furnished holiday lettings.

- Property income also includes premiums from a short lease. You need to able to calculate how much of the lease premium will be classified as property income and will be included in the income tax computation.

Calculation of property income

All rental income received by an individual from UK properties is assessed under s264 IT(T&OI)A 2005, whether the property is let as furnished or unfurnished.

The income from a UK property business is determined using normal accountancy principles. Income is accounted for on a receivable basis i.e. include the proportion of rent earned in the year from the tenants use of the property in that year. An adjustment will be required where rent is receivable in advance or arrears.

Expenses are allowed to the extent that they are incurred wholly and exclusively for business purposes and this rule applies to interest just as for any other expense.

Income from a UK property business is assessed on a tax year basis and is taxed as non-savings income.

Where more than one property is held, the rents and expenses for all properties are pooled to give a single profit or loss.

	£
Rent receivable in the tax year (accrued)	X
Less allowable expenses (accrued)	(X)
Property income/(loss)	X/(X)

Allowable expenses

These are expenses incurred by the landlord and reduce the property income. Allowable expenses include:

- repairs;

- decorating;

- council tax and water rates

- insurance premiums payable in the fiscal year;

- irrecoverable debts;

- advertising costs;

- cost of replacing the windows and boiler;

- interest payable on a loan to buy or improve a property;

- premiums paid (see more later)

- wear and tear allowance if landlord has furnished the property:

> wear and tear allowance calculation:
>
> 10% x {rent − (water rates and council tax paid by landlord)}

Note, that any substantial repairs carried out shortly after the landlord has acquired a property to put it in a fit state are generally disallowed as constituting capital expenditure. These costs would then be treated as enhancement costs for CGT purposes.

London
School of Business
& Finance
shaping success in business and finance

Legal fees are generally disallowed. However, there are some cases where the deduction is allowable namely:

* granting of a lease of < 1 year;

* renewal of lease provided it is < 50 years in length;

* fees incurred in evicting a tenant, appealing against a compulsory purchase order or in drawing up accounts/tax returns

Capital allowances are given on plant and machinery used in a UK property business in the same way as they are for a trading business, although they are not normally given on plant and machinery used in a dwelling. However, if the plant and machinery is used partly in a dwelling and partly for other purposes, a just and reasonable apportionment of the expenditure can be made.

Disallowable expenses

These are expenses not incurred wholly and exclusively by the landlord for business purposes and they will not reduce the taxable property business profits. Disallowable expenses include:

* Cost of furniture (this is capital expenditure)

* Cost of capital improvements;

* Personal use of expenses.

Learning example 6.1

Nathan owns two properties in School Lane. Details of income and expenditure in respect of each in 2011/12 are as follows:

No 12: An unfurnished house which was rented for £1,200 per month, payable monthly in advance until 31 January 2012. The tenant left owing two months rent which Nathan was unable to recover. The property remained empty until 1 April 2012 when it was rented for £1,250 per month, payable quarterly in advance. Allowable expenses amounted to £1,750.

No 17: A furnished house which Nathan acquired on 1 September 2011 He paid mortgage interest of £200 per month on a loan which he took out to acquire the property. On 1 September 2011 Nathan incurred advertising fees of £650 and paid an insurance premium of £400 for the year to 31 August 2012. He paid decorating costs of £1,200 on 15 September 2011. The house remained empty until 1 November 2011 when it was rented for £600 per month, payable monthly in advance.

Required

Calculate Nathan's property income assessment for 2011/12.

Property income losses

If an individual lets out properties and the allowable expenses are greater than the rent receivable, the individual makes a property income loss.

If this is the case, the property income figure in the income tax computation is NIL. There is no property income in the tax year.

The property income losses can be carried forward and offset against the first available property income in the future.

Learning example 6.2

Hitesh owns two flats which he rents out to tenants. The rental income and expenses for each flat are as follows:

	Income £	Expenses £
Flat 1	10,000	4,000
Flat 2	4,000	5,500

He has a property income loss brought forward of £3,500.

Required

Calculate Hitesh's property income assessment for 2011/12.

London
School of Business
& Finance
shaping success in business and finance

Rent a room relief (RARR)

Special relief is available to an individual who receives payment for letting furnished accommodation in a qualifying residence. A qualifying residence is a residence that is the individual's only or main residence at some time in the basis period for the tax year of assessment in relation to the lettings.

Availability of relief

Rent-a-room relief is available automatically where the gross sums received (before expenses or capital allowances) do not exceed £ 4,250 per tax year. This limit is reduced to £2,125 if during the same basis period someone else received income from letting accommodation in the same property. The rent-a-room relief limits are not pro-rated within a tax year i.e. where a room is let in say December 2011, the full relief of £4,250 (or £2,125 if applicable) will be available for tax year 2011/12.

Where the rents are within these limits, they are wholly exempt from income tax and any expenses (including capital allowances) are ignored. Losses cannot be created under the Rent-a-room scheme.

However, a taxpayer can claim to ignore Rent-a-room relief where a loss has been made (expenses greater than rental income).

Where the gross sums received exceed £ 4,250 per tax year (or £ 2,125 if applicable), the taxpayer can choose between paying tax on:

- The actual profit (gross rents minus actual expenses and capital allowances), or

- Gross receipts (and any balancing charges) minus £ 4,250 (or £ 2,125 if applicable) – with no deduction for expenses or capital allowances.

The second option is known as the 'alternative basis'.

An election to be taxed under the 'alternative basis' or to ignore the rent-a-room relief, must be made by the 31 January, which is 22 months from the end of the tax year concerned (2011/12 = 31.1.2014).

Method 1: use RARR

	£
Rent receivable	X
Less: Rent a room relief	(4,250)
Property income (RARR cannot create a loss)	X/Nil

Method 2: normal calculation

	£
Rent receivable	X
Less: Allowable expenses	(X)
Property income/(loss)	X/(X)

Worked example

A landlord lets out a furnished room in their own home for £100 per week. Calculate their property income for 2011/12 assuming they take RARR.

	£
Rental income (100 x 52)	5,200
Less RARR	(4,250)
Property income	950

A landlord lets out a furnished room in their own home for £250 per month. Calculate their property income for 2011/12 assuming they take RARR

	£
Rental income (250 x 12)	3,000
Less RARR	(4,250)
Property income	nil

Choice of method

- If rental income ≤ £4,250, RARR is automatic. Can elect to use normal method instead. Would do so to generate a loss

- If rental income > £4,250, normal method is automatic. Can elect to use RARR instead. Would do so if expenses < £4,250

Learning example 6.3

Chris rents out a furnished room in his own home and receives rental income of £5,200 for the tax year. He has expenses in connection with the room totalling £2,500.

Required

Should Chris make the election to claim rent a room relief?

Furnished holiday lettings (FHLA)

Definition and conditions

Where a person lets FHLA (including caravans), it may be treated as a trade provided certain conditions are satisfied:

- The property must be situated in the UK or the European Economic Area.

- It must be let on a commercial basis with a view to the realisation of a profit.

- It must be let as furnished accommodation.

- It must be available for commercial letting to the public as holiday accommodation for at least 20 weeks (140 days) in a 12-month period – the availability condition

- It must be let for at least 70 days in a 12-month period – the letting condition

- It must not normally be occupied by the same person for more than 31 consecutive days at any time during a 7-month period within the 12-month period – the pattern of occupation condition

Consequences of an investment property meeting the conditions

A FHLA is treated as a trade, and subsequently is taxed in a different way from other business properties – these differences are highlighted below.

Relief for interest

Interest on loans used to purchase the FHLA should qualify as an expense incurred in the trade. In some cases, the inclusion of such interest will give rise to a loss for tax purposes.

Capital allowances

Capital allowances may be available on equipment, furniture and fittings.

Relief for losses

Relief can be gained for losses by carrying forward against the individual's future profits from furnished holiday lettings.

Profits classed as earned income

Profits arising from a FHLA are treated as earned income, meaning that it qualifies as relevant earnings for pension purposes.

Lease premiums

When an individual grants (gives) a short lease (< 50 years) on a building, part of the premium received up front is subject to income tax in the tax year it is received.

Premiums are only received once, at the very start of the lease. It is subject to income tax in the tax year the premium is received by the landlord.

Tax treatment of the lease premium

The lease premium is treated as follows for tax purposes:

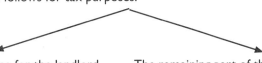

Part is taxed as property income for the landlord in the year the lease is granted	The remaining part of the premium becomes proceeds in a gain calculation
You MUST be able to calculate this for the purposes of your F6 exam	This calculation is NOT required for the F6 paper

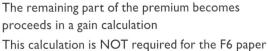

Amount of lease premium assessable as property income is:

	£
Lease premium	x
Less 2% x (years on lease – 1) x premium	(x)
Premium taxed as property income for landlord	x

Worked example

Tom received a premium of £14,700 for a 9 year lease on the offices on the 1st June 2011 from his tenant.

What will Tom's property income be in 2011/12?

Amount of lease premium assessable as property income is:

	£
Lease premium	14,700
Less 2% x (years on lease – 1) x premium:	
2% x (9-1) x 14,700	(2,352)
Premium taxed as property income for landlord 2011/12	12,348

Learning example 6.4

Henry rents out a retail shop for £1,000 per month payable quarterly in advance. On 1 January 2012 the tenant left the property and on 1 March 2012 Henry granted a 10 year lease to a new tenant for a premium of £12,000 and a monthly rent of £450 payable quarterly in advance.

Required

Calculate Henry's property income assessment for 2011/12.

Implications for the tenant paying the lease premium

The tenant that pays the lease premium can get a deduction from trading profits and treat some of the premium as rent expense:

$$\frac{\text{property income for landlord}}{\text{no of years of lease}} = \text{deduction from trading profits p.a.}$$

Worked example

Tom received a premium of £14,700 for a 9 year lease on the offices on the 1st June 2011 from his tenant.

What would be the annual deduction from trading profits for the tenant in respect of the premium?

In our previous worked example, we calculated that Tom, the landlord, would have a property income figure in respect of the premium of £12,348. This would all be taxed in 2011/12, the year the lease is granted.

The tenant who pays the lease premium to Tom can also get a deduction from trading profits by treating some of the premium as rent expense:

$$\frac{12,348}{9} = 1,372$$

The tenant paying the premium to Tom will be entitled to a deduction from trading profits of £1,372 each year over the life of the lease.

Learning summary

- Property income is computed for a tax year on the accruals basis.
- Losses arising on a property business can be aggregated against profits from another property business, or carried forward for relief against future property business profits.
- Where a premium is received or given on the grant of a short lease, part of the premium is taxed as rent on the recipient. The tenant can deduct part of the premium each year as a deductible expense.
- Rent-a-room relief is available where gross rents for the tax year do not exceed £4,250.
- Special rules exist where the property qualifies as a furnished holiday lettings.

Learning solution 6.1

Property		£	£
No 12	Rent: 10 x £1,200	12,000	
	Bad debt	(2,400)	
	Allowable expenses	(1,750)	
			7,850
No 17	Rent: 5 x £600	3,000	
	Mortgage interest £200 x 7	(1,400)	
	Advertising	(650)	
	Insurance £400 x 7/12	(233)	
	Decoration	(1,200)	
	Wear & tear allowance (10% x £3,000)	(300)	
			(783)
Property income 2011/12			7,067

London School of Business & Finance
shaping success in business and finance

Learning solution 6.2

Flat 1

	£	£
Rental income	10,000	
Expenses	(4,000)	
		6,000

Flat 2

	£	£
Rental income	4,000	
Expenses	(5,500)	
		(1,500)
		4,500
Less: Property loss b/f		(3,500)
Property income 2011/12		1,000

Learning solution 6.3

Method 1: use RARR	£	Method 2: normal calculation	£
Rent receivable	5,200	Rent receivable	5,200
Less: Rent a room relief	(4,250)	Less: Allowable expenses	(2,500)
Property income	950	Property income	2,700

Chris should claim the rent a room relief as this produces lower Property income for inclusion in his tax return.

Learning solution 6.4

Henry – Property income assessment 2011/12

	£	£	£
Rent: (9 x £1,000) + £450		9,450	
Lease premium:			
Premium	12,000		
Less: £12,000 x 2% x (10 – 1)	(2,160)		
		9,840	
Property income 2011/12			19,290

TAXATION

TAXATION

7

Trading Profits

Context

In order to understand income tax it is important to know what constitutes income. One type of income which is being studied in this chapter comes from running a business, this is trading profit.

Income tax computations are used to compute the total income tax payable by a person each tax year and are a very important area of the syllabus .They will always be tested in question one of the paper.

A person who has self employed income will pay income tax on their trading income.

Exam hints

In question 1 of the exam, you may have to calculate the trading profits for a sole trader. The areas covered in the following chapters are crucial in enabling you to calculate trading income correctly

Key learning points

- You may need to decide if an individual is trading or not. This will determine whether they pay income tax on their trading profits or capital gains tax on the profit.

- Accounting profits need to be adjusted to calculate tax adjusted profits. To do this, you will need to produce a working showing your adjustments to profit.

- The main adjustment to profit is to add back any disallowed expenses, such as depreciation.

- You may also need to adjust for stock drawings, income taxed elsewhere and deductible expenditure not included in the accounts.

Badges of trade

Badges of trade are tests used by HMRC to help them determine whether an individual is trading or not. The badges of trade help to decide how a transaction should be taxed. For example, imagine that an individual sells a clock. Does this constitute trading or not?

This decision has a big impact in terms of the tax the individual would pay. If HMRC decide it constitutes trading, the individual will pay income tax on their trading profits. If it is not trading, the individual will pay capital gains tax on the profit from the sale.

Badges of trade are tests that HMRC would look at to help them make a decision. This is very subjective, generally the more badges which are found to be present then the greater is the probability that a trade exists.

However in some cases the existence of only one badge can be sufficient, this was found to be the case in CIR v Rutledge. (You do not need to remember the case names for your exam)

The badges of trade are:

- Subject matter

- Length of period of ownership

- Frequency of similar operations

- Subsequent work (improvements)

- Circumstances (reason)

- Motive

Subject matter

HMRC will look at the subject matter of the transaction. There are a number of reasons for acquiring something:

- Buy for personal use and enjoyment (unlikely to be trading)

- Buy as an investment (unlikely to be trading)

- Buy for the purposes of making a profit (likely to be trading)

Length of period of ownership

Normally trading stock is held for a short period of time, i.e. rapid turnover. The shorter the period of ownership, the more likely it is to be trading.

Frequency of similar operations

The more often a deal takes place the greater the presumption that it is a disposal of trading stock. One off or infrequently sales are less likely to constitute trading.

Subsequent work (improvements)

Change of character of an asset is likely to be an indication of trading. For example, buying bulk and breaking down into smaller saleable units hence increasing profitability. Advertising and making the item more marketable may also indicate trading.

Circumstances (reason)

HMRC will also look at the reason behind the sale. For example, a sudden emergency for ready money (cash flow) can negate a presumption of trading.

Motive

Intention to trade is trading. Intention to make a profit is necessary for trading but a lack of profit will not necessarily negate trading.

Badges of trade can be remembered by the mnemonic **"SO FIRM"**:

Subject Matter
Ownership Length
Frequency of Transactions
Improvements
Reason
Motive

Calculation of Trading Profits

A sole trader pays income tax on his trading income but how is this trading income figure calculated?

To calculate trading profits, we start with the net profit from the sole trader's income statement. This net profit figure however, contains items that the tax man may not be happy with. For example some of the expenses that have been deducted from net profit are subjective, such as depreciation. Each sole trader can chose their own depreciation rate and this could be used to manipulate the profit figure, to try and pay less tax.

As a result, to calculate your trading profit, you must adjust your net accounting profit for any items that the tax man is not happy with.

Accounting profit	$\longrightarrow$	Trading profit

Calculation of tax adjusted trading profit

Tax computations start with 'net profit per income statement and are then adjusted for items specifically not allowed (for tax deduction) in legislation.

Accounts should be prepared on an accruals basis, rather than a receipts basis. The complexity of the accounts depends on the nature of the business.

Adjustment of Accounting Profit to Give Tax Adjusted Accounting Profit

	£	£
Net profit per income statement		X
Add:		
Expenditure charged in the accounts not allowed for tax purposes (disallowed items)	X	
Income taxable as trade profits but not credited to the accounts	X	
		X
Less:		
Profits included in the accounts not taxable as trade profits (e.g. bank interest receivable, dividends)	(X)	
Expenditure deductible for tax purposes but has not been charged in the accounts (e.g. capital allowances)	(X)	
		(X)
Trade profits adjusted for tax purposes		X

Disallowed expenses

Certain expenditure is disallowed through legislation and case law, although it may be acceptable to include the expense in calculating the accounting profits of the business. In these circumstances, the deduction is required to be 'added back' into the accounting profit. Chapter 18 contains a detailed review of the main items which, either through case law or legislation, are allowed or disallowed in calculating business profits for tax purposes. To introduce, the disallowed items are summarised below.

(1)   Expenses that are not wholly and exclusively incurred for trade.

(2)   Dual purpose expenses – if business and private elements can be split, allowed business element. You may need to apportion these in the exam

(3)   Withdrawals of profit by the owners of the business.

(4)   Depreciation and amortisation, profit or loss on disposal of a fixed asset

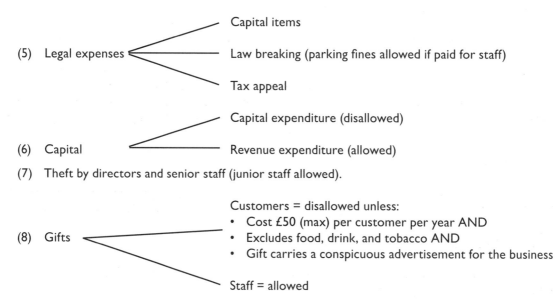

(5)   Legal expenses
- Capital items
- Law breaking (parking fines allowed if paid for staff)
- Tax appeal

(6)   Capital
- Capital expenditure (disallowed)
- Revenue expenditure (allowed)

(7)   Theft by directors and senior staff (junior staff allowed).

(8)   Gifts
- Customers = disallowed unless:
  - Cost £50 (max) per customer per year AND
  - Excludes food, drink, and tobacco AND
  - Gift carries a conspicuous advertisement for the business
- Staff = allowed

(9)   Loans to employees, customers and suppliers written off

(10) Charitable gifts under gift aid

(11) Donations to national charities and political parties (local charities allowed if there is a 'commercial purpose' for donation)

(12) Lease premiums (see more later)

(13) Hire car charges. Where the lease contract commenced after 1 April 2009, the amount disallowed is a flat 15% for cars with CO_2 emissions exceeding 160g/km hired for a period exceeding 45 days. The lease costs should exclude any maintenance charges but include the 50% VAT charge where the company is VAT registered. The restriction will not apply to the hire of low CO_2 emission cars or electric cars.

(14) Entertaining of customers/suppliers (entertaining of staff is however allowable provided it is not excessive).

Other adjustments to profit

Income taxed elsewhere

The income statement may contain income that does not relate to trade. You will need to remove this from your trading profits by DEDUCTING it in your adjustments to profit.

For example, the income statement may contain rental income. This is not to do with trade, so needs to the removed from trading profits and reclassified as property income in the main income tax computation.

Sole trader stock drawings

Where the sole trader has taken goods for their own use during the period of account, an adjustment to profits will be required. The nature of the adjustment depends on how the transaction was initially accounted for:

- If the goods have been adjusted for (the cost of the goods has been removed from cost of sales), add back the profit element

- If the goods have not been adjusted for, add back the selling price

Deductible expenditure not included in the accounts

Certain tax deductible expenses may not have been included in the accounts simply as they were paid personally by the sole trader. For example, a telephone bill may have been paid by the sole trader out of his personal bank account. Where this is a genuine business expense, it should be deducted as an allowable trade expense.

Pre-trading expenditure, is expenditure incurred in the seven years before the trade started and is treated as incurred on the day trade commenced. It is therefore treated as an allowable expense provided it would qualify as deductible under the normal rules for expenses.

Adjustments for lease premiums paid

The sole trader may pay a lease premium during the year. We studied lease premiums from the landlord's perspective in the property income chapter.

We are now going to think in more detail about the tenant that pays the lease premium to the landlord. In the property income chapter, we learnt that the tenant that pays the lease premium can get a deduction from trading profits and treat some of the premium as rent expense:

$$\frac{\text{property income for landlord}}{\text{no of years of lease}} = \text{deduction from trading profits p.a.}$$

In your adjustments to profit, you may therefore need to make the following adjustment:

- Add back the lease premium paid during the year (as you do not get a deduction for the full premium paid)

- Deduct the allowable amount for the year, calculated using the formula

$$\frac{\text{property income for landlord}}{\text{no of years of lease}} = \text{deduction from trading profits each year}$$

Worked example

Billy Bunter has decided to lease a shop for 10 years. To acquire the lease, Billy is required to pay a lease premium of £10,000. This lease premium is an upfront payment made to the owner of the shop. Billy is also charged annual rent by the owner.

The annual rent paid to the landlord is deductible from Billy's trading profits as an allowable expense. The lease premium is however, more difficult to deal with. To determine how much of the premium is an allowable deduction, a formula is used:

$$\frac{\text{property income for landlord}}{\text{no of years of lease}} = \text{deduction from trading profits each year}$$

Recap on calculating the property income for the landlord (from the property income chapter)

	£
Lease premium	x
Less 2% x (years on lease – 1) x premium	(x)
Premium taxed as property income for landlord	x

So in this case, the property income for the landlord would be:

	£
Premium	10,000
Less: 2% x (10 -1) x 10,000	(1,800)
Property income for landlord	8,200

For Billy, the deduction from his trading profits would be:

$$\frac{\text{property income for landlord}}{\text{no of years of lease}} = \text{deduction from trading profits each year}$$

8,200/10 = £820

Billy will be able to deduct £820 each year from his trading profits for 10 years.

London
School of Business
& Finance

shaping success in business and finance

Learning example 7.1

Cato has been in business for many years, preparing accounts to 30 September annually. His income statement for the year ended 30 September 2011 is as follows:

	£		£
		Gross profit b/f	40,409
Light and heat	885	Bank deposit interest	77
Office salaries	11,240	Dividends (net)	173
Repairs to premises (a)	2,670	Interest from National Savings Bank	20
Motor expenses (f)	1,200		
Depreciation			
Motor vans	1,250		
Equipment	920		
Rent and rates (g)	2,540		
Amortisation of lease (g)	200		
Loss on sale of equipment	160		
Impaired debts (b)	570		
Professional charges (c)	1,255		
Loan interest	450		
Sundry expenses (d)	1,590		
Salary			
Cato	5,000		
Wife, as secretary	2,450		
Net profit	8,299		
	40,679		40,679

The following information is given.

(a) Repairs to premises comprise:

	£
Installation of new covered walkway	2,000
Redecorations	670
	2,670

(b) Impaired debt

The figure of £570 for impaired debts includes a loan to an employee of £170, which was written off.

(c) Professional charges:

	£
Accountancy	500
Cost of action for contravening health and safety rules	450
Cost of tax appeal (successful)	220
Cost of renewing short lease	80
	1,250

(d)   Sundry expenses:

	£
Fine for contravening health and safety rules	250
Subscription to trade association	70
Donation to local hospice	25
Entertaining	
UK customers	120
Customers resident in France	300
Staff Christmas party – 25 staff	400
Diaries sent to 25 customers bearing firm's name	300
Miscellaneous allowable expenses	125
	1,590

(e)   During the year Cato had withdrawn goods from stock for his own consumption. The cost of this stock was £180. The business makes a uniform gross profit of 25% on selling price. No entry had been made in the books in respect of the goods taken.

(f)   Motor expenses include hire charges of £800 for a Ford Focus costing £15,000.The emissions value is 170g/km.

(g)   Rent includes a lease premium of £2,000 for a 10-year lease from 1 October 2010.

(h)   Capital allowances for the year ended 30 September 2011 are agreed at £1,200.

Required

Compute Cato's tax adjusted trading profit for the year ended 30 September 2011.

Learning summary

- In deciding whether or not a trade exists, the badges of trade can be used.

- Accounts profits are adjusted for a number of items in reaching taxable profits.

London
School of Business
& Finance
shaping success in business and finance

Exam standard question

Jasper Conran, a sole trader, has prepared draft accounts for the year ended 31 March 2012, which show a net profit of £42,000. He has written to you and extracts from his letter are as below:

(1) I have been paying myself a salary of £15,000 per year and Mrs Conran, who is the business secretary, a salary of £16,000. My other secretary doing the same job is paid £12,000 per year.

(2) During the year I took stock costing £500 that would normally be sold for £800. This has not been reflected in the accounts.

(3) I had to meet my bank manager, so I bought a suit, costing £300 and have included this in sundry expenses.

(4) The repairs include £20,000 for repair work to the roof of a workshop that I bought very cheap. I had to fix the roof before I could use the building.

(5) I spend £45 per head on a summer banquet for 12 members of staff. In addition, I gave 250 customers diaries costing £3 each, and for 25 selected customers, bottles of sherry costing £15 each at Christmas.

(6) Sundry expenses include:

	£
Parking fines paid on behalf of staff while on business	720
Subscriptions to Trade Association	150
Donation to National Charity	200
Donation to Labour Party	400

(7) Legal fees charged in the accounts include the following expenses:

	£
Defending action for defective goods	420
Defending breach of Trading Act: Verdict – Guilty	750
Bad debt recovery	1,740
Recovery of loans to employees	200
Renewal of short lease	500

(8) A machine costing £5,000 was purchased on 3 May 2011. Depreciation of £2,000 has been charged in the accounts. Capital allowances have been agreed at £5,000 for the year ended 31 March 2012.

(9) Sundry expenses include £500 relating to patent royalties paid in the period.

Required

(a) Draft notes in preparation for a meeting with Jasper responding to the points raised by him. Give full explanations to support your reasoning.

(b) Compute Jasper's tax adjusted trading profit for the year ended 31 March 2012.

Your answer should start with the net profit figure of £42,000 and use nil or zero (0) when no adjustment is required for items in notes 1 to 9.

Learning solution 7.1

Tax adjusted trading profits for year ended 30 September 2011	£	£
Net profit per accounts		8,299

Step 1: adjustments to profit

Add disallowed expenses:

	£	£
Motor expenses (W2)	120	
New covered walkway	2,000	
Depreciation (1,250 + 920)	2,170	
Amortisation of lease	200	
Lease premium	2,000	
Capital loss (equipment)	160	
Loan to employee written off	170	
Professional fees ref health and safety	450	
Professional fees ref tax appeal	220	
Fine ref health and safety	250	
Entertaining – UK customers	120	
Entertaining – Foreign customers	300	
Cato's salary	5,000	13,160
		21,459

Less income taxed elsewhere:

	£
Bank deposit interest	(77)
Dividends (net)	(173)
NSB interest	(20)
Less: deductible expenditure not included in the accounts	
Lease premium paid on the grant of a short lease (W1)	(164)
Add: adjustments due to sole trader stock drawings (W3)	240

Step 2: Deduct capital allowances on plant and machinery (1,200)

Tax adjusted trading profits	20,065

Workings:

(1) Lease premium

	£
Premium received	2,000
Less: 2% (10 − 1) x 2,000	(360)
	1,640
Rent in advance	

Deductible expense for tenant = $\dfrac{1,640}{10}$ = £164

(2) Motor expenses

£800 x 15% (disallowed) = £120

(3) Goods withdrawn from stock at selling price

	£	%
Selling price	240	100
Cost	(180)	(75)
Gross profit	60	25

London
School of Business
& Finance
shaping success in business and finance

Solution to exam standard question

(a) Notes for meeting with Jasper Conran

(1) Wages are allowable only to the extent that they are reasonable in relation to the work performed. The salary paid to Jasper's wife is in excess of the salary paid to the other secretary in performing the same job, so £4,000 (16,000 – 12,600) of the wife's salary is disallowable. Jasper is the owner of the business and his salary will be a disallowable expense.

(2) Trading stock withdrawn must be added back to profit at selling price and not cost, therefore, increasing profit by £800.

(3) The suit is for a dual purpose expense. It has a personal element, which is warmth and decency, and a professional element, which is the business use. As it is impossible to quantify the business and professional elements, the whole amount should be disallowed, £300.

(4) The repair work to the building relates to its condition pre-acquisition and was reflected in its purchase price. The building could not be used until the repair work was carried out. Therefore, the repair should be treated as capital expenditure as in Law Shipping v CIR (the ship case), which has the result of disallowing the expenditure.

(5) While entertaining is generally disallowed, reasonable staff entertaining is specifically allowed. Thus the cost of the summer banquet is allowable. Gifts to customers/suppliers costing up to £50 per person are allowable as long as they have a conspicuous advertisement. However, this specifically excludes food, drink or tobacco. Therefore, the diaries would be an allowable expense as long as they have an advertisement but the cost of the sherry is disallowed.

(6) Sundry expenses

Parking fines – specifically allowed
Subscription – normal trade expense – allowed

Donations to national charity and political parties are disallowed

(7) Legal fees are allowable except for 'law-breaking' items and non-trade items. Legal fees for a renewal of a short lease are specifically allowed. The defective goods – normal trade expense – allowable. Breach of Trading Act – 'Law Breaking' – disallowed. Bad debts recovery – normal trade expense – allowable. Loans to employees – non-trade item – disallowed.

(8) Depreciation is a disallowed expense. Instead HMRC gives tax depreciation called capital allowances. The machine was bought on 3 May 2011 thus the annual investment allowance (100%) is available. Capital allowances of £5,000 are available in the year ended 31 March 2012.

(9) Patent royalties are allowable in computing taxable profit.

(b) Tax adjusted trading profit year end 31 March 2012

	£
Net profit per the question	42,000

Step 1: adjustments to profit

Add disallowed expenses:

(1) Jasper's salary	15,000
(2) Wife's salary	4,000
(3) Suit	300
(4) Repairs to roof	20,000
(5) Sherry (25 x 15)	375
Entertaining staff	Nil
Diaries	Nil
(6) Sundry expenses:	
Parking fines staff	Nil
Trade subscription	Nil
Donation to national charity	200
Donation to political party	400
(7) Legal fees:	
Defending action re defective goods	Nil
Bad debt recovery	Nil
Renewal of short lease	Nil
Breach of trading act	750
Loans to employees	200
(8) Depreciation	2,000
(9) Patent royalties	Nil
	85,225

(2) Add: adjustments due to sole trader stock drawings	800
Step 2: Deduct capital allowances	(5,000)
Tax adjusted trading profits	81,025

8

Capital
Allowances

Context

As we saw in the previous chapter, deprecation must be added back as a disallowed expense as it is too subjective. Instead, the taxman gives us his own version of depreciation, known as "capital allowances". This ensures that the tax relief given to businesses on their capital expenditure is standardised. This chapter covers how capital allowances are calculated.

Capital allowances are given on plant and machinery. In the exam, you may have to decide which assets meet the definition of plant and machinery and give capital allowances accordingly.

Exam hints

Capital allowances are available to all types of businesses: sole traders, partnerships and companies. As a result, you may be required to calculate capital allowances in more than one question in the exam. It is common for the examiner to ask you to calculate capital allowances in both question 1 and question 2 of the exam. It is very likely to be tested in your exam, making it an important topic area.

Key learning points

- Capital allowances are the tax version of depreciation, designed to give tax relief on types of plant and machinery.

- There is not set definition of plant and machinery. This has lead to a number of court cases about whether certain assets can be classified as plant and machinery.

- Capital allowances are calculated for each accounting period.

- There are various types of capital allowances available that you need to be able to calculate in the exam. These include the annual investment allowance (AIA) and writing down allowance (WDA).

- Most plant and machinery is pooled together in the capital allowances working, either in the main pool or the special rate pool.

- Certain assets have their own column, such as expensive cars, assets with private use and short life assets.

Capital allowances – plant and machinery

Capital allowances are a deduction in the trading income working of a sole trader. In the exam, you will be required to calculate this figure and deduct it from your working to get the tax adjusted trading profits figure

Capital allowances are calculated for each accounting period of the sole trader.

Trading income working recap:

	£
Net profit per sole trader accounts	X
Step 1: adjustments to profit	X/(X)
Add: disallowed expenses	
Add: adjustments due to sole trader stock drawings	
Less: income taxed elsewhere	
Less: deductible expenditure not included in the accounts	
Step 2: capital allowances (w)	(X)
Tax adjusted trading profit	X

Definition of plant and machinery

The definition of plant and machinery is not as straight forward as you may think. An asset can be considered to be plant if it performs an 'active function' in the business. It would not be considered plant if it has a 'passive function' i.e. it is part of the setting in which business takes place

Items which would be considered to be plant and machinery include:

- Machinery

- Equipment

- Computers

- Motor vehicles

- Fixtures and fittings

- Furniture

As there is no set definition, there have been a number of challenges through the courts which has led to the following assets also meeting the definition of plant and machinery via case law.

Capital allowances given as per case law

- Swimming pool installed by owners of a caravan park

- The law books of a barrister

- Moveable office partitioning

- Light fittings, décor and murals of a hotel and pub business

- Free-standing screens used in a window display by building society

- Fire regulation expenditure

- Thermal insulation of industrial building

- Sports ground safety requirement expenditure

- Expenditure on a security asset, such as alarms, bullet proof windows to improve personal security of those under special threat, e.g., from terrorists.

- Computer, telecommunication and surveillance systems, including wiring, etc

- Safes and burglar alarm systems

- Advertising hoardings, signs and displays, etc

- Refrigeration/cooking equipment, washbasins, sinks, sanitary ware and furniture/furnishings

- Display equipment, counters and checkouts

- Lifts and escalators

- Space/water heating, ventilation and air conditioning systems, including floors/ceilings therein

- Electric, cold water, gas and sewerage systems which are specific to trade requirements or connected with specific trade plant items

- Any machinery and expenditure on altering buildings to accommodate plant or machinery which qualifies for capital allowances.

Not qualifying as plant – No capital allowances given as per case law

- Laboratory and gymnasium of a school

- Canopy over petrol station

- Ship used as a floating restaurant

- Football club's spectator stand

- False ceiling containing conduits, ducts and lighting apparatus

- Lighting in department store

Capital allowances working – for each accounting period

Proforma capital allowances on plant and machinery

	AIA/ FYA	Main pool (MP)	Short life asset	Special Rate Pool (SRP)	Private use assets	Expensive Car	BU%	Total Capital Allowances
	£	£	£	£	£	£		£
Tax WDV b/f (at beginning of accounting period)		X	X		X	X		
Add: Additions AIA in SRP and MP	X							
Less: AIA (UL = £100,000 for 12m)	(X)	X/Nil						X
Add: High CO$_2$ cars				X				
Add: Medium CO$_2$ cars		X						
Less:								
Disposal proceeds (lower of SP and cost)		(X) X	(X)	— X	(X)	— X		
Balancing allowance					X		xBU%	X
Balancing charge			(X)					(X)
Small balance relief if the balance on the main pool or special rate pool is < £1,000								
Writing down allowance (WDA)								
@ 20%		(X)						X
@ 10%				(X)				X
@ 20% restricted to max of £3,000 pa for expensive cars						(X)		X
Add: Low CO$_2$ cars	X							
FYA @ 100%	(X)	—	—	—	—	—		X
Tax WDV c/f		X	Nil	X	Nil	X		
Allowances to be claimed								X

London School of Business & Finance
shaping success in business and finance

Categories of plant and machinery

Plant and machinery will be included under one of the following column headings:

- Main pool (general pool)
- Expensive cars
- Private use assets
- Special rate pool
- Short life assets

We will look at each of these columns in turn.

Main Pool

Capital expenditure on plant and machinery is generally placed in a main pool of expenditure.

Some items are not included in the main pool. These are:

- Cars already owned at 6 April 2009 and costing > £12,000.
- Short-life assets (if the election is made)
- Long-life assets (if qualified)
- Assets with a private use element (if an unincorporated business)

On disposal of assets from the main pool, proceeds are used as the disposal value. However, the disposal value cannot exceed the original purchase price.

Capital allowances given in the main pool

There are three types of capital allowances that plant and machinery could receive. These are:

- Annual investment allowance (AIA)
- Writing down allowance (WDA)
- First year allowance (FYA)

Annual investment allowance (AIA)

The first £100,000 per annum of expenditure on plant and machinery (other than cars) qualifies for the annual investment allowance (AIA). In effect, the AIA provides a 100% allowance for the first £100,000 invested in plant and machinery each year.

A business is free to allocate the AIA between different types of expenditure in any way that it sees fit. For example, a business which invests £80,000 in general plant and machinery and £60,000 in "integral features" in a 12-month accounting period might allocate £40,000 of the AIA to general plant and machinery and the remaining £60,000 to the special rate pool. This would maximise allowances for the period, since general plant and machinery attracts the WDA at 20%, whereas the special rate pool attracts a WDA at only 10%.

The £100,000 allowance is for qualifying expenditure in a 12 month accounting period. If the accounting period is < 12 months, or > 12 months then the £100,000 allowance is reduced or increased accordingly.

If a business spends more than £100,000 then the expenditure beyond the £100,000 enters the main pool or special rate pool and is eligible for the WDA.

Writing down allowance (WDA)

In general, a business may claim a WDA for each of its pools of plant and machinery in each accounting period. The WDA is given after the AIA.

The WDA is a set % given on the tax written down value (TWDV) of the plant and machinery. The WDA is calculated as follows:

$$20\% \times \textbf{TWDV} = \textbf{WDA}$$

The WDA must be increased or reduced if the accounting period is greater than or less than 12 months.

Learning example 8.1

Sally is a new sole trader and produces accounts to 31 December 2011. During the year she has purchased the following assets:

		£
2 January	Medium CO_2 car	8,500
5 May	machinery	15,000
8 June	machinery	35,000
19 October	van	14,000

Required

Calculate Sally's capital allowances for the year ended 31 December 2011.

Learning example 8.2

Jeff is a new sole trader and his first set of accounts cover 18 months to 31 December 2012. Jeff has purchased the following assets:

		£
1 July 2011	machinery	50,000
6 September 2011	Medium CO_2 car	5,500
18 September 2011	machinery	17,600
16 January 2012	fixtures	5,400
15 March 2012	equipment	3,200

Required

Calculate Jeff's capital allowances for the 18 months ended 31 December 2012.

First year allowance (FYA)

Certain expenditure still qualifies for a 100% first year allowance. The main 100% FYAs are as follows:

(a) Expenditure on low emission motor car is eligible for a 100% FYA so long as the expenditure is incurred on or before 31 March 2013. The definition of a low emission car for the purposes of the 100% FYA is one with an emission rating not exceeding 110 g/km. An exam question will state the emissions of the car.

(b) Expenditure by businesses on energy-saving or environmentally beneficial plant and machinery qualifies for enhanced capital allowances (ECA) of 100%.

The FYA will not apply to expenditure on long-life assets or motor vehicles, unless covered by (a) above.

The FYA is never increased or decreased if the accounting period is more or less than 12 months and can never be claimed if the activity of the company ceases in the accounting period.

* The FYA for low emission cars is available to all businesses whether they are small, medium or large. Low emission cars should be included in the main pool.

Learning example 8.3

Paula is a sole trader with a year end 30 June 2012. During the year, she purchased the following assets:

		£
5 August 2011	machinery	35,000
9 October 2011	low emission car	20,000
17 March 2012	machinery	8,000

She has a brought forward balance on the main pool at 1 July 2011 of £6,500

Required

Calculate Paula's capital allowances for the year ended 30 June 2012.

Expensive cars

Prior to 6 April 2009 for individuals, an expensive car, one costing £12,000 or more, would be allocated to a separate expensive car pool and a writing down allowance of 20% , up to a maximum of £3,000 per annum, would be given.

Where a motor car is already owned at 6 April 2009, the tax treatment, as described above, is to continue for five tax years. CO_2 emissions will not be relevant.

From 6 April 2009 for individuals, the writing down allowances on expensive cars will depend upon its CO_2 emissions:

* Motor cars with CO_2 emissions of between 111 – 160g/km (medium CO_2 cars) qualify for WDA of 20% on the full purchase price – included in main pool.

* Motor cars with CO_2 emissions of more than 160g/km (high CO_2 cars) qualify for WDA of 10% on the full purchase price – included in special rate pool.

* Motor cars with CO_2 emissions of 110g/km and less (low CO_2 cars) qualify for FYA of 100% on the full purchase price – included in the main pool.

Learning example 8.4

Joe is a sole trader, with a year end 31 March 2012. During the year he purchases the following assets:

		£
19 May 2011	equipment	48,600
5 December 2011	car	17,800

The car has CO_2 emissions of 165g/km.

Required

Calculate Joe's capital allowances for the year ended 31 March 2012.

Private use assets

If an asset has private use by the sole trader, there is a restriction in the amount of capital allowances available to the business. A separate column is used for each asset with private use. The tax implications of a private use asset are as follows:

- Although the full amount of WDA is deducted from the private use column, only the business % of the WDA may be claimed by the business

- The private use restriction only applies to private use by the SOLE TRADER only. There is no adjustment if it is private use by an employee

Learning example 8.5

Karina has the following balances on 1 January 2011:

	£
Main pool	23,700
Expensive car (25% private use by Karina)	25,400

Required

Karina prepares accounts to 31 December 2011. Calculate the capital allowances for this period.

Special rate pool

This is a pool of assets which includes the following types of expenditure:

- Assets which are acquired as an integral feature of a building, such as:

  - Electrical systems and lighting systems

  - Cold water systems

  - Central heating systems

  - Air conditioning and ventilation systems

  - Lifts and escalators

- Thermal insulation in a building.

- Long life assets costing at least £100,000 per annum and have a life of at least 25 years.

- The special rate pool also includes expenditure on a high CO_2 car.

The tax implications of the special rate pool are as follows:

- The plant and machinery in the special rate pool can get the AIA of up to £100,000. It is more tax efficient to allocate the AIA to the special rate pool than the main pool, as the WDA in the special rate pool is only 10%, compared to 20% in the main pool.

- The WDA is limited to 10%.

Learning example 8.6

Freddie has been a sole trader for many years and has a year end of 31 December. During the year, he made the following acquisitions:

		£
23 April 2011	New escalator	40,000
15 May 2011	Equipment	10,000
29 September 2011	New cold water system	60,000

Required

Calculate Freddie's capital allowances for the year ended 31 December 2011.

Short life assets

A short-life asset is an asset which is expected to be sold within an eight year period for less than its tax written down value. Once an election is made to treat an asset as a short-life asset this is irrevocable.

A balancing charge or allowance will arise on the disposal of the asset if it is made within eight years. This can greatly enhance the speed at which the asset allowance is matched against its useful life.

For example, where an asset costing £100,000 is added to the pool, it will qualify for WDA and be pooled with other assets. If in year four, it is sold for say £5,000, the proceeds of £5,000 will be deducted from the main pool. The tax written down value of the asset would have been £52,000 (approximately).

Had the asset been included in the short-life pool, the WDA would have been the same. However, in year four, no WDAs would have been given and instead, the proceeds would have been deducted from the tax written down value of the asset, leaving a balancing allowance of £47,000.

If a short-life election is made, the balancing allowance is obtained when the asset is sold. Under the main pool, the allowance would only be received if the business ceases.

An asset which has a short-life election and is still used in the trade after eight years is transferred into the main pool in year nine.

Disposal of plant and machinery

If a business sells an asset from a single asset column, such as expensive car, private use or short life asset, then a balancing allowance or balancing charge will arise.

There is no balancing allowance if the business sells an asset from the main or special pool. This is because assets in the pool have 'lost their identity'. If the disposal proceeds of the asset being sold exceed the balance of expenditure in the main rate or special rate pool there will be a balancing charge equal to the excess.

A balancing allowance or balancing charge on a single asset column is calculated as follows:

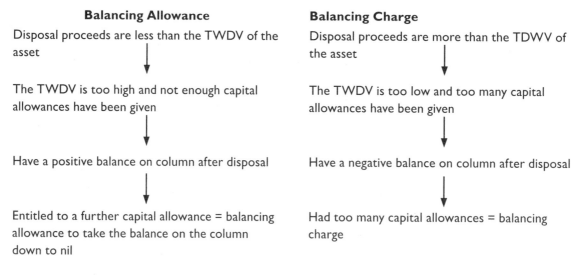

Balancing Allowance	Balancing Charge
Disposal proceeds are less than the TWDV of the asset	Disposal proceeds are more than the TDWV of the asset
The TWDV is too high and not enough capital allowances have been given	The TWDV is too low and too many capital allowances have been given
Have a positive balance on column after disposal	Have a negative balance on column after disposal
Entitled to a further capital allowance = balancing allowance to take the balance on the column down to nil	Had too many capital allowances = balancing charge

Points to note

- There is no balancing allowance on the disposal of an asset from the main or special rate pool unless the business is ceasing.

- No WDA is given in the year of disposal

Learning example 8.7

A sole trader buys a car, with an emissions value of 145g/km for £18,000 on 1 January 2009. The car is then sold on 25 May 2012. The car is the sole trader's only asset and is used 85% for business.

Required

Calculate the capital allowances for the year ended 31 December 2012 assuming the car is sold for:

a) £11,000

b) £7,000

Small pools of plant and machinery

If the TWDV brought forward at the beginning of the accounting period plus additions less disposals during the accounting period on the main pool or the special rate pool is £1,000 or less, the business may claim a small balance relief equal to the value of the balance, instead of claiming the WDA.

Learning example 8.8

Bo Peep trades as a landscape gardener, making up accounts to 31 March each year. Bo Peep started trading on 1 April 2011. During the first two accounting periods the following transactions were undertaken:

Purchases:

		£
1 April 2011	Car with CO_2 emission 145g/km (used 20% privately)	17,000
4 June 2011	Computer and peripherals	3,000
17 July 2011	Car with CO_2 emission 180g/km (used by employee 80% for business)	18,000
21 August 2011	Equipment	2,000
11 September 2011	Office furniture	5,200
12 December 2011	Machinery	38,000
14 March 2012	Tools	9,000
5 July 2012	Car with CO_2 emission 180g/km (used 20% privately)	18,000
12 September 2012	Machinery	22,000
19 February 2013	New car for employee with CO_2 emission 105g/km (used 80% for business	15,000

Sales:

		£
5 July 2012	Car (used 20% privately)	9,000

The tax adjusted trading profits for the first two accounting period before deducting capital allowances are:

	£
Year ended 31.3.2012	59,000
Year ended 31.3.2013	71,000

Required

Compute Bo Peep's capital allowances for her first two accounting periods.

Learning summary

- Capital allowances are available for expenditure on capital equipment used in the trade of the business. The rate of capital allowances depends on the type of asset.

- An Annual Investment Allowance of £100,000 is available for qualifying expenditure in the main pool or special rate pool with the exception of motor vehicles.

- Writing down allowances (WDA) of 20% are available for main pool assets, 10% for special rate pool assets.

- 100% First year allowances are available for low emission cars.

- Assets with an element of private use are treated as separate assets for capital allowances.

- An adjustment for private use of assets is made to restrict capital allowances.

- It may be beneficial to make an election for a short-life asset to enhance the availability of balancing allowances.

Exam standard question

Humpty trades as a management consultant, making up accounts to 31 March each year. At 1 April 2011 the tax written down value of plant and machinery was:

Main pool	£8,720
Car (acquired 1 August 2008)	£17,000

The following transactions have taken place:

Purchases

		£
1 May 2011	Furniture for reception area	9,500
4 June 2011	Car high CO_2 emissions	18,000
	(Used 20% privately by Humpty's personal assistant)	
27 July 2011	Laptop computer	900
18 August 2011	Car with CO_2 emission 107g/km (30% private use by Humpty)	18,200
26 September 2011	Painting for Humpty's office	5,600
30 November 2011	Van	20,000
17 December 2011	Computers and peripherals	9,700
25 March 2012	Car for business use (CO_2 = 156g/km)	12,500

Required

Compute Humpty's capital allowances for the period of account ending 31 March 2012.

London
School of Business
& Finance

shaping success in business and finance

Learning solution 8.1

Capital allowances – year ended 31 December 2011

	AIA/FYA £	Main pool £	Capital allowances £
Additions - no AIA		8,500	
Additions - AIA:			
Machinery	15,000		
Machinery	35,000		
Van	14,000		
Less: AIA	(64,000)	Nil	64,000
		8,500	
WDA @ 20%		(1,700)	1,700
WDV c/f		6,800	
Capital allowances			65,700

Learning solution 8.2

Capital allowances – 18 months to 31 December 2012

	AIA/FYA £	Main pool £	Capital allowances £
Additions - no AIA		5,500	
Additions - AIA:			
Machinery	50,000		
Machinery	17,600		
Fixtures	5,400		
Equipment	3,200		
Less: AIA	(76,200)	Nil	76,200
		5,500	
WDA @ 20% x 18/12		(1,650)	1,650
WDV c/f		3,850	
Capital allowances			77,850

Learning solution 8.3

Capital allowances – year ended 30 June 2012

	AIA/FYA £	Main pool £	Capital allowances £
TWDV b/f		6,500	
Additions - AIA:			
Machinery	35,000		
Machinery	8,000		
Less: AIA	(43,000)	Nil	43,000
		6,500	
WDA @ 20%		(1,300)	1,300
Additions with FYA	20,000		
FYA @ 100%	(20,000)	–	20,000
WDV c/f		5,200	
Capital allowances			64,300

Learning solution 8.4

Capital allowances – year ended 31 March 2012

	AIA/FYA £	Main pool £	Special rate pool £	Capital allowances £
Additions - AIA:				
Equipment	48,600			
Less: AIA	(48,600)	Nil		48,600
Additions – high CO_2 car			17,800	
WDA @ 10%			(1,780)	1,780
WDV c/f		–	16,020	
Capital allowances				50,380

Learning solution 8.5

Capital allowances – year ended 31 December 2011

	Main pool £	Expensive Car 25% private use £	Capital allowances £
WDV b/f	23,700	25,400	
WDA @ 20%	(4,740)		4,740
WDA @ 20% (restricted to £3,000 for expensive car)		(3,000) x 75%	2,250
WDV c/f	18,960	22,400	
Capital allowances			6,990

London
School of Business
& Finance

shaping success in business and finance

Learning solution 8.6

Capital allowances – year ended 31 December 2011

	AIA/FYA £	Main pool £	Special rate pool £	Capital allowances £
Additions - AIA:				
Equipment	10,000			
Escalator	40,000			
Cold water system	60,000			
Less: AIA	(100,000)		_____	100,000
		10,000	=	
WDA @ 20%		(2,000)	_____	2,000
WDV c/f		8,000	=	
Capital allowances				102,000

Although the equipment is also eligible for the AIA, it is more tax efficient to allocate the AIA to the special rate pool than the main pool, as the WDA in the special rate pool is only 10%, compared to 20% in the main pool.

Learning solution 8.7

Year ended 31 December 2009 (year of acquisition)

	Expensive Car £	Capital allowances £
Addition – no AIA	18,000	
WDA @ 20% (restricted to £3,000 for expensive car)	(3,000) x 85%	2,550
WDV c/f	15,000	
Capital allowances		2,550

As the car was purchased 1 January 2009, it still has the 'old' treatment of restricted WDA of £3,000 per annum. Had the car been purchased after 1 April 2009, it would have been placed in the main pool.

Year ended 31 December 2010

	Expensive Car £	Capital allowances £
WDV b/f	15,000	
WDA @ 20% (no need to restrict as = £3,000)		
	(3,000) x 85%	2,550
WDV c/f	12,000	
Capital allowances		2,550

Year ended 31 December 2011

	Expensive Car £	Capital allowances £
WDV b/f	12,000	
WDA @ 20% (no need to restrict as < £3,000)	(2,400) x 85%	2,040
WDV c/f	9,600	
Capital allowances		2,040

Year ended 31 December 2012 (year of disposal)

Part a – car is sold for £11,000

	Expensive Car £	Capital allowances £
WDV c/f	9,600	
Disposal (lower of cost and proceeds)	(11,000)	
	(1,400)	
Balancing charge	(1,400) x 85%	(1,190)
WDV c/f	Nil	
Capital allowances		(1,190)

Part b – car is sold for £7,000

	Expensive Car £	Capital allowances £
WDV c/f	9,600	
Disposal (lower of cost and proceeds)		
	(7,000)	
	2,600	
Balancing allowance	2,600 x 85%	2,210
WDV c/f	Nil	
Capital allowances		2,210

Learning solution 8.8

Year ended 31 March 2012

	£	Main Pool £	Car with private use (20%) £	Special rate pool £	Capital allowances £
Additions – no AIA					
Medium CO_2 car			17,000		
High CO_2 car				18,000	
Additions - AIA					
Computer	3,000				
Equipment	2,000				
Furniture	5,200				
Machinery	38,000				
Tools	9,000				
	57,200				
Less: AIA	(57,200)				57,200
		Nil	____	____	
		Nil	17,000	18,000	
Less: WDA					
20% x 17,000			(3,400) x 80%		2,720
10% x 18,000				(1,800)	1,800
Tax WDV c/f			13,600	16,200	
Total allowances to be claimed					61,720

Year end 31 March 2013

	Main Pool	Car with private use (20%)	Special rate pool	Car with private use (20%)	Capital allowances
	£	£	£	£	£
TWDV b/f		–	13,600	16,200	
Additions – no AIA					
High CO_2 car				18,000	
Additions AIA					
Machinery	22,000				
Less: AIA	(22,000)				22,000
		–			
Disposals (lower of cost and proceeds)					
Car used privately	_____	(9,000)	_____	_____	
		–	16,200	18,000	
Balancing allowance		4,600 x 80%			3,680
Balancing charge					
Less: WDA					
10% x 16,200			(1,620)		1,620
10% x 18,000				(1,800) x 80%	1,440
Additions FYA					
Low emission car	15,000				
FYA (100% x 15,000)	(15,000)	_____	_____	_____	15,000
Tax WDV c/f	–	–	14,580	16,200	
Total allowances to be claimed					43,740

Solution to exam standard question

Period of account 1.4.11 – 31.3.12

	Main Pool	Expensive car	Special rate pool	Car with private use (30%)	BU 70%	Capital allowances
	£	£	£	£	£	£
TWDV b/f		8,720	17,000			
Additions – no AIA:						
Car for assistant				18,000		
Medium CO_2 car		12,500				
Additions – AIA:						
Furniture	9,500					
Laptop	900					
Van	20,000					
Computers	9,700					
	40,100					
Less: AIA	(40,100)					40,100
		21,220	17,000	18,000		
WDA						
21,220 x 20%		(4,244)				4,244
17,000 x 20% (max £3,000)			(3,000)			3,000
18,000 x 10%				(1,800)		1,800
Addition FYA						
Low emission car					18,200	
FYA (100%)					(18,200)	x 70%	12,740
TWDV c/f	16,976	14,000	16,200		–	
Capital allowances						61,884

Note: The painting does not satisfy the functional test and is not used in the business but rather contributes to the setting thus is not plant and machinery and no capital allowances can be claimed on it.

9

Basis Periods

Context

Now that the tax adjusted trading profit has been calculated, we need to fit this figure into tax years, using special rules known as basis periods. This is the final step in our trading income working, as shown below:

Trading income working:

Net profit per sole trader accounts	X
Step 1: adjustments to profit	X/(X)

Add: disallowed expenses
Add: adjustments due to sole trader stock drawings
Less: income taxed elsewhere
Less: deductible expenditure not included in the accounts

Step 2: capital allowances(w)	(X)
Tax adjusted trading profit	X

Step 3: fit into tax years using basis periods

Exam hints

The problems covered in this chapter are firstly to determine how much of the tax adjusted trading profits will be subject to tax in the first tax year of trading and this will require knowledge of the opening year rules and secondly to determine how much of the tax adjusted trading profits will be subject to tax in the final tax year, this will require knowledge of the closing year rules. These rules are very frequently examined and could appear in question 1, question 4 and question 5 of the exam paper

Key learning points

- Basis periods are the rules that are used to fit the tax adjusted trading profit for a set of accounts into tax years.

- There a different basis period rules depending on whether you are a new sole trader (opening year rules), if you have been trading for many years (current year basis) or if you are ceasing to trade (closing year rules).

- A sole trader can also change their accounting date, by producing a long or short set of accounts. Special basis period rules apply in this instance.

Basis period rules

There are three types of basis periods that you need to know for your exam. You must look at the scenario in the question and decide which is the appropriate basis period to use for the sole trader.

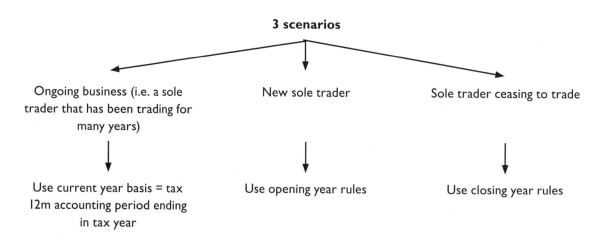

Current year basis

If a sole trader has been trading for many years, then we use the current year basis to decide which profits to tax.

Current year basis: Tax the 12 month accounting period ending in the tax year

For example, a sole trader has a year end of 31 December 2011, this ends in the tax year 2011/12.

Learning example 9.1

Josh has been trading for many years and has a year end of 30 June. His recent tax adjusted trading profits are as follows:

	£
30 June 2010	16,000
30 June 2011	9,600
30 June 2012	13,500

Required

In which tax year will the profits be assessed?

London
School of Business
& Finance

shaping success in business and finance

Learning example 9.2

The following sole traders have been trading for many years. Their recent tax adjusted trading profits are as follows:

		£
Tom	Year ended 31 May 2010	10,000
Janice	Year ended 28 February 2010	19,000
Sammy	Year ended 31 December 2011	50,000
Ricky	Year ended 31 March 2011	35,000

Required

In which tax year will the profits be assessed?

Opening year rules

When a sole trader starts to trade, we apply the opening year rules. First, you must identify the tax year that the sole trader starts to trade in. Then follow the rules below.

You MUST learn these rules for your exam.

First tax year of trade:
from start of trade to end of tax year   **Actual basis – tax profits**

Second tax year of trade onwards:

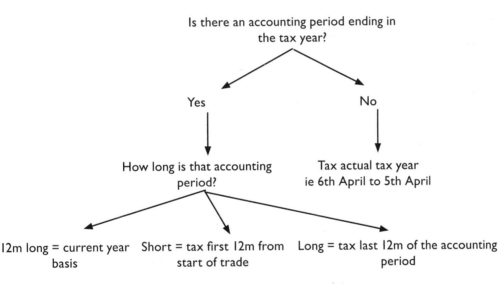

Overlap profits

If a business chooses an accounting date of 5 April which coincides with the end of the tax year there will be no overlap profits. If any other accounting date is chosen then some of the sole trader's tax adjusted trading profits will be taxed in more than one tax year.

The profits which are taxed twice are called overlap profits and relief is given on change of accounting date and on cessation of trading, when the taxable trading profits of the final tax year are reduced by the overlap profits.

Learning example 9.3

Scooby started trading on 1 November 2009, making up accounts to 31 October each year. His tax adjusted profits are as follows:

	£
Year ended 31 October 2010	36,000
Year ended 31 October 2011	75,000

Required

Calculate the taxable trading profits for all relevant tax years.

Learning example 9.4

Percy started trading on 1 January 2010 making up accounts to 31 July each year. His tax adjusted trading profits are as follows:

	£
7 months to 31 July 2010	21,000
Year ended 31 July 2011	67,200

Required

Calculate the taxable trading profits for all relevant tax years.

Learning example 9.5

Vlad started trading on 1 December 2009 making up accounts for 16 months to 31 March 2011 and annually thereafter to 31 March. His tax adjusted trading profits are as follows:

	£
16 months to 31 March 2011	24,000
Year ended 31 March 2012	13,300

Required

Calculate the taxable trading profits for all relevant tax years.

Learning example 9.6

Keynes started trading on 1 February 2010 making up accounts for 18 months to 31 July 2011 and annually thereafter to 31 July. His tax adjusted trading profits are as follows:

	£
18 months to 31 July 2011	27,000

Required

Calculate the taxable trading profits for all relevant tax years.

Cessation of trade

When the sole trader/partnership ceases trading, there are special closing year rules for calculating (T) in the final tax year.

The closing year rules apply to a sole trader in the following circumstances:

(1) When the sole trader sells the business to another sole trader.

(2) When the sole trader sells the business to a company.

(3) When the sole trader gifts the business. The donor applies the closing year rules and the donee applies the opening year rules.

(4) When a partner leaves the partnership.

On cessation the sole trader must prepare a final set of accounts for the period up to the date of cessation. In the final accounting period there is no AIA, WDA or FYA, only balancing allowances and balancing charges.

The final tax year in which trading profits are assessable is the tax year in which the cessation occurs.

Closing year rules

In tax year of cessation:

	£
Tax all profits not yet taxed	x
Less overlap profits	(x)
Trading profits	x

Learning example 9.7

Polo ceased trading on 31 January 2012 making up a final set of accounts for seven months. Previously he prepared accounts to 30 June each year. His tax adjusted profits were:

	£
Year end 30 June 2010	24,000
Year end 30 June 2011	20,000
7 months to 31 January 2012	7,280

Polo had £4,200 of overlap profits.

Required

Calculate taxable trading profits for all relevant tax years.

Learning example 9.8

Bunyan ceased trading on 31 May 2011 making up a final set of accounts for five months. Previously he prepared accounts to 31 December each year. His tax adjusted profits were:

	£
Year end 31 December 2010	22,600
5 months to 31 May 2011	7,500

Bunyan had £3,600 of overlap profits.

Required

Calculate the taxable trading profits for all relevant years.

Learning example 9.9

Marco started trading on 1 August 2007 and prepared accounts to 31 July. He ceased trading on 31 July 2011.

	£
Year end 31 July 2008	30,000
Year end 31 July 2009	46,000
Year end 31 July 2010	54,000
Year end 31 July 2011	71,200

Required –

Calculate the taxable trading profits assessable in all relevant years.

Change of accounting date

Choice of accounting date

The choice of an appropriate accounting date at the commencement of a business can affect the level of profits to be taxed in a particular tax year, the overlap profits created and the timing and amount of tax payments. Over the life of the business, the individual will be charged on all the profits earned but planning can have an advantageous impact.

The debate is usually between early in the tax year (e.g. 30 April) and late in the tax year (e.g. 31 March).

Some factors to take into account are:

a) A date early in tax year provides the longest period between earning profits and payment of tax.

b) A date late in tax year reduces the overlap profits to be carried forward (often to nil, i.e. 31 March).

c) Alternative dates can determine the level of profits to be taxed in the early years.

d) Seasonal trading conditions may make it easier to prepare accounts if the year end is at a quiet time of the year.

If conditions change the trader may decide to change his accounting date.

Basis periods on a change in accounting date

Where a trader decides to change their accounting date, special rules apply for fixing basis periods. The rules depend on whether there is:

- A long (> 12 months) period of account after the change in date; or

- A short (< 12 months) period of account after the change in date; or

- No period of account in the tax year after the change in date; or

- Two periods of account in the tax year after the charge in date.

Long period of account

The basis period for the tax year ends on the new accounting date. This means that the basis period is over 12 months in length.

As over 12 months of profits are taxed in one tax year, the trader is able to obtain relief from any unused overlap profits. The relief for overlap profits is restricted to the number of months' taxable profit in excess of 12 months.

For example, where the basis period is sixteen months, relief can be given for up to four months of unused overlap profits.

Learning example 9.10

Reggie has been a sole trader for many years, with an accounting year end of 30 June. He has now decided that he would like to change his year end to 31 December.

His recent tax adjusted profits are as follows:

	£
Year end 30 June 2010	15,000
Period end 31 December 2011	27,000
Year end 31 December 2012	18,000

He has overlap profits from commencement of trade of £6,000, relating to a 6 month period.

Required

Calculate Reggie's taxable trading income for all the relevant tax years

No accounting date in the tax year

A basis period usually ends on an accounting date. If there is no accounting date ending in the basis period this presents a problem. A basis period is artificially created by taking the new accounting date and deducting one year. The basis period is then 12 months to this date. This will create overlap profits, which must be added to any previous overlap profits.

For example, a trader has always prepared accounts to 31 January, the last accounts being 31 January 2011 (2010/11). The accounts date was changed to the 17 months to 31 May 2012. No basis period arises in 2011/12, therefore, the artificially created basis period is 31 May 2011.

Overlap profits for the period 1 June 2010 – 31 January 2011 arise.

Two accounting dates in the tax year

The basis period ends on the new accounting date. It begins immediately after the end of the previous basis period. The basis period will exceed 12 months and overlap profits can be used to ensure that only 12 months of profits are assessed in the tax year.

For example, a trader prepares accounts to 31 August 2011. He then decide to change his year-end to 5 April to fit in with the end of the tax year. The new accounting date is 5 April 2012. This is also the end of the basis period for 2011/12. The start of the basis period for 2011/12 is 1 September 2010, which gives a basis period for 2011/12 of 1 September 2010-5 April 2012 (17 months). Five months of overlap profits can be taken against this basis period in 2011/12.

Short period of account

The basis period must always be the 12 months to the new accounting date.

For example, a trader who previously prepared accounts to 30 September, changes his accounting date to 30 June. The first set of accounts covered is the nine month period to 30 June 2011. This leads to the creation of a short period of account in 2011/12, with the basis period for 2011/12 being the 12 months to 30 June 2011.

Overlap profits will arise as the basis period for 2010/11 was the period of account (12 months accounts) to 30 September 2010, and the basis period for 2011/12 will include the period 1 July 2010-30 September 2010.

Learning example 9.11

Steve has been sole trader for many years, with an accounting year end of 31 December. He has now decided that he would like to change this to a 31 May year end. His recent tax adjusted profits are as follows:

	£
Year end 31 December 2010	63,000
Period end 31 May 2011	7,600
Year end 31 May 2012	82,000

Required

Calculate Steve's taxable trading profits for all the relevant years and state any overlap profits arising.

Application and conditions

The rules are automatically applied where a trader changes his accounting date in the first 3 years of trading. After this, certain conditions have to be met before a change in basis periods is allowed:

*   Trader must notify HMRC by 31 January following the tax year in which the change is made (31 January 2013 for 2011/12)

*   The period of account must not exceed 18 months

*   There must not have been a change of accounting period in the previous 5 tax years. A second change is only allowed for genuine commercial reasons

Learning summary

*   Accounting periods are linked to tax years through basis periods.

*   Special rules apply in fixing basis periods for opening and closing years and where there is a change in accounting date.

*   The choice of accounting date will impact a number of issues including length of time between end of period and payment of tax.

Exam standard question

Cecil commenced self employment as an art critic on 6 June 2007 and initially prepared accounts to 5 November each year, but then changed his accounting date to 5 January.

The adjusted trading profits after capital allowances have been as follows:

	£
Five months to 5 November 2007	7,400
Year ended 5 November 2008	23,700
Year ended 5 November 2009	36,100
Fourteen month period ended 5 January 2011	50,300
Year ended 5 January 2012	41,900

Required

(a)   Compute Cecil's trading income assessments for each of the tax years 2007/08 to 2011/12.

(b)   State the qualifying conditions that must be met for a change of accounting date to be valid.

(c)   Advise Cecil of the advantages and disadvantages for tax purposes of changing his accounting date.

Learning solution 9.1

Tax year	Basis period	Trading profit £
2010/11	Year end 30 June 2010	16,000
2011/12	Year end 30 June 2011	9,600
2012/13	Year end 30 June 2012	13,500

Learning solution 9.2

	Tax year	Basis period	Trading profit £
Tom	2010/11	Year ended 31.5.10	10,000
Janice	2009/10	Year ended 28.2.10	19,000
Sammy	2011/12	Year ended 31.12.11	50,000
Ricky	2010/11	Year ended 31.3.11	35,000

Learning solution 9.3

Scooby

Tax year	Basis period	Trading profit £
2009/10	Actual: 1.11.09 - 5.4.10 $5/12 \times 36,000$	15,000
2010/11	CYB 31.10.10	36,000
2011/12	CYB 31.10.11	75,000

Overlap profits = £15,000

Learning solution 9.4

Percy

Tax year	Basis period	Trading profit £
2009/10	Actual: 1.1.10 - 5.4.10 $3/7 \times 21,000$	9,000
2010/11	First 12 months (1.1.10 - 31.12.10) $21,000 + 5/12 \times 67,200$	49,000
2011/12	CYB 31.7.11	67,200

Overlap profits = £37,000 (8 months)

Learning solution 9.5

Vlad

Tax year	Basis period	Trading profit £
2009/10	Actual: 1.12.09 - 5.4.10	
	4/16 x 24,000	6,000
2010/11	Last 12 months	
	(1.4.10 - 31.3.11)	
	12/16 x 24,000	18,000
2011/12	CYB 31.3.12	13,300

No overlap profits

Learning solution 9.6

Keynes

Tax year	Basis period	Trading profits £
2009/10	Actual: 1.2.10 - 5.4.10	
	2/18 x 27,000	3,000
2010/11	Actual: 6.4.10 - 5.4.11	
	12/18 x 27,000	18,000
2011/12	Last 12 months	
	(1.8.10 - 31.7.11)	
	12/18 x 27,000	18,000

Overlap profits = 8/18 x 27,000 = £12,000

Learning solution 9.7

Polo

Tax year	Basis period	Trading profits £
Penultimate 2010/11	CYB 30.6.10	24,000
Final 2011/12	1.7.10 - 31.1.12	
	Remaining profits	
	20,000 + 7,280	27,280
	Less: Overlap relief	(4,200)
		23,080

Learning solution 9.8

Bunyan

Tax year	Basis period	Trading profits £
Penultimate 2010/11	CYB 31.12.10	22,600
Final 2011/12	Remaining profits	
	1.1.11 - 31.5.11	7,500
	Less: Overlap relief	(3,600)
		3,900

Learning solution 9.9

Marco

Tax year	Basis period	Trading profits £
First 2007/08	Actual: 1.8.07 - 5.4.08	
	8/12 x 30,000	20,000
Second 2008/09	CYB 31.7.08	30,000
Third 2009/10	CYB 31.7.09	46,000
Fourth 2010/11	CYB 31.7.10	54,000
Fifth – Final 2011/12	1.8.10 - 31.7.11	
	Remaining profits	71,200
	Less: Overlap profits	(20,000)
		51,200

Learning solution 9.10

Tax year	Basis period	Trading profit £
2010/11	CYB: year end 30 June 2010	15,000
2011/12	1.7.10 - 31.12.11 (18m)	27,000
	Less overlap (6 months)	(6,000)
		21,000
2012/13	CYB: year end 31 December 2012	18,000

Learning solution 9.11

Tax year	Basis period	Trading profit £
2010/11	CYB: year end 31 December 2010	63,000
2011/12	1.6.10 - 31.5.11 (12 months):	
	7/12 x 63,000	36,750
	5m to 31 May 2011	7,600
		44,350
2012/13	CYB: year end 31 May 2012	82,000

Overlap profits are £36,750 relating to a 7 month overlap

Solution to exam standard question

(a) Trading income assessments:

2007/08

6 June 2007 to 5 April 2008	£
5/5 x £7,400	7,400
5/12 x £23,700	9,875
Assessable	17,275

2008/09

Year ended 5 November 2008	23,700

Overlap profits £9,875 – 5 months

2009/10

Year ended 5 November 2009	36,100

2010/11

Period ended 5 January 2011	50,300
Less overlap relief	
£9,875 x (14 – 12)/5 months	(3,950)
Assessable	46,350

2011/12

Year ended 5 January 2012	41,900

Overlap profits to carry forward are 3 months = £5,925 (9,875 – 3,950)

(b) Conditions for a change of accounting date

The change must be notified to HMRC by 31 January following the tax year of the change

The new accounting period must not be longer than 18 months

There must be no other change of accounting period within five years, unless it is for a commercial reason

(c)

Advantages

Overlap relief can be used on changing the accounting date.

Disadvantages

The additional two months profit would be assessable in 2010/11.

There is a shorter interval between the accounting date and the due date for tax and the due dates for filing tax returns.

10

Trading Losses

Context

So far in our calculation of trading income, we have always seen that the sole trader has made a trading profit. However, in reality, this is not always the case. Imagine your trading income working looked like this:

	£
Net loss per sole trader accounts	(X)
Step 1: adjustments to profit	X/(X)
Add: disallowed expenses	
Add: adjustments due to sole trader stock drawings	
Less: income taxed elsewhere	
Less: deductible expenditure not included in the accounts	
Step 2: capital allowances (w)	(X)
Tax adjusted trading loss	(X)

In the exam, you may be required to deal with this trading loss.

The trading income for the year in the income tax computation is entered as NIL.

You then need consider the different options available for utilising the loss.

Exam hints

This is not a frequently tested area but is still potentially examinable. You must be able to deal with the calculation of a trading loss for a sole trader and then importantly, know how to use the loss in the most efficient way to give the best possible tax relief.

Each loss relief has a section number, relating to the tax legislation. You do not need to know the section numbers for your exam.

Key learning points

- The trading loss can be carried forward against first available future trading profits.

- The trading loss can be used in the current tax year and/or the prior tax year against the individual's total income.

- The loss should be used in the tax year when the individual is paying the highest rate of tax.

- Additional loss reliefs are available for new sole traders , sole traders that have ceased to trade and sole traders that have incorporated into a company.

If a sole trader has a trading loss for the period, the trading income in the income tax computation is entered as NIL.

We then need to consider the different loss relief options available to the sole trader. The different loss relief options are as follows:

Carrying forward loss (s83)

The trading loss may be carried forward and offset against the first available future trading profits of the same trade.

You must use as much of the loss as possible. Restricted claims are not possible in order to preserve the personal allowance.

This loss relief is automatic. No claim is required

Disadvantage

Carrying forward the loss gives relief in the future which is not cash flow efficient.

Advantages

The trading loss is offset against one source of income. If the taxpayer has sufficient other income it may be possible to preserve the personal allowance by carrying the loss forward and leaving the other income to cover the PA.

If the taxpayer expects profits to rise in the future or expects tax rates to increase, it may be tax efficient to claim relief under S83 and benefit from tax relief at the increased rate.

Learning example 10.1

Patrice is a sole trader who has been trading for many years. His recent tax adjusted profits are as follows:

	£
Year ended 30 June 2011	(15,000)
Year ended 30 June 2012	8,000
Year ended 30 June 2013	15,000

He has no other sources of income.

Required

Calculate Patrice's taxable income, assuming he wishes to carry forward his loss

Assume the rate of PA continues unchanged in the future

Current year/prior year loss relief (s64)

s64 relief is available for a maximum of two tax years: the tax year of the loss and/or the previous tax year.

The loss can be used in the following ways:

- In current year only

- In prior year only

- In current year and then the prior year

- In the prior year and then the current year

You must use as much of the loss as possible. Restricted claims are not possible in order to preserve the personal allowance.

The trading loss is offset against the taxpayer's total income i.e. before the personal allowance (PA)

Where there are still losses not relieved against general income, these are carried forward under s83 – see above.

Losses cannot be relieved under s83 unless the business is conducted on a commercial basis with a view to the realisation of profits. The tax payer must make a claim for loss relief on the anniversary from 31 January after the end of the tax year in which loss occurs i.e. for 2011/12, the latest date for a claim is 31 January 2014.

The taxpayer cannot choose the amount of loss to relieve. This can lead to the loss of use of personal allowances, which is not tax efficient. However, by taking relief against general income, tax relief is taken at the earliest opportunity. If s64 is claimed in the prior year this will give rise to a repayment of income tax previously paid.

The trading loss is offset against the taxpayer's total income, in the order of non-savings income, then savings income, then dividend income.

Disadvantage

s64 relief involves setting the trading loss against the total income, which may result in wasting of the PA.

Advantage

s64 gives earlier relief for the loss than carrying it forward (cash flow advantage to the taxpayer). If s64 is claimed in the year prior to that in which the assessable trading profit is nil, this will give rise to a repayment of income tax previously paid.

Learning example 10.2

Edwin is a sole trader who has been trading for many years. His recent tax adjusted profits are as follows:

	£
Year ended 31 December 2009	11,500
Year ended 31 December 2010	4,500
Year ended 31 December 2011	(20,000)
Year ended 31 December 2012	12,500

He also has savings income of £3,500 each year (gross)

Required

Calculate Edwin's taxable income, assuming he wishes to use the loss as soon as possible.

Assume the rate of PA is £7,475 throughout

Decision of loss relief option

There are a number of factors that an individual would take into consideration when deciding the best use of the loss. These are:

*   The taxpayer wants to optimise his tax saving by reducing his liability at his highest marginal rate (saving tax at 50% is better than saving tax at 40% is better than 32.5% is better than 20% is better than 10%). This is usually the KEY consideration.

*   The taxpayer wants relief for the loss as early as possible.

*   The taxpayer wants to preserve the personal allowances whenever possible.

Approach to losses questions

1. set up losses proforma with years across the top

2. put in numbers from the question

3. put losses into losses memo

4. look at rate of tax paid in each year to decide best use of the loss

Proforma losses working

	2010/11 (py)	2011/12 (cy)	2012/13 (c/f)
Trading income c/f	x	-	x
Savings income	x	x	x
Dividend income	x	x	-
Total income	x	x	x
PA	(x)	(x)	(x)
Taxable income	x	x	x

Learning example 10.3

Cheryl is a sole trader who has been trading for many years. Her recent tax adjusted profits are as follows:

	£
Year ended 31 December 2010	44,500
Year ended 31 December 2011	(28,000)
Year ended 31 December 2012	25,600

She also has dividend income of £3,500 each year (gross)

Required

Calculate Cheryl's taxable income, assuming she wishes to use the loss as efficiently as possible

Assume the rate of PA is £7,475 throughout

Trading loss used against capital gains (s261)

If a claim has been made under s64 in a particular year then additionally it is possible to make a claim to reduce capital gains in the same year and hence reduce CGT.

The value of capital gains against which relief is available is the gains net of current and brought forward losses but prior to applying any annual exemption.

The taxpayer cannot decide how much of the loss to relieve against capital gains. This may lead to the loss or partial loss of the annual exemption for capital gains tax.

Learning example 10.4

Nicola is a sole trader who has been trading for many years. Her recent tax adjusted profits are as follows:

	£
Year ended 31 March 2012	(78,000)

She has savings income of £9,800 each year (gross)

In 2011/12, she also has a chargeable gain of £50,000

Required

Calculate Nicola's taxable income and taxable gain, assuming she wishes to use the loss in the current year.

Assume the rate of PA is £7,475 throughout

Loss on commencement of trade (s72)

Trading losses incurred in any of the first four tax years of trading can be relieved under s72. The trading loss can be carried back for three years on a FIFO basis and offset against the total income of the previous three years.

You must use as much of the loss as possible. Restricted claims are not possible in order to preserve the personal allowance.

The claim applies to all three previous tax years and you cannot miss out a year.

Disadvantage

s72 relief involves setting the loss against total income which may result in wastage of the PA.

Advantage

s72 gives earliest relief for the trading loss (cash flow advantage to the taxpayer). If s72 relief is claimed it will give rise to a repayment of income tax previously paid.

Learning example 10.5

Vanilla is a sole trader running a music business. She started trading on 1 June 2010 and her first accounts are prepared for the 15 months to 31 August 2011 and show a tax adjusted loss of £75,000.

Required

Show the trading losses for 2010/11 and 2011/12 and discuss the various methods of loss relief available to Vanilla.

Terminal loss relief (s89)

In normal circumstances a trader who incurs a trading loss may choose between carrying the loss forward against future profits of the same trade or relieving the loss against total income.

But if a trading loss is incurred in the final 12 months of trading, it is not possible to carry forward the loss so instead s89 terminal loss relief is available.

The trading loss incurred in the final 12 months of trading can be carried back for three years on a LIFO basis and offset against the trading profits of the previous three years.

London
School of Business
& Finance

shaping success in business and finance

Learning example 10.6

Cheung has been self-employed since 1999, but ceased trading on 30 September 2011. She has always prepared accounts to 30 September. Her results for the final five years of trading were as follows:

		£
Year ended 30 September 2007	Trading profit	24,800
Year ended 30 September 2008	Trading profit	20,600
Year ended 30 September 2009	Trading profit	18,200
Year ended 30 September 2010	Trading profit	1,600
Year ended 30 September 2011	Trading loss	(19,200)

For each of the years 2007/08 to 2011/12 Cheung has rental income of £5,000. Cheung has unused overlap profits brought forward of £4,600.

Required

Assuming that Cheung claims terminal loss relief (under s89), calculate her taxable income for each year 2007/08 to 2011/12 after claiming the relief.

Transfer of a Business to a Company (s86)

Background

If the owner of a business transfers that business to a limited company, there is a change in the legal ownership of the business and the vendor is deemed to have ceased trading. In consequence, any trading loss sustained by the vendor before the date of transfer cannot be carried forward and set against the company's trading profits.

Mechanism Of Relief

A further relief is available to the sole trader which provides that If the business is transferred to a limited company and the following conditions are met:

1. The consideration is wholly or mainly in exchange for shares in that company (80% of the consideration must be in shares),

2. The vendor of the business continues to hold those shares,

3. The company continues to carry on the transferred business,

then the vendor may set unrelieved trading losses against the first available income, in the order of non-savings income such as salary, savings income such as interest, dividend income, that they receive from the company.

Learning summary

- The calculation of trade losses and the main uses of trade losses including consideration of the impact of the various reliefs (loss of personal allowances, timing of tax refund, claim periods, marginal rate of tax saved).

- Opening years rules where special provisions allow for the carry back of losses arising in the first four years against total income of the previous three years.

- Terminal loss relief including use of any overlap profits which arose on the opening years or on a change of accounting date.

Exam standard question

Piers commenced business as a freelance journalist on 1 June 2011, preparing annual accounts to 31 May. The following tax adjusted figures (before capital allowances) have been ascertained:

		£
Year ended 31 May 2012	Loss	(19,000)
Year ended 31 May 2013	Profit	11,000

Piers acquired plant and machinery on 1 June 2011 at a cost of £5,000. There have not been any subsequent purchases or sales of plant.

Before starting his business, Piers was a reporter for his local newspaper.

Details of other incomes of Piers and his wife are as follows:

	2008/09 £	2009/10 £	2010/11 £	2011/12 £	2012/13 £	2013/14 £
Piers						
Salary from employment	17,000	20,000	5,500	5,000	-	-
Interest (gross)	1,000	2,000	2,000	1,000	1,000	1,000
Wife						
Salary	-	-	-	-	8,000	8,500

Required

Advise, with the aid of computations, how Piers should relieve his trading loss. Use 2011/12 rates and allowances throughout.

Learning solution 10.1

	2011/12 (cy)	2012/13 (c/f)	2013/14 (c/f)
Trading income	-	8,000	15,000
c/f		(8,000)	(7,000)
Savings income	-	-	-
Dividend income	-	-	-
total income	-	-	8,000
PA	(7,475)	(7,475)	(7,475)
Taxable income	-	-	525

London
School of Business
& Finance

shaping success in business and finance

Learning solution 10.2

	2010/11 (py)	2011/12 (cy)	2012/13 (c/f)
Trading income	4,500	-	12,500
c/f			(8,500)
			4,000
Savings income	3,500	3,500	3,500
Dividend income	-	-	-
Total income	8,000	3,500	7,500
cy	-	(3,500)	
py	(8,000)		
PA	(7,475)	(7,475)	(7,475)
Taxable income	-	-	25

Learning solution 10.3

First, we need to decide the highest rate of tax that Cheryl would pay before the loss is considered:

	2010/11 (py)	2011/12 (cy)	2012/13 (c/f)
Trading income	44,500	-	25,600
Dividend income	3,500	3,500	3,500
Total income	48,000	3,500	29,100
cy			
py			
PA	(7,475)	(7,475)	(7,475)
Taxable income	40,525	-	21,625
Rate of tax	40%	-	20%

Decision

So we can see that if Cheryl wishes to save tax at the highest rate, the best use of her loss is to use it in the prior year and then carry any remaining loss forward to 2012/13. She should not use any loss in the current year as her income is already covered by the personal allowance.

Finally, work the £28,000 of loss through the question:

	2010/11 (py)	2011/12 (cy)	2012/13 (c/f)
Trading income	44,500	-	25,600
Dividend income	3,500	3,500	3,500
Total income	48,000	3,500	29,100
cy			
py	(28,000)	-	-
PA	(7,475)	(7,475)	(7,475)
Taxable income	12,525	-	21,625

Learning solution 10.4

Income tax:

	2011/12 £
Trading income	-
Savings income	9,800
Dividend income	-
Total income	9,800
Cy	(9,800)
PA	(7,475)
Taxable income	-

Note the wastage of personal allowances

Loss remaining to be used against capital gains: 78,000 − 9,800 = £68,200

Capital gains tax:

Chargeable gain	50,000
Less: s261	(50,000)
Annual exemption	(10,600)
Taxable gain	-

Note the wastage of annual exemption

Nicola still has £18,200 of trading loss to be carried forward to 2012/13

London
School of Business
& Finance
shaping success in business and finance

Learning solution 10.5

Vanilla

Year	tax year	basis period	Trading loss £
1	2010/11	1.6.10-5.4.11 10/15 x 75,000	(50,000)
2	2011/12	Does an accounting date fall in 2011/12 Yes (31.8.11) Y/e 31.8.11 (75,000 – 50,000)	(25,000)

Methods of relieving the losses

Carry forward the loss (s83)

The trading losses can be carried forward and offset against the first available taxable trading profits of the same trade in 2012/13 etc.

Current year/prior year (s64)

The trading loss can be relieved against total Income in the tax year in which the trading loss is made and/or the previous tax year.

2010/11 (50,000) - This loss can be relieved in 2010/11 and/or 2009/10
2011/12 (25,000) - This loss can be relieved in 2011/12 and/or 2010/11

Loss on commencement of trade (s72)

A trading loss incurred in any of the first four tax years of trading may be carried back for three years on a FIFO basis and offset against the total income for the previous three years.

2010/11 (50,000) - This loss may be carried back to 2007/08, 2008/09 and 2009/10
2011/12 (25,000) - This loss may be carried back to 2008/09, 2009/10 and 2010/11

Learning solution 10.6

Convert the tax adjusted profits into trading income by applying the closing year rules

Tax year	Basis period	Loss £	Trading income £
2007/08	CYB: Year ended 30.9.07		24,800
2008/09	CYB: Year ended 30.9.08		20,600
2009/10	CYB: Year ended 30.9.09		18,200
2010/11	CYB: Year ended 30.9.10		1,600
2011/12	Closing year rules:		
(final tax year)	1.10.10-30.9.11 (19,200)		
	Less: Overlap profits (4,600) (23,800)		-
	(23,800)		

The terminal loss is also £(23,800) as this is the loss of the final 12 months of trading.

Set up the income tax computations for all tax years and show relief for the trading loss.

	2007/08	2008/09	2009/10	2010/11	2011/12
Trading profits	24,800	20,600	18,200	1,600	-
TLR (s89)	-	(4,000)	(18,200)	(1,600)	-
Rental income	5,000	5,000	5,000	5,000	5,000
Total income	29,800	21,600	5,000	5,000	5,000
PA	(7,475)	(7,475)	(7,475)	(7,475)	(7,475)
Taxable Income	22,325	14,125	-	-	-

The terminal loss is carried back on a LIFO basis and offset against trading profits and leaves other income to cover personal allowances.

This will result in a repayment income tax previously paid.

Solution to exam standard question

First: Determine the capital allowances for each accounting period.

	AIA FYA £	Capital allowances £
Y/e 31.5.12		
Addition 1.6.11	5,000	-
AIA: 5,000 x 100%	(5,000)	5,000
TWDV c/f 31.5.12	-	
Capital allowances		=
Y/e 31.5.13		
	-	-
TWDV c/f 31.5.13	-	
Capital allowances		-

Next: Deduct the capital allowances from the tax adjusted profit/(loss).

	Tax adjusted profit/(loss) £	Capital allowances £	Tax adjust profit/loss £
Y/e 31.5.12	(19,000)	(5,000)	(24,000)
Y/e 31.5.13	11,000	-	11,000

Then: Fit tax adjusted profit into tax years using basis periods

Year	tax year	Basis periods	Trading profit/loss £
1	2011/12	1.6.11-5.4.12	
		10/12 x (24,000)	(20,000)
2	2012/13	CYB Y/e 31.5.12	
		(24,000 – 20,000)	(4,000)
3	2013/14	CYB Y/e 31.5.13	11,000

Now: Consider the various methods of loss relief available to Piers.

Current year/prior year (S64)

2011/12(Loss)   £(20,000)

This can be relieved in 2011/12 and/or 2010/11 against the Total Income. It is not possible to make partial or restricted claims to preserve personal allowances. By claiming in 2011/12 and 2010/11 he will waste his personal allowances.

2012/13 (Loss)   £(4,000)

This can be relieved in 2012/13 and/or 2011/12 against Piers' Total Income.

By claiming in 2011/12 and 2012/13 he will waste his personal allowances. Therefore S64 is not the best option for this loss.

Loss on commencement of trade (s72)

This method of loss relief is available where a loss is incurred in any of the first four fiscal years of a new trade.

The loss can be carried back for three years on a FIFO basis.

2011/12 (Loss)   £(20,000)

This can be carried back to 2008/09, 2009/10, 2010/11. The loss must be relieved against the Total Income of each year. It is not possible to make partial or restricted claims.

2012/13 (Loss)   £(4,000)

This can be carried back to 2009/10, 2010/11 and 2011/12.

This appears to be a better use of his loss as relief is obtained as early as possible. Personal allowances will be wasted in 2008/09, but are preserved in all other years.

Piers will get a repayment of income tax previously paid in 2007/08 and 2008/09.

Finally: Set up personal tax computations for all relevant years.

	2008/09 £	2009/10 £	2010/11 £	2011/12 £	2012/13 £
Employment income	17,000	20,000	5,500	5,000	-
Interest income	1,000	2,000	2,000	1,000	1,000
Net income	18,000	22,000	7,500	6,000	1,000
s72 (1)	(18,000)	-	-	-	-
s72 (2)	-	(2,000)	-	-	-
s72 (3)	-	(4,000)	-	-	-
	-	16,000	7,500	6,000	3,000
PA	-	(7,475)	(7,475)	(7,475)	(7,475)
Taxable income	-	8,525	25	-	-

Loss memo

	(1) £	(2) £
	20,000	4,000
s72 (1)	(18,000)	-
	2,000	-
s72 (2)	(2,000)	-
s72 (3)	-	(4,000)
	-	-

London
School of Business
& Finance
shaping success in business and finance

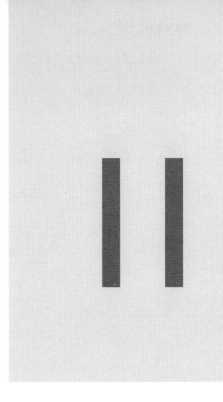

Partnerships

Context

A partnership is simply a single trading entity for a number of sole traders in business together; where each partner is treated as an individual for income tax purposes (they complete their own tax returns based on an apportionment of partnership profits). The easiest way of dealing with partnerships is to calculate the partnership profits, apportion to each partner, and then tax each partner as if he were a sole trader running his own business.

Exam hints

Although not as commonly examined as sole traders, you could potentially get a question on partnerships in your exam. You must therefore be able to calculate the trading profits of a partner in a partnership.

Key learning points

- The tax adjusted profit figure for a partnership is calculated in the same way as that of a sole trader.

- In a partnership, the tax adjusted profit needs to be shared out amongst the partners using a profit sharing arrangement (PSA).

- Each partner will then have their own share of the tax adjusted profit and will fit this into a tax year using the relevant basis period rules.

Calculation of trading profits for a partner in a partnership

The approach to working out each individual partner's share of the trading profits is very similar to the way that we calculate trading profits for a sole trader.

Approach:

1. take net profit per partnership accounts and adjust profits as normal (step one in trading income working)

2. calculate capital allowances as normal for the set of accounts and deduct them to get tax adjusted profits of partnership (step two in trading income working)

Trading income working	£
Net profit per partnership accounts	X
Step 1: adjustments to profit	X/(X)
Step 2: capital allowances (w)	(X)
Tax adjusted trading profit	X

Now we have a problem. Previously, with our sole trader all the tax adjusted profit belonged to one person, and so we simply had to fit this figure into tax years using the basis period rules. Now however, this tax adjusted profit figure belongs to more than one person and needs to be shared out between the different partners. The tax adjusted profit is shared out between the partners using the profit sharing arrangement (PSA)

The PSA is a legal document, drawn up by the partnership, agreeing how the profits should be shared out. The profit can be shared out using the following tools:

- Salary to partner (NB this is not actual salary, simply a guaranteed share of the profit)

- Interest on capital

- Profit sharing ratio

The PSA is usually laid out as follows:

		Total £	Partner A £	Partner B £
Salary		X	X	X
Interest on capital (10%)		X	X	X
Balance	(PSR 2:1)	X̲	X̲	X̲
Tax adjusted figure per partnership accounts		X̲	X̲	X̲

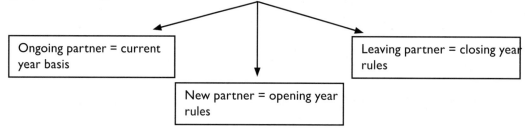

3.   allocate tax adjusted profits to each partner using profit sharing agreement eg salaries, interest on capital, PSR (new extra step)

4.   now each partner has own share of profits, chose appropriate basis period for each partner (step 3 in trading income working)

> Ongoing partner = current year basis

> New partner = opening year rules

> Leaving partner = closing year rules

Learning example 11.1

Trish, Simon and Kate have for many years shared profits in the ratio 5:3:2, after charging salaries of Trish £4,000 and Simon £5,000, with interest at 6% per annum on the capitals of Trish £10,000, Simon £9,000 and Kate £11,000.

The profits for the firm were £25,000 for 31 December 2011 and capital allowances agreed at £4,200.

Required

Calculate each partner's share of taxable trading profits for 2011/12.

Loss reliefs

Partners are entitled to the same loss reliefs as sole traders. These are:

*   Carry forward relief – available to new and continuing partners

*   Offset against general income and capital gains – available to all partners

*   Loss on commencement of trade – available against general income for new partners, for the fist four years

*   Terminal loss relief – available to ceasing partners

*   Carry forward on incorporation – available to ceasing partners if the business is incorporated.

However, where the partner is a limited partner or not active in the business (works for < 10 hours per week), such a partner can only use loss relief against general income and capital gains up to an amount which is equal to their contribution to the partnership. Their contribution includes capital contributed and undrawn profits. There is an overriding cap of £25,000.

Investment income

Where a partnership has non-trading income (dividends, bank interest), these items are treated separately from the partnership's trading income. Any non-income which arises is shared according to the PSR and Partnership Agreement.

Change in profit sharing arrangements

If the profit sharing arrangement is changed during an accounting period, then the profits will need to be time apportioned, before and after the arrangement changed. The time apportioned profits are then allocated to each partner.

Learning example 11.2

Castle and Ford have traded since 1990 sharing profits 3:2 after charging salaries of £4,500 and £3,000 respectively. From 1 April 2011 they altered their agreement, the new terms being that the salaries should be doubled, the balance of profit being shared 2:1.

The adjusted profit for the year ended 30 September 2011 was £37,000 and capital allowances were agreed at £4,000.

Required

You are required to show the amounts to be included in respect of each partner's income for 2011/12.

Partner joins or leaves the partnership

Each partner has is taxed as a sole trader and consequently, has their own trading cycle.

Scenario	Tax treatment
Partner joins	Opening year's rules apply to the joining partner. Overlap profits may arise on the joining partner only. All other existing partners treated as if continuing a trade.
Partner leaves	Closing year's rules apply to leaving partner. Use of overlap profits, potential terminal loss relief may apply. All other existing partners treated as if continuing a trade.

Learning example 11.3

Perry and Tom commenced in partnership on 1 July 2009 and decided to produce their accounts to 30 June annually. On 1 January 2011 Harvey joined the partnership.

The partnership's accounts show the following adjusted profits:

	£
Year ended 30 June 2010	20,000
Year ended 30 June 2011	27,000
Year ended 30 June 2012	36,000

Required

Show the amounts assessed on the individual partners assuming profits are shared equally for each relevant tax year.

Learning summary

- A partnership is a source of profits and losses for trades being conducted by individual partners. Each partner is treated as a sole trader (for tax purposes), with opening years rules applying individually to each partner when they join the partnership, and cessation rules applying when they leave.

- Profits and losses of the partnership are allocated to the partners in accordance with the profit sharing ratio. The profit sharing ratio is applied after any apportioning any salaries or interest due to individual partners.

Exam standard question

Harry and Erica have commenced in partnership on 1 July 2011 as publishing consultants.

Profit and loss account for the year ended 30 June 2012

The partnership's summarised profit and loss account for the year ended 30 June 2012 is as follows:

	Note	£	£
Sales	1		340,000
Expenses			
Depreciation		20,800	
Motor expenses	2	13,900	
Other expenses	3	38,050	
Wages and salaries	4	60,000	
Gifts and donations	5	8,500	
Professional fees	6	5,400	
			146,650
Net profit			193,350

(1)   The sales figure of £340,000 is exclusive of output value added tax (VAT) of £68,000.

(2)   The figure of £13,900 for motor expenses includes £6,000 in respect of the partners' motor cars, with 40% of this amount being in respect of private journeys.

(3)   The figure of £38,050 for other expenses includes £1,720 for entertaining employees and £4,000 for entertaining suppliers. The remaining expenses are all allowable.

(4)   The figure of £30,000 for wages and salaries includes the annual salary of £14,000 paid to Harry (see the profit sharing note below), and the annual salary of £16,000 paid to Erica's husband, who works part-time for the partnership. Another part-time employee doing the same job is paid a salary of £8,000 per annum.

(5)   The figure of £8,500 for gifts and donations includes:

Gifts to customers – bottle of wine at Christmas, costing £5 each bottle	£3,000
Gifts to customers – diaries displaying the partnership branding, costing £10 each	£1,200
Donation to local charity – where the partnership received free advertising in the charity magazine	£200

(6)   The figure of £5,400 for professional fees includes £1,600 for accountancy work and £250 for some capital gains tax advice for Erica on a matter not relating to the partnership.

Plant and machinery

The following transactions took place during the year ended 30 June 2012:

		Cost/(Proceeds) £
1 August 2011	Purchased a van	15,000
1 November 2011	Purchased equipment	162,000
15 December 2011	Purchased a motor car (1)	22,100
19 March 2012	Purchased a motor car (2)	12,000

Motor car [1] has a CO_2 emission rate of 155 grams per kilometre. It is used by Harry and 60% of the mileage is for business journeys.

Motor car [2] had a CO_2 emission rate of 108 grams per kilometre. It is used by one of the partnership employees.

Profit sharing

Profits are shared 70% to Harry and 30% to Erica. This is after paying an annual salary of £14,000 to Harry, and interest at the rate of 8% on the partners' capital account balances.

The capital account balances are:

	£
Harry	50,000
Erica	100,000

Required

(a) Calculate the partnership's tax adjusted trading profit for the year ended 30 June 2012.

Note: Your computation should commence with the net profit figure of £193,350, and should also list all of the items referred to in notes (1) to (6) indicating by the use of Nil or zero (0) any items that do not require adjustment.

(b) Calculate the trading income assessments of Harry and Erica for the tax years 2011/12 and 2012/13 and any overlap profits arising.

Learning solution 11.1

Trish, Simon and Kate

	Total £	5 T £	:	3 S £	:	2 K £
Salary	9,000	4,000		5,000		-
Interest	1,800	600		540		660
Balance	10,000	5,000		3,000		2,000

£25,000 (tax adjusted profit) less £4,200 (capital allowances) →

	Total £	T £	S £	K £
	20,800	9,600	8,540	2,660

All partners will be using the current year basis (year ended 31 December 2011)

		£
2011/12:	Trish	9,600
	Simon	8,540
	Kate	2,660

Learning solution 11.2

Castle and Ford

	Total £	C £	:	F £
1.10.10-31.3.11 (6 months)				
Salary (6/12)	3,750	2,250		1,500
Balance	12,750	7,650		5,100

£33,000 x 6/12 →

	16,500	9,900		6,600

	Total £	2 C £	:	1 F £
1.4.11 – 30.9.11 (6 months)				
Salary (6/12)	7,500	4,500		3,000
Balance	9,000	6,000		3,000

£33,000 x 6/12 →

	16,500	10,500		6,000

Totals	33,000	20,400		12,600

£37,000 (tax adjusted profit) less £4,000 (capital allowances) →

Both partners will be using the current year basis (year ended 30 September 2011)

		£
2011/12:	Castle	20,400
	Ford	12,600

London
School of Business
& Finance

shaping success in business and finance

Learning solution 11.3

You should start by allocating the profits between the partners. Remember that as Harvey joins the partnership part of the way through the accounting year ended 30 June 2011, the profits for that year will need to be time-apportioned prior to allocation.

	Total £	Perry £	Tom £	Harvey £
A/cs to 30.6.10	20,000	10,000	10,000	-
A/cs to 30.6.11				
(6/12)	13,500	6,750	6,750	-
(6/12)	13,500	4,500	4,500	4,500
	27,000	11,250	11,250	4,500
A/cs to 30.6.12	36,000	12,000	12,000	12,000

Once the profits have been allocated between the partners, each partner is then treated as if he is carrying on a business alone.

Perry and Tom will both be assessed on the following figures:

		£
2009/10	opening year rules (1.7.09 - 5/4/10) £10,000 x 9/12	7,500
2010/11	CYB:A/cs to 30.6.10	10,000
2011/12	CYB: A/cs to 30.6.11	11,250
2012/13	CYB:A/cs to 30.6.12	12,000

They will both be entitled to overlap relief to £7,500.

Harvey is treated as commencing trading on 1 January 2011. He will therefore be assessed as follows:

		£
2010/11	opening year rules (1.1.11 - 5.4.11) £4,500 x 3/6	2,250
2011/12	opening year rules £4,500 + (£12,000 x 6/12)	11,500
2012/13	CYB:A/cs to 30.6.12	12,000

Harvey's 2011/12 assessment is based on the profits of the first 12 months of trading as his share of the accounts to 30.6.11 does not cover a full 12 months.

Harvey will be entitled to overlap relief of £8,250 which is made up as follows:

	£
1.1.11 to 5.4.11	2,250
1.7.11 to 31.12.11	6,000
	8,250

Solution to exam standard question

(a) Adjusted trading profit for the year ended 30 June 2012

	£	£
Net profit		193,350
Depreciation	20,800	
Input VAT	Nil	
Motor expenses (6,000 x 40%)	2,400	
Entertaining employees	Nil	
Entertaining suppliers	4,000	
Appropriation of profit	14,000	
Excessive salary (16,000 – 8,000)	8,000	
Gifts of wine to customers (food and drink)	3,000	
Gifts of diaries to customers	Nil	
Donation to local charity	Nil	
Professional fees – accountancy	Nil	
Professional fees – capital gains tax work	250	
		52,450
Capital allowances (W1)		(130,052)
Tax adjusted trading profit		115,748

Tutorial notes:

No adjustment is required in respect of the input VAT as the expense figures are already exclusive of VAT.

Working – Capital allowances y/e 30 June 2012

	Main Pool £	Motor car [1] £	Bus Use 60%	Allowances £
WDV brought forward	0	0		
Additions – Medium CO_2				
Motor car [1]		22,100		
Additions - AIA				
Van 15,000				
Plant and machinery				
162,000				
177,000				
Less AIA (100,000)				100,000
	77,000			
	77,000	22,100		
WDA - 20%	(15,400)			15,400
WDA – 20%		(4,420)	x 60%	2,652
	61,600			
Addition - FYA				
Motor car [2]	12,000			
FYA - 100%	(12,000)			12,000
WDV carried forward	61,600	17,680		
Total allowances				130,052

London
School of Business
& Finance

shaping success in business and finance

Tutorial notes:

- Motor car [2] has CO_2 emissions of no more than 110 grams per kilometre and therefore qualifies for the 100% first year allowance.

- Motor car [1] has CO_2 emissions between 111 and 160 grams per kilometre, and therefore qualifies for writing down allowances at the rate of 20%.

(b) Trading income assessments 2011/12 & 2012/13

	Total £	Harry £	Erica £
Salary	14,000	14,000	
Interest (50,000 at 8%)	4,000	4,000	
Interest (100,000 at 8%)	8,000		8,000
Balance (70%/30%)	89,748	62,824	26,924
	115,748	80,824	34,924

Harry

2011/12
1 July 2011 to 5 April 2012
£80,824 x 9/12 = £60,618

2012/13
Year ended 30 June 2013 = £80,824

Overlap profits of £60,618

Erica

2011/12
1 July 2011 to 5 April 2012
£34,924 x 9/12 = £26,193

2012/13
Year ended 30 June 2012 = £34,924

Overlap profits £26,193

12

National
Insurance
Contributions
(NICs)

Context

National insurance contributions (NICs) are payable by employees, employers, and those who are self employed.

NICs are payable by individuals aged 16 years or over up to the state pension age. Employees who continue to work after reaching state pension age pay no further contributions but employers must still pay secondary contributions for such employees.

State pension age is 65 for men, and for women is being increased from age 60 to age 65 over the ten years from April 2010.

NICs are collected by HMRC, and audited and checked by the National Insurance Contributions Office (NICO), which is a part of HMRC.

Exam hints

The rates of NICs will be provided to you in the exam. You will however need to know how to apply these rates correctly to get the right answer.

It is unlikely that you would see a whole question just covering NICs. It is more likely to be examined as a small part of a bigger question, for example as part b of question 1. It can be tested in more than one question. The key is to know which type of NIC is relevant and to calculate it correctly

Key learning points

- Class 1 primary is paid by employees on their earnings and class 1 secondary is paid by employers, also based on earnings.

- Class 1A is paid by employers only on non-cash benefits in kind.

- Class 2 and class 4 are paid by individuals who are self employed, based on trading profits.

Class 1 NICs - employees

Class 1 primary – employee

Employees are liable for class 1 (primary) NICs on their earnings, which comprises gross pay, excluding benefits which cannot be turned into cash (holiday entitlement). In general terms, if an item is an exempt benefit for income tax, it will be exempt from inclusion in the earnings calculation for NICs.

Businesses expenses are not treated as earnings for NIC purposes. Mileage allowances are also excluded if below the AMAP limits. For cars, the less than 10,000 mile rate is used, regardless of total mileage.

Vouchers are liable to Class1 NICs even if they cannot be exchanged for cash, unless they are exempt from income tax.

For the tax year 2011/12 the rates of employee class 1 primary NIC have changed to 12% and 2%. The rate of 12% is paid on earnings between £7,225 per year and £42,475 per year, and the rate of 2% is paid on all earnings over £42,475 per year.

Class 1 secondary – employers

In addition to the 'primary' contributions paid by the employee, employers are required to pay 'secondary' contributions. The rate of employer class 1 secondary NIC is 13.8%, and is paid on all earnings over £7,072 per year. There is no ceiling on the amount of an employee's earnings that attracts secondary contributions. No liability for secondary contributions can arise unless there is a liability for primary contributions.

Class 1A – employers

Class 1A NICs apply to most benefits. The rate of Class 1A NIC that employers pay on taxable benefits is 13.8%. The payment date of Class 1A NICs is 19 July after the end of the year of assessment. The Class 1A liability is an employer's only charge and is a tax-deductible expense.

Class 1A NICs are not paid where:

- Class 1 NICs are already due (on expense payments);
- The expense payment is covered by a P11D dispensation or specific exemption;
- The expenses payment is subject to Class 1B NICs (through a PAYE Settlement Agreement);
- The benefit-in-kind is provided to an excluded employee

The class 1 and class 1A NIC information will be given in the tax rates and allowances section of the examination paper. For the June and December 2012 sittings the rates are shown below and will be reproduced for you in the exam.

Earnings periods for NICs

NICs are based on earnings periods. For most employees, this is the period to which the earnings relate i.e. monthly, weekly.

Directors have an annual earnings period. In broad terms, this means that directors do not start to pay NICs until the annual exemptions, as given above, are exceeded. Once exceeded, all earnings are subject to NICs. Conversely, the payment of a large bonus or lump sum payment could attract the maximum contributions for a year, rather than for one week or one month.

For an employee, the annual exemption limits are divided by 12 (if monthly earnings) or 52 (if weekly earnings) and this fraction is allowed against earnings before NIC is payable.

NICs rates and limits

	Class I Primary		Class I Secondary		Class IA	
Paid by:	Employees		Employers		Employers	
Paid on:	Cash earnings: e.g. salary, bonus and taxable benefits convertible into cash, such as payments in excess of mileage allowance limits and vouchers.		Cash earnings (same as primary)		Taxable benefits (not convertible into cash)	
Limits and rates of NICs:	**Annual limit**	**Rate**	**Annual limit**	**Rate**	**Annual limit**	**Rate**
	£1 - £7,225 £7,226 - £42,475 £42,475 and above	Nil 12% 2%	£1 - £7,072 £7,073 and above	Nil 13.8%	No limit	13.8%

Learning example 12.1

Samuel Ltd has one employee Samuel who is paid a salary of £48,000 per year.

Required

Calculate the class 1 primary national insurance payable by the employee and the class 1 secondary payable by the employer in 2011/12.

Learning example 12.2

Hari is an employee of Trigger Ltd, with a gross salary of £50,000. He also receives a company car, with a taxable benefit of £6,600.

Required

Calculate the NICs contributions payable by Hari and Trigger Ltd in 2011/12.

Class 2 and Class 4 NICs – self-employed

A self-employed individual is liable to class 2 NICs of £2.50 per week unless their earnings are below the exemption limit of £5,315, and they have applied for a Certificate of Exemption. Where the individual has commenced self-employment, they have three months to inform NICO, otherwise a penalty may be levied.

A self-employed individual is liable to class 4 NICs at a rate depending on their profit levels as determined for income tax purposes. The rates of class 4 NIC are 9% and 2%. The rate of 9% is paid on profits between £7,226 and £42,475, and the rate of 2% is paid on all profits over £42,475.

Class 2 is paid in two equal installments by 31 January during the tax year and by 31 July following the end of the tax year. Class 4 NICs are paid to HMRC as part of the payments on account of income tax made in July and January each year

The class 4 NIC information that will be given in the tax rates and allowances section of the examination paper is as follows:

Self employed:

	Class 2	**Class 4**	
Paid by:	Self employed	Self employed	
Paid on:	Only paid if accounting profit for the tax year is > £5,315	Taxable trading profits for accounting period ending in tax year	
Limits and rates of NICs	Flat rate of £2.50 per week	**Annual limit**	**Rate**
		£1 - £7,225	Nil
		£7,226 - £42,475	9%
		£42,475 and above	2%

Learning example 12.3

Samuel is self-employed has trading income of £48,000 per year.

Required

Calculate the class 2 and class 4 national insurance payable by Samuel in 2011/12.

Learning summary

- Class 1 National insurance is payable by employees and employers on employment earnings.

- Class 2 and 4 National insurance is payable by self-employed individuals. Class 2 National insurance is a fixed weekly payment, whereas Class 4 National insurance is based on the self-employment business profits.

London
School of Business
& Finance

shaping success in business and finance

Learning solution 12.1

Class I primary (payable by Samuel)

		£
$(42,475 - 7,225) \times 12\%$	=	4,230
$(48,000 - 42,475) \times 2\%$	=	111
		4,341

Class I secondary (payable by Samuel Ltd)

$(48,000 - 7,072) \times 13.8\%$	=	5,648

Learning solution 12.2

NICs payable by Hari

		£
Class I primary:		
$(42,475 - 7,225) \times 12\%$	=	4,230
$(50,000 - 42,475) \times 2\%$	=	151
		4,381

NICs payable by Trigger Ltd

Class I secondary:		
$(50,000 - 7,072) \times 13.8\%$	=	5,924
Class IA		
$6,600 \times 13.8\%$	=	911

Learning solution 12.3

Class 2

Samuel pays £2.50 x 52 weeks = £130

Class 4

Taxable trading profit for the tax year 2011/12 = £48,000

		£
$(42,475 - 7,225)$	$= 35,250 \times 9\%$	3,173
$(48,000 - 42,475) = 5,525 \times 2\%$		111
Class 4		3,284
Total NICs		3,414

13

Capital Gains Tax

Context

In previous chapters, we have considered income tax, paid by individuals on their regular income. We are now about to meet a new tax, capital gains tax (CGT). CGT is not payable on your regular income.

It arises when you sell certain assets and make a profit. It is this profit that CGT is payable on.

Exam hints

The tax implications of disposing of assets are a very important area of the syllabus and will be tested frequently. This will always be tested in question 3 for 15 marks.

The capital gains implications of making disposals of assets can also be tested in question 1 and 2 as was demonstrated in the pilot paper.

Key learning points

- CGT is payable when there is a chargeable disposal of a chargeable asset by a chargeable person.

- A gain must be calculated for each chargeable asset disposed of. A gain is calculated by deducting the original cost of the asset from the proceeds from sale.

- Each individual is entitled to an annual exemption for the tax year (2011/12: £10,600) and CGT is payable at 18% or 28% on the taxable gain depending on other taxable income levels.

- An asset may be sold at a loss. Capital losses must be used against gains in the current year. Unused capital losses are carried forward to be used against gains in future years.

- The transfer of assets between spouses/civil partnership are at no gain, no loss.

- Part disposal of an asset also gives rises to CGT. A special calculation must be used to determine the cost figure to be deducted in the gain calculation.

- Special rules apply to wasting and non wasting chattels. Non wasting chattels are subject to the special £6,000 rule when determining the gain.

Scope of capital gains tax

For capital gains tax to be payable, there must be a **chargeable disposal** of a **chargeable asset** by a **chargeable person**.

Chargeable disposal

- the sale or gift of the whole or part of an asset
- loss or destruction of an asset

Of a chargeable asset

Anything that is not exempt

Exempt assets:
- Motor cars
- Cash
- Types of chattel
- Gilts and qualifying corporate bonds
- National Savings Certificates and Premium Bonds.
- Shares in an ISA
- Racehorses
- Trading stock

By a chargeable person

Individual resident or ordinarily resident in the UK

Residence and ordinary residence

An individual is resident in the UK for a tax year where:

a)   he is present for 183 days or more in the UK; or

b)   substantial visits are made to the UK. This is defined as averaging 91 days a year over four or more consecutive years.

An individual is ordinarily resident in the UK where residence is of a habitual nature or settled nature.

Normally an individual is treated as resident and/or ordinarily resident for a whole tax year. However the year of arrival may be split if the individual had not been resident or ordinarily resident in any of the five previous tax years, and the year of departure may be split provided that the individual had not been resident and ordinarily resident for the whole of at least four out of the seven years prior to the year of departure.

Rates and basis of assessment

- A person's CGT liability for a tax year is based upon the chargeable disposals made by that person during the tax year.

- The gain or loss arising on each disposal made during the year is calculated separately.

- Total chargeable gains are reduced by the amount of the annual exemption (AE) £10,600. Any excess is called the taxable gain.

- The taxable gain is subject to tax at 18% or 28%.

- The rate of capital gains tax depends on the level of the individual's income. If the individual is a higher or additional rate taxpayer the gains are taxed at 28%. If the individual is a basic rate taxpayer and the chargeable gains do not exceed the individual's unused basic rate band the gains are taxed at 18%. If they do exceed the individual's unused basic rate band then gains up to the amount of the unused basic rate band are taxed at 18% and the excess are taxed at 28%.

- The basic rate band is extended if a person pays personal pension contributions or makes a gift aid donation

- The due date for paying the tax to HMRC is 31 January following the tax year of assessment

Capital Gains Tax computation

Asset 1	X
Asset 2	X
Less: current year capital loss	(X)
Less: b/f capital loss	(X) (note)
Net gains	X
Less AE	(10,600)
Taxable gain	X
CGT rate = 18%/28%	

Note: Bought forward capital losses are restricted the level of the annual exemption.

Calculating gain or loss on disposal

The computation of the capital gain or loss arising on the disposal of a chargeable asset begins by subtracting the acquisition cost of the asset from its disposal value.

The basic proforma that you need to use to compute the capital gain or loss for individuals is:

	£	£	NOTES
Consideration (or proceeds)		X	Disposal proceeds or market value if gift
Less Incidental costs of sale		(X)	Legal expenses, valuation fees, advertising costs, stamp duty, auctioneers fees
Net sale proceeds		X	
Less Allowable expenditure			
- Acquisition cost	X		If bought = purchase price If gift = market value at date of gift If inherited = probate value
- Incidental costs of acquisition	X		
		(X)	
- Enhancement expenditure		(X)	Expenditure that enhances the value of the asset e.g. new extension on a house
gain/(loss)		X / (X)	

Learning example 13.1

Mr Gates disposed of an investment property on 31 December 2011. He incurred legal costs and estate agents fees of £7,000. Mr Gates had purchased the property originally on 12 March 1986 for £27,000 and incurred acquisition costs of £2,000.

Mr Gates spent £35,000 on an extension to property on 31 July 2003.

Required

Assuming the sale proceeds were:

(a) £130,000
(b) £55,000
(c) £80,000

Compute the chargeable gain assessable on Mr Gates in 2011/12.

Capital losses

A taxpayer may dispose of an asset in the year and make a loss on the asset. For example:

	£
Proceeds	5,000
Cost	(8,000)
Loss	(3,000)

In the exam, you need to be able to calculate and use a capital loss correctly.

Use of capital losses

Current year losses

If a loss on disposal of an asset in the current tax year is made, it must be used against current year gains. You must use as much of the loss as possible. Any remaining capital loss that cannot be used in the current year is then carried forward against gains in future years.

Current year capital losses are offset before brought forward capital losses.

Learning example 13.2

Sabine has sold two assets during the 2011/12 tax year, with the following gains and losses:

	£
Asset 1: Gain	20,000
Asset 2: Loss	(8,000)

Required

Calculate her capital gains tax for the year, assuming she has employment income of £22,000

London
School of Business
& Finance

shaping success in business and finance

Brought forward losses from previous years

Brought forward capital losses are deducted after current year capital losses. They must be used against current year gains. However, they do not have to be used in full. Can restrict amount of loss used to preserve annual exemption, as demonstrated by the worked example below:

Worked example

Sarah has the following gains and losses in the tax year 2011/12:

	£
Gains	17,500
Current year losses	6,000

She also has a capital loss brought forward of £7,500

Required

Calculate Sarah's taxable gain for 2011/12

Approach:

- Set up a basic CGT computation and put in the gains and losses given in the example.

- The current year capital loss MUST be used in full against the gains

- The brought forward capital loss can be restricted to preserve the annual exemption of £10,600 as follows:

Capital Gains Tax computation

	£
Gain	17,500
Less current year capital loss	(6,000)
Less b/f capital loss	(900)
Net gains	10,600
Less AE	(10,600)
Taxable gain	nil

> Only have to use enough brought forward loss to take net gain down to £10,600. The remaining brought forward loss can be carried forward to the next year

Learning example 13.3

Ruth has disposed of the following assets during the tax year 2011/12:

	£
Asset 1: gain	35,000
Asset 2: loss	2,000

Ruth also has a brought forward capital loss of £10,000

Required

Calculate her capital gains tax payable for 2011/12. Assume Ruth has employment income of £41,000 in 2011/12.

Capital gains tax complications

Transfers between spouses/civil partnership

Each spouse (or civil partner) is taxed as a separate individual, with their own CGT computation and annual exemption. However, when assets are transferred between a husband and a wife (or civil partners), a special CGT rule applies.

The transfer of assets between spouses occurs at no gain, no loss (NGNL). This means that one spouse takes over the asset and is treated as if they acquired the asset at the same date and the same cost as the original spouse, who first acquired the asset.

When the asset is eventually sold, the gain calculation would be as follows:

	£
Proceeds	x
Cost (when first acquired by husband or wife)	(x)
	x

Learning example 13.4

Doris and Henry have been married for many years. On 1st March 1996 Doris bought an antique painting for £37,000. On 25th December 2005, she gave it to Henry as a Christmas present. On 7 July 2011, Henry sold the painting for £65,000.

Required

Calculate the gain arising on Henry when he sells the painting

Part disposal of an asset

If only part of an asset is disposed of, then the full original acquisition cost cannot be deducted in the gain calculation, as the full asset has not been disposed of.

To calculate how much of the original acquisition cost can be deducted, use the following formula:

Cost x $\dfrac{A}{A + B}$

- A = market value of part disposed of

- B = market value of part retained

Any incidental costs of disposal are still deductible in full.

Learning example 13.5

Patrick buys a house with a garden for £48,000 in October 1995. He sells the garden for £120,000 in August 2011, incurring selling costs of £2,000.

The value of the remaining house is £200,000 in August 2011.

Patrick has £25,000 of capital losses brought forward from 2003/04.

Required

Calculate the taxable gain on the disposal of the garden in 2011/12 and calculate the CGT payable by Patrick in 2011/12. Patrick has employment income of £60,000 in 2011/12.

Chattels rules

Chattels are defined as 'tangible, moveable property'. There are two types of chattels:

Wasting chattel	**Non wasting chattel**
Expected life ≤ 50 years	Expected life > 50 years
E.g. animals, computers, clocks, watches, caravans and boats	E.g. antiques, jewellery, works of art
Exempt from CGT	Subject to £6,000 rule

The £6,000 rule

Cost / Proceeds	≤ £6k	> £6k
≤ £6k	Exempt	Get a capital loss but the loss is limited: Ignore actual sale proceeds and use a deemed gross proceeds figure of £6,000 in gain calculation
> £6k	1. calculate gain as normal 2. calculate 5/3 (gross proceeds – 6000) 3. gain is the lower of the two	Chargeable in full

Learning example 13.6

Sylvia bought an antique table for £3,500 in May 1990.

In September 2011 she sold the table for gross proceeds of

(a) £4,900 (incurring selling costs of £100)
(b) £7,500 (incurring selling costs of £100)

Required

Calculate the chargeable gain arising in each case.

Learning example 13.7

During December 2011 Venetia disposed of an oil painting for £240, its market value. She had bought the painting for £9,500 in July 1986 believing it to be a collector's item.

Required

Compute Venetia's capital loss in 2011/12 and explain how Venetia can use her capital loss.

Wasting assets

A wasting asset is defined as an asset with an expected life of ≤ 50 years.

If a wasting asset is disposed of an adjustment is made to the amount of the allowable expenditure that is deductible in the computation to reflect the decline in value of the asset as its life expires.

The cost of acquisition must be written down on a straight line basis, as must any enhancement expenditure.

These rules are modified for leases, but this is outside the scope of the syllabus.

Learning Example 13.8

Maria sold a copyright for £12,000. At the date of sale it had 9 years to run. She had acquired it 6 years earlier for £15,000.

Required

Calculate the chargeable gain.

Learning summary

- CGT applied where there is a chargeable transfer of a chargeable asset by a chargeable person.

- Chargeable gains are calculated using proceeds minus cost. Enhancement expenditure is included in calculating the chargeable gain, as are incidental costs of sale and acquisition.

- Where the disposal is to a connected party, market value must be used as instead of actual proceeds.

- Transfers between spouses/civil partners are at nil gain/nil loss.

- Each chargeable person is allowed an annual exemption of £10,600 against chargeable gains.

- CGT is paid at a rate of either 18% or 28% on chargeable gains depending on a person's taxable income levels.

- Part disposals involve the apportioning of the cost of the asset between the part retained and the part disposed.

- Gains of the majority of wasting chattels (assets with a life of 50 years or less) are not subject to CGT.

Learning solution 13.1

(a) Sale proceeds £130,000	£	£
Gross sale proceeds		130,000
Less: Costs of sale		(7,000)
Net sale proceeds		123,000
Less: Cost	27,000	
Incidental acquisition costs	2,000	(29,000)
Enhancement expenditure		(35,000)
Gain		59,000

(b) Sale proceeds £55,000		
Gross sale proceeds		55,000
Less: Costs of sale		(7,000)
Net sale proceeds		48,000
Less: Cost	29,000	
Enhancement expenditure	35,000	(64,000)
Allowable loss		(16,000)

(c) Sale proceeds £80,000		
Gross sale proceeds		80,000
Less: Costs of sale		(7,000)
Net sale proceeds		73,000
Less: Cost	29,000	
Enhancement expenditure	35,000	(64,000)
Gain		9,000

Learning solution 13.2

	£
Asset 1	20,000
Less: Current year capital loss	(8,000)
Less: b/f capital loss	(-)
Net gains	12,000
Less: AE	(10,600)
Taxable gain	1,400

CGT rate = 18% as employment income is £22,000 and, therefore, the entire basic rate band is not fully utilised

CGT payable = £252

Learning solution 13.3

Ruth's taxable income is £33,525 (41,000 - 7,475), so £1,475 (35,000 − 33,525) of her basic rate band is unused. The capital gains liability on Ruth's capital gain of £12,400 (see working below) is calculated as follows:

	£
1,475 x 18%	266
10,925 x 28%	3,059
	3,325

Capital gain

	£
Asset 1	35,000
Less: Current year capital loss	(2,000)
Less: b/f capital loss	(10,000)
Net gains	23,000
Less: AE	(10,600)
Taxable gain	12,400

Learning solution 13.4

Gain arising on Henry:

	£
Proceeds	65,000
Cost (to Doris)	(37,000)
Gain	28,000

There is no gain/no loss arising on 25th December 2005 when Doris gives the painting to Henry

Learning solution 13.5

	£
Sale proceeds	120,000
Less: Selling costs	(2,000)
Net sale proceeds	118,000
Cost	
$\frac{48,000 \times 120,000}{120,000 + 200,000}$	(18,000)
Gain	100,000

Capital gains tax payable in 2011/12

	£
Gain	100,000
Less: Current year capital loss	(-)
Less: b/f capital loss	(25,000)
Net gains	75,000
Less: AE	(10,600)
Taxable gain	64,400

CGT rate = 28% as employment income is £60,000 and, therefore, the entire basic rate band is fully utilised.
CGT payable = £18,032

London
School of Business
& Finance

shaping success in business and finance

Learning solution 13.6

(a)   Consideration = £4,900, cost = £3,500.

This is the disposal of an exempt asset for CGT, therefore any gain is exempt.

(b)   2011/12

		£
	Consideration	7,500
	Less: Selling costs	(100)
	Net sale proceeds	7,400
	Less: Cost	(3,500)
	Gain	3,900
	But gain cannot exceed 5/3 (£7,500 − £6,000)	2,500
	Chargeable gain	2,500

Learning solution 13.7

2011/12	£
Deemed consideration	6,000
Less: Cost	(9,500)
Allowable loss	(3,500)

The capital loss must be carried forward and reduce future capital gains

Learning solution 13.8

	£
Sale proceeds	12,000
Less acquisition cost	
9/(9 + 6) x £15,000	(9,000)
Chargeable gain	3,000

14

Capital Gains
Tax and Shares

Context

The disposals of shares by an individual gives rise to a gain on which CGT is payable, as shares are a type of chargeable asset.

There are complications surrounding the disposal of shares, such as establishing a value for the disposal and identifying which shares have been disposed of.

Exam hints

The tax implications deriving from disposing of assets is a very important area of the syllabus and will be tested very frequently as seen in all the recent exam papers.

This particular chapter is going to build on the previous chapters and will concentrate on the situation where an individual disposes of shares and securities.

Capital gains aspects of disposing of shares can be tested in question two and question three of the F6 exam.

Key learning points

- There are special valuation rules for quoted shares. Shares should be valued at the lower of the ¼ up rule and the average method.

- To identify which shares have been disposed of by an individual, the matching rules must be applied to the disposal.

- If shares are acquired via a bonus issue, this will impact the number of shares owned by the individual but not the cost, as the shares are free.

- If shares are acquired via a rights issue, this will impact both the number of shares owned by the individual and the cost, as the shares must be paid for.

- Shares may be acquired as a result of a takeover. If this is the case, the cost of the original shares will need to be apportioned using the market value of the consideration received.

Valuation rules for quoted shares and securities

If it is necessary to establish a market value figure for quoted shares and securities, their value is taken from the price quoted on the Stock Exchange Daily Official List.

The figure is the LOWER of:

Method one – ¼ up method

This method is used if the examiner gives the market values as a range of values on a particular day.

The lower quoted value in the range plus one-quarter of the difference between the lower and the higher prices in the range

Lower value + ¼ (Higher value - Lower value)

Method two – average method

This method is used if the examiner gives the individual market values on a particular day.

Take the higher of the individual market values and add it to the lower of the individual values and get the average value by dividing by two.

$$\text{Average value} = \frac{\text{Higher value + Lower value}}{2}$$

Learning example 14.1

The shares in Sanctus plc are quoted on the Stock Exchange at 560p – 640p. On the same day the individual market values are quoted as 652p, 600p and 548p

Required

Compute the market value of the shares for capital gains tax purposes.

Disposal of shares

Shares are a chargeable asset for CGT purpose and their disposal will give rise to a capital gain.

The gain calculation for the disposal of shares causes no problems unless a taxpayer disposes of part of a shareholding which was originally acquired over a period of time in several separate transactions.

If this happens it is necessary to identify the shares which are being disposed of in order to establish the cost and acquisition date of the shares concerned.

Matching rules for shares

When an individual disposes of shares, the share disposal is matched with shares in the following order:

1. Acquisitions made on the same day.

2. Acquisitions made in the next 30 days (FIFO basis).

3. Any shares in the s104 pool (all shares acquired pre disposal) (sometimes referred to as the 1985 pool).

Learning example 14.2

Justin has purchased shares in X plc over a number of years. The details of his acquisitions are as follows:

8 January 1991	purchased 1,000 shares
10 September 2001	purchased 50 shares
15 February 2012	purchased 40 shares
9 March 2012	purchased 100 shares

Required

On 15 February 2012, Justin sold 300 shares in X plc. Which shares have been disposed of?

Section 104 share pool

The section 104 pool contains all shares acquired pre disposal. The shares that go into the share pool loose their identity, so when we sell a share out of the pool, we must use a weighted average cost in our gain calculation.

The section 104 pool working is laid out as follows:

	No of shares	Cost £
Acquisition	X	X
	X	X
Acquisition	X	X
	X	X
Disposal	(X)	(X)
	X	X

Exam technique for share disposals

1. identify which shares have been disposed of using the matching rules

2. set up a gain calculation for each group of shares disposed of

3. if shares from the section 104 pool have been disposed of, set up a section 104 pool working to identify the cost of the shares sold

Learning example 14.3

Brenda sold 15,000 shares in Ossie plc, a quoted company on 19 October 2011 for £75,000. She had bought the ordinary shares in the company on the following dates:

	Number of shares	Cost of the shares £
1 May 2002	9,600	8,940
12 December 2002	4,800	6,600
19 October 2011	1,200	3,900
10 November 2011	2,400	7,200

Required

Calculate the chargeable gain assessable on Brenda in 2011/12.

Bonus and rights issues

Bonus issue

This is an issue of FREE shares to existing shareholders in proportion to the number of shares owned at the date of the bonus issue.

These shares are deemed to be acquired on the same date as the original shares they relate to and have no cost.

Rights issue

A rights issue occurs when a company offers its shareholders the right to buy extra shares, usually at a preferential price (i.e. below market value). Rights issues are similar to bonus issues in that the number of shares offered to each shareholder is generally in proportion to his or her existing shareholding.

These shares are deemed to be acquired on the same date as the original shares they relate to and have will have a cost, which is the price paid.

Learning example 14.4

Miss Hokitika sold 900 shares in Musgrave Ltd, an unquoted trading company, on 10 February 2012 for £36,000.

She acquired 500 shares in the company on 21 April 1998 for £6,000 and a further 400 shares on 4 September 2008 for £5,000. On 8 May 2005 there was a 1:5 rights issue for £14 per share.

Miss Hokitika purchased all of the shares she was entitled to under the rights issue.

Required

Calculate gain arising on the sale of the shares.

Takeovers and reorganisations

A takeover occurs when one company acquires the shares in another company. Shareholders of the target company exchange their shares in return for cash, or shares of the acquiring company, or a combination of both cash and shares. The CGT treatment of such disposal is as follows:

- If a takeover is entirely for cash the shareholders of the target company have sold their shares and have made a normal chargeable disposal.

- If a takeover is entirely for shares (a "paper for paper" takeover), no chargeable disposal has taken place. A shareholder's newly-acquired shares in the acquiring company replace the shares originally held in the target company and are deemed for all CGT purposes to have been acquired on the same date and at the same cost as the original holding.

- If a takeover is partly for cash and partly for shares, a part disposal has taken place and a part disposal calculation is usually required. The value of the part disposed of is the amount of cash received and the value of the part remaining is the value of the shares received

Exam technique for takeovers which are a mixture of cash and shares

As the shareholder has received a mixture of cash and shares as a result of the takeover, the part of the gain that relates to the cash proceeds is chargeable immediately and a part disposal has occurred. The element of the gain that related to the shares received continues to be deferred until the shares are sold.

To compute the cost needed for the part disposal, an extra working is necessary. The total cost of the original shares must be apportioned between the cash and share elements of the consideration, using the market value of the elements of the consideration.

Description of exchanged assets	Market value of exchanged assets at the date of exchange	Original cost
Cash	MV1	
Shares	MV2	____
	Total MV	Cost of original shares

Learning example 14.5

In June 1994, Richard bought 2,000 shares in Rectangle plc for £12,000. In November 2011, Square plc made a takeover bid for Rectangle plc, offering two ordinary shares and one preference share in Square plc for each ordinary share in Rectangle plc.

This offer was accepted on 21 November 2011 when the market value of ordinary shares in Square plc was £6 per share and the market value of preference shares in Sphere plc was £3 per share.

Required

Show how Richard's cost of £12,000 should be allocated between the shares which he received by virtue of the takeover.

Gilt edged securities and qualifying corporate bonds

Gilt-edged securities and qualifying corporate binds are exempt from capital gains tax, so that gains arising are not taxable and losses arising are not allowable.

Gilt-edged securities, or "gilts", are loan stocks issued by the Government, such as Treasury Loan or Exchequer Stock.

Qualifying corporate bonds are securities which:

- are normal commercial loans. This excludes bonds which are convertible into shares,

- are expressed in sterling and do not contain any provision allowing them to be converted into any other currency,

- do not have a redemption value linked to any share price index and

- were acquired after 13 March 1984.

Learning summary

- The valuation methods of shares.

- Shares disposed of are matched in a specific order with those shares purchased. Shares are matched with shares acquired on the same day, then those acquired in the next 30 days on a FIFO basis and then from the 's104 share pool'.

- The 'share pool' is used for shares acquired after March 1985.

- Special rules exist for the acquisition of shares issued under a bonus or rights issue.

- Where cash is received on a restructuring, the cash element is taxable immediately.

- Where shares and cash are received in a restructuring, the new shares sit in the place of the old shares.

Learning solution 14.1

¼ up method:

560 + ¼ (640 – 560)   = £5.80 per share

Average method:

$$\frac{548 + 652}{2}$$ = £6 per share

Take LOWER of the two. Each share is valued at £5.80 per share

Learning solution 14.2

Matching rules:

First, match with any shares purchased the same day as disposal.

Then with any shares purchased in the next 30 days following the date of disposal

Finally match with any shares in the section 104 pool (all shares acquired before the disposal date). This will be a balancing amount of shares.

15 February 2012	40 shares
9 March 2012	100 shares
Section 104 pool (contains 1,050 shares – take balancing figure)	160 shares
	300 shares

London
School of Business
& Finance

shaping success in business and finance

Learning solution 14.3

The shares disposed of are identified with the following acquisitions:

- Firstly – 19 October 2011 – on the same day
- Secondly – 10 November 2011 – within the following 30 days
- Thirdly – section 104 pool

Note: As we have identified the 15,000 shares sold to THREE different acquisitions, the actual computation must also be done in THREE stages.

		£
1	**19 October 2011 acquisition**	
	Proceeds (1,200/15,000 x £75,000)	6,000
	Less: Acquisition cost	(3,900)
	Gain	2,100
2	**10 November 2011 acquisition**	£
	Proceeds (2,400/15,000 x £75,000)	12,000
	Less: Acquisition cost	(7,200)
	Gain	4,800
3	**Section 104 pool**	£
	Proceeds (11,400/15,000 x £75,000)	57,000
	Less: Acquisition cost (W1)	(12,302)
	Gain	44,698

Total chargeable gain on disposal of 15,000 shares:
£2,100 + £4,800 + £44,698 = £51,598

(W1)   section 104 pool

	Number	Cost £
1 May 2002	9,600	8,940
12 December 2002	4,800	6,600
	14,400	15,540
Disposal	(11,400)	(12,302)*
	3,000	3,238

The third disposal identified to the section 104 pool requires us to remove less than the total number of shares in this 'pool' – we therefore use the 'average cost' method.

*To deduct cost of 11,400 shares: 15,540/14,400 x 11,400 = £12,302

Learning solution 14.4

Gain on sale of Musgrave Ltd shares

Matching rules. All shares in the section 104 pool

	£
Disposal from section 104 pool	
Proceeds	36,000
Cost (W1)	(11,160)
Gain	24,840

Section 104 pool working

	Number	Cost
		£
21 April 1998	500	6,000
Right Issue	100	1,400
4 September 2008	400	5,000
	1,000	12,400
Disposal identification	(900)	(11,160)
	100	1,240

To deduct cost of 900 shares: 12,400/1,000 × 900 = £11,160

Learning solution 14.5

Description of exchanged assets	Market value of exchanged assets at the date of exchange	Original cost
4,000 ordinary shares	24,000	
2,000 preference shares	6,000	————
	30,000	12,000

Since 80% of the total value of the exchanged assets is ordinary shares in Square plc, these shares are treated as costing 80% of the original cost of £12,000 which is £9,600.

Similarly the preference shares in Square plc are deemed to have cost him 20% of £12,000 = £2,400. All of these shares are treated as if acquired in June 1994.

15

Capital Gains
Tax Reliefs

Context

The tax implications deriving from disposing of assets is a very important area of the syllabus. This chapter is going to cover the very important topic of CGT reliefs.

Firstly it is important to know when and where to apply these reliefs and secondly it is necessary to know how to apply them and the conditions necessary to apply them. After computing the gains on disposal of individual chargeable assets the next stage is to consider the availability of any possible reliefs. It is the gain AFTER reliefs which is taken to the CGT computation.

There are a number of different CGT reliefs that you need to be able to deal with in your exam. You need to be able to identify which reliefs are available in certain circumstances and apply the relief accordingly.

Exam hints

This topic will normally be tested in question three of the F6 exam but could also appear in question two where the examiner sometimes examines rollover relief, available to individuals and companies. CGT reliefs are unlikely to be a question in their own right but it is highly likely they will form part of the CGT question on the paper.

Key learning points

- Rollover relief is available to both individuals and companies. It defers the gain arising on the disposal of a business asset.

- Entrepreneurs' relief (lifetime limit of £10m) is available to individuals disposing of a business asset. This relief reduces the amount of the gain that is chargeable to CGT.

- Gift relief is available if an individual gives away a business asset. It allows the gain to be deferred until a later date.

- Incorporation relief is available if an individual incorporates their sole trader business into a company. The relief enables the gains arsing on incorporation to be deferred until a later date.

- Principal Private Residence relief is available for individuals disposing of property. The relief reduces down the amount of the gain chargeable to CGT.

Overview of CGT reliefs

There are two types of reliefs; complete exemptions, where the capital gain is reduced to nil by a complete exemption, for example, Principal Private Residence relief (PPR), and deferral reliefs, where the CGT due on the disposal of a chargeable asset is deferred until some future event, for example, holdover relief.

Complete Exemptions	Deferral Exemptions
− Principal Private Residence Relief (PPR relief)	− Gifts holdover relief
− Letting relief	− Rollover relief/ holdover relief
− Entrepreneurs' relief	− Incorporation relief

Rollover relief (ROR)

Roll-over relief may be available where a taxpayer sells an asset used by him in a trade and reinvests in replacement assets used for business purposes.

The asset disposed of must have been used in a business and have fallen into one of the following categories:

- Land and buildings

- Fixed plant and machinery

- Ships

- Milk and potato quotas

- Aircraft

- Hovercraft

- Lloyd's syndicate rights

The replacement asset must also fall into one of the above categories. It can however be used in a different trade carried on by the business.

Roll-over relief is not available on the disposal of shares in a family company.

The replacement asset must normally be acquired within a period starting one year before and ending three years after the date of disposal of the original asset.

Nature of roll-over relief

A gain which arises is said to be rolled over in that it is not charged to tax but is deducted from the person's acquisition cost of the new asset. Therefore the disposal of the old asset is deemed to give rise to neither a gain nor a loss.

The roll-over relief is either a full deferral or partial deferral of the gain depending on whether or not the proceeds from the original sale are fully reinvested in the replacement asset.

Full roll-over relief

Full roll-over relief is available only if the disposal proceeds of the old asset are wholly reinvested in the new asset.

Partial roll- over relief

If only part of the disposal proceeds are used to acquire the new asset, the effect of a claim for roll-over relief is that the chargeable gain on the disposal of the old asset is partly chargeable in the period of disposal and part of the old asset gain is deferred and reduces the cost of the new asset.

The amount of the gain which is chargeable on the disposal of the old asset is equivalent to the sale proceeds not reinvested (so long as this is less than the gain).

Reinvested **ALL** proceeds		£		Partial reinvestment of proceeds		£
1.	Calculate gain as normal	X	1.	Calculate gain as normal		X
2.	Calculate rollover relief (full amount)	(x)	3.	Calculate rollover relief (balancing figure)		(β)
3.	Gain remaining	nil	2.	Gain remaining = proceeds not reinvested		x

Learning example 15.1

On 2 July 2011 Foot sold a freehold office building for £257,000. The office building had been purchased on 3 January 1993 for £124,000. Foot has made a claim to rollover the gain on the office building against the replacement new freehold office building that was purchased on 14 January 2011.

Both office buildings have always been used entirely for business purposes in a wholesale business run by Foot as a sole trader.

Assume the cost of the replacement office building was:

- £270,000

- £230,000

- £112,000

Required:

Compute the chargeable gain under each alternative and the new base cost of the replacement office building.

Rollover relief and non-trade use

Assets used partly for business

Partial roll-over and hold-over relief can also occur where part of an asset is used for trade purposes. Only the gain attributable to the trade use is eligible for roll-over/holdover relief..

Learning example 15.2

On 8 November 2011 Ms Rainbow sold a freehold factory for £250,000. The factory was purchased on 3 January 2000 for £102,000. 80% of the factory has been used in a manufacturing business run by Ms Rainbow as a sole trader. However the remaining 20% of the factory has never been used for business purposes.

Ms Rainbow has claimed roll-over relief on the factory against the replacement cost of a new freehold factory that was purchased on 10 November 2011 for £260,000.

The new factory is used 100% for business purposes by Ms Rainbow.

Required

Compute the CGT assessable on Ms Rainbow in 2011/12 and the base cost of the replacement factory. Assume Ms Rainbow has no other taxable income in 2011/12.

Depreciating assets

Roll-over relief is modified where the replacement expenditure consists of the purchase of a wasting asset (also known as a depreciating asset). This is an asset with an expected life of 60 years or less at the time of acquisition. The most common examples of depreciating assets are leasehold buildings and fixed plant and machinery. The gain arising on the disposal of the old asset cannot be rolled-over and is not deducted from the cost of the new asset. Instead, the gain is temporarily deferred or "held-over" until it becomes chargeable on the earliest of the following:

(a)   The date on which the new asset is disposed of.

(b)   The date on which the new asset ceases to be used in the trade.

(c)   The 10th anniversary of the acquisition of the new asset.

Clearly a gain which is held-over in these circumstances will become chargeable no more than ten years after the date of acquisition of the depreciating asset. However, if a suitable non-depreciating asset is acquired at any time before the earliest of the above three dates, the held-over gain may be transferred to this new asset, so converting a held-over gain into a rolled–over gain.

Entrepreneurs' relief

Entrepreneurs' relief is available when an individual disposes of a business asset or part of a business. For 2011/12, the lifetime qualifying limit has increased to £10m (2010/11: £5m).

Qualifying gains are now taxed at 10% irrespective of a person's taxable income.

Entrepreneurs' relief is available to individuals only, NOT companies

Conditions for entrepreneurs' relief

- It must be a disposal of a **qualifying business asset:**

- The disposal of the whole or part of a business run by a sole trader. It is not available if a sole trader merely disposes of a business asset. Relief is only available in respect of capital gains arising on the disposal of assets in use for the purpose of the business.

- The disposal of shares in a trading company where an individual has a 5% shareholding in the company AND is also an employee of the company. Provided the company is a trading company, there is no restriction to the amount of relief if it holds non-trading asset such as investments.

- The asset must have been owned for at least one year prior to the date of disposal.

- Relief applies to the first £10m of net gains (over lifetime). Excess taxed at CGT rates of 18% or 28% depending on the person's taxable income levels.

- An election must be made one year from the 31 January following the tax year of disposal (disposal in 2011/12 election by 31 January 2014).

Optimal operation of entrepreneurs' relief

1. Calculate the gains and losses from business assets and then net off gains and losses from business disposals

2. Deduct any capital losses and the annual exemption from any gains arising on non-qualifying assets. This approach will save CGT at either 18% or 28% compared to just 10% if used against capital gains which do qualify for relief. If no other disposals are made, the annual exemption and capital losses can be used against any excess.

3. Any remaining gain is then subject to CGT at a rate of 10%.

4. When calculating the rate applicable to gains which do not qualify for Entrepreneurs' relief, any qualifying gains must be taken into account. Capital gains qualifying for relief reduce the amount of any unused basic rate tax band.

Learning example 15.3

Mr Brown is a sole trader and disposed of three chargeable assets during 2011/12 and realised the following gains and loss:

- The disposal of his entire sole trader business making a gain of £350,000. He has owned the business for 3 years.

- The disposal of a chargeable asset (painting) which realised a capital gain of £45,000.

- The disposal of a 30% shareholding in Pink Ltd an unquoted trading company making a gain of £380,000, he has owned these shares for 2 years. Mr Brown is an employee of Pink Ltd.

Mr Brown has £15,000 of capital losses brought forward and no other taxable income in 2011/12.

Required

(a) Compute the CGT payable in 2011/12.

(b) Evaluate how much of Mr Brown's entrepreneurs' relief is available to carry forward to 2012/13.

Gift relief (holdover relief)

The gift of a chargeable asset is a chargeable disposal and this is the case whether or not the asset is used in the business.

One of the disadvantages of making a gift of a chargeable asset is that the donor will possibly pay CGT in the tax year in which the gift is made.

It is possible for the donor to defer paying CGT in the tax year of the gift, by claiming to defer the gain using gift relief. However this is only possible if it is a gift of a qualifying asset and provided all the necessary conditions are satisfied.

Gift relief is available to individuals only, NOT companies

Conditions

Available to **individuals only** if they give away a **business asset**

Definition of a business asset for gift relief:

- Assets used in the trade of donor (i.e. a sole trader) or by donor's personal company (where donor has ≥ 5% voting rights)

- Shares in unquoted trading company

- Shares in donor's personal company

Operation of gift relief

Gift relief has implications for both the donor that gives away the business asset and the recipient of the gift.

The donor is able to reduce the gain arising on the gift down to nil, using gift relief. The gain on the asset is then deferred against the base cost of the asset for the recipient.

This means that when the recipient sells the asset in the future, they will get a bigger gain. For this reason, gift relief must be a joint claim between the donor and the recipient.

Donor	£	Donee	£
Gain	X	Base cost of asset	X
Less: Gift relief (balancing figure)	(X)	Less: Gift relief	(X)
Chargeable gain	X	Revised base cost	X

Learning example 15.4

Warren is a sole trader and has decided to gift his shop to his son, Calvin. The shop cost Warren £150,000 when he bought it in July 2001 and when he gifts the shop to Calvin in July 2011, it has a market value of £350,000.

Both Warren and Calvin have agreed to make a joint gift relief claim.

Required

Calculate the gain arising on Warren in 2011/12 when he gifts the asset and state the base cost of the shop for Calvin.

Gift relief complications

Sale at undervalue

Where the recipient gives the donor consideration (> cost to the donor but < market value) for the asset this is called a "sale at undervalue"

In this case, gift relief is modified as follows: part of the gain remains chargeable in the tax year in which the gift is made, and the balance of the gain is deferred by gift relief.

	Donor		Recipient	
1.	Calculate gain as normal:		base cost of asset (market value)	X
	Proceeds (still use market value)	X		
	Cost	(X)		
		X		
3.	Less: Gift relief (balancing figure)	(β)	Less: Gift relief	(X)
2.	Gain remaining =			
	excess of consideration over cost	X	revised base cost	X

Learning example 15.5

Rich gave his daughter Richenda an office building that he uses in his business on 1 October 2011 when its market value was £200,000. Rich paid £90,000 for the offices on 17 May 2001. Richenda sells the asset for £250,000 on 1 December 2012.

Required

(a) Compute the taxable gain arising on the disposals if gift relief is not claimed.

(b) Compute the gains arising on the disposals if gift relief is claimed.

(c) If Richenda gave Rich £99,000 what effect would this have?

Gift of shares in personal company

If the gift is shares in the donor's personal company, there may be assets owned by the personal company which are not business assets (e.g. the company may hold investments). In this case, the gift relief is modified as follows:

The proportion of the gain which qualifies for gift relief on shares is restricted to:

$$\text{gain} \times \frac{\text{MV of chargeable business assets (CBA) of the company}}{\text{MV of chargeable assets (CA) of the company}}$$

Learning example 15.6

On 17 May 2011 Churchill made a gift of his entire holding of 10,000 £1 ordinary shares (a 100% holding) in Chequers Ltd, an unquoted trading company, to his daughter.

The market value of the shares on that date was £210,000. The shares had been purchased on 21 January 2007 for £120,000. On 17 May 2011 the market value of Chequers Ltd's chargeable assets was £150,000, of which £100,000 was in respect of chargeable business assets.

Churchill and his daughter have elected to hold over the gain on this gift of a business asset.

Assume Churchill has capital losses brought forward of £4,000.

Required

Compute the CGT assessable on Churchill in 2011/12 and state the due date by which the tax must be paid. Assume Churchill is not a full time employee of Chequers Ltd and does not have any other taxable income in 2011/12.

Incorporation relief

Where a person transfers a business to a company (he incorporates his business), there is a disposal of assets held by the business that are transferred to the company. Not all the assets become chargeable assets for CGT purposes, specifically stocks, cash and debtors are excluded, but a gain may arise on assets such as land, buildings and goodwill.

Subject to certain conditions, the gain arising on the disposal of a business by a sole trader/ partners to a company is not chargeable in the tax year of disposal; the gain is deferred until the donor disposes of the shares in the limited company. The deferred gain realised on the disposal of the business is held over and reduces the cost of the shares in the company.

Operation of incorporation relief

1. calculate gains on any chargeable assets disposed of (land and buildings and goodwill) using market value as proceeds

2. calculate the incorporation relief

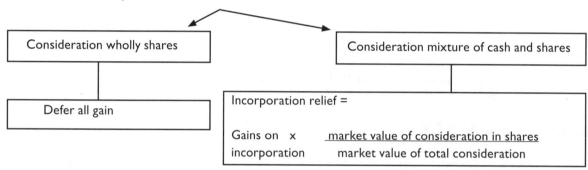

Consideration wholly shares	Consideration mixture of cash and shares
Defer all gain	Incorporation relief = Gains on x market value of consideration in shares incorporation market value of total consideration

3. deduct incorporation relief from base cost of new shares

Conditions for incorporation relief

For incorporation relief to apply, certain conditions must be met:

(1)   The business must be transferred as a going concern.

(2)   All the assets of the business (other than cash) are transferred to the company.

(3)   The consideration received by the donor should consist wholly or partly of shares in the company. These not need be ordinary shares.

Incorporation relief applies automatically so there is no need for the donor to claim that the gain should be held-over. However the donor may elect that incorporation relief should not apply. Such an election might be made if the donor wishes to preserve his or her entitlement to an annual exemption and wants earliest relief for any capital losses brought forward.

Learning example 15.7

Ricky, a sole trader has decided to incorporate his business into a company, Ricky Ltd. At the date of incorporation, Ricky owns the following assets:

	Market value on incorporation £	Gain arising on incorporation £
Goodwill	150,000	150,000
Freehold office	250,000	170,000
Stock	20,000	-
Debtors	30,000	-
Property	100,000	80,000
Cash	50,000	-
	600,000	

In return for transferring the assets into the company, Ricky receives shares worth £500,000 and cash worth £100,000

Required

Calculate the gains remaining after incorporation relief

Interaction with entrepreneurs' relief

Incorporation relief is applied automatically where the above conditions are met. Where the election is made to disclaim incorporation relief, entrepreneurs' relief can be claimed.

A claim for entrepreneurs' relief can also be made where the consideration is partly in shares, with entrepreneurs' relief applying to the gain remaining after incorporation relief.

Learning example 15.8

On 8 January 2012 Cindy incorporated a wholesale business that she had run as a sole trader since 1 June 2003. The market value of the business on 8 January 2012 was £280,000.

All of the business assets were transferred to a new limited company, with the consideration consisting of 210,000 £1 ordinary shares valued at £210,000 and £70,000 in cash.

The only chargeable asset of the business was goodwill and this was valued at £120,000 on 8 January 2012. The goodwill has a nil cost.

Required

Calculate the CGT arising from Cindy's disposals during 2011/12. You should assume that Cindy has made the necessary election to claim entrepreneurs' relief on this disposal.

Disadvantages of claiming incorporation relief

If the consideration is wholly in shares then the entire gain is deferred which may mean wasting the annual exemption, delaying relief for any capital losses and not taking advantage of entrepreneurs' relief. This problem can be solved by the sole trader receiving partly cash/ loan and partly shares up to an amount which leaves the gain remaining equal to annual exemption plus any losses plus any entrepreneurs' relief claimed.

Also in order to claim incorporation relief, the donor must be willing to transfer all of the assets to the company; it is not possible to retain any of the assets. This may lead to a double CGT charge on the sale of property held by the company as when the property is sold it will be subject to corporation tax on the gain. When the shares are sold, any gain at the time of the transfer to the company, will be chargeable on the individual, subject to entrepreneurs' relief.

An alternative route – Gift relief

If the trader is to retain any assets of the business other than cash, incorporation relief is denied and gains may therefore crystallise on incorporation.

As an alternative, the taxpayer could use the gift relief provisions.

The sole trader then gifts the assets to the company. Gift relief then defers the gains on the chargeable assets used in the business. This leads to a low base cost of assets in the company. It allows the trader to defer gains whilst retaining some assets of his business

Principal private residence relief

There is a total exemption from CGT where a gain is realised by an individual on the disposal of property that has been his sole or main residence throughout the period of ownership. The legislation also provides exemption for land that forms part of the property (gardens or grounds) up to the 'permitted area'. The permitted area is always at least 0.5 hectares but may be more where the land is required for the reasonable enjoyment of the property.

If a person sells part of the garden attached to their main residence and keeps the house and a smaller garden the disposal of the garden is exempt from CGT and a subsequent disposal of the remaining house and garden is also exempt from CGT.

If a person disposes of their main residence and keeps the land attached to the garden and then sells the land later on this second disposal is chargeable.

Occupation test

A summary of the occupation exemptions and rules is provided below. An occupancy exemption may be deemed as conditional or unconditional. For a conditional exemption, generally the property has to have been occupied at some point before and after the exemption is claimed. These are explained in more detail below.

Conditional
- Up to 3 years for any reason
- Any period working abroad

- Up to 4 years working in the UK

Unconditional
- Last 36 months of ownership
- Any periods where the property is occupied as the individual's main residence

A gain arising will be wholly exempt where the owner has occupied the whole of the residence throughout the period of ownership. A proportion of the gain will arise where the property has not been occupied by the owner throughout the period of ownership.

Provided the property has at some time qualified as the owner's main residence, the last 36 months of ownership qualify for exemption. This applies even where the owner has another house which has been nominated as his principal private residence.

Deemed occupation

Other periods of absence are also considered to be deemed occupation for the purposes of PPR relief. To qualify, there has to have been some actual occupation before and after the periods of absence.

Periods spent working abroad

If, during a period when his property was used as his main residence, the owner was required to work abroad, the property continues to be considered as his main residence. The owner has to be employed abroad under a contract of employment and the employment duties performed overseas.

The condition requiring actual occupation after the period abroad is relaxed where the owner is unable to resume residence because the terms of his new employment require him to work elsewhere.

Periods spent working elsewhere in the UK

A period of up to 4 years during which the owner's employment necessitated his living elsewhere in the UK is also a qualifying period.

The condition requiring actual occupation after the period elsewhere in the UK is relaxed where the owner is unable to resume residence because the terms of his new employment require him to work elsewhere.

Other qualifying periods

A further period of absence of up to 3 years can be treated as qualifying for exemption, provided it is preceded and succeeded by a period of actual occupation.

Business use

If part of the property is used exclusively for business throughout the period of ownership, the gain on this part of the property is taxable. Also, the final 36 months exempt rule does not apply to the part used for business.

If part of the property is used for business for only a part of the period of ownership, the gain is apportioned on the basis of months used for business/total months occupied. In this case, the last 36 months exemption will apply.

Calculation of PPR

(i)   Calculate the gain on the property using normal CGT rules.

(ii) Set-up a table showing periods of ownership separated into exempt months and chargeable months

(iii) Calculate all the exempt periods using the rules detailed above.

(iv) Apply the formula:

Gain   x $\dfrac{\text{Exempt periods}}{\text{Total period of ownership}}$

For example, a house sold in May 2011 had the following periods of occupation:

Description	Total months	Exempt	Non-exempt
30 April 1995 – 31 May 1998 (main residence)	37	37	-
1 June 1998 – 31 May 2003 (working abroad)	60	60	-
1 June 2003 – 31 May 2008 (working in the UK)	60	48	12
1 June 2008 – 31 May 2011 (main residence)	36	36	-
	193	181	12

The last 36 months of ownership are exempt. Up to four years working in the UK is exempt and any period working abroad, as long as property is occupied before and after as main residence. This leaves 12 months chargeable (60 months less 48 months UK work period exempt).

The PPR relief would be:

Gain x $\dfrac{181}{193}$

Any chargeable gain after PPR will be reduced by annual exemption and any capital losses.

Learning example 15.9

Caroline buys a property on 28 February 2002 and uses it as her main residence for the first 5 years of ownership until she moved out on 28 February 2007.

Caroline sells the property on 28 February 2012. The gain on the disposal of the property has been calculated as £100,000.

The property was empty from 1 March 2007 until it was sold on 28 February 2012.

Required

Calculate the gain after PPR relief

Letting relief

Where an individual lives in a property as their main residence and lets all or part of the residence for residential purposes, on the disposal of this property, in addition to claiming the PPR relief, letting relief is also available to reduce the gain.

This is the lower of:

*   £40,000

*   The PPR relief

*   The gain attributable to the chargeable period when the property was let.

Learning example 15.10

Gilly Gold bought a house on 1 April 1984.

1.4.1984 - 31.3.1986	- lived in as PPR
1.4.1986 - 30.9.1993	- travels the world and lets the house
1.10.1993 - 31.3.2005	- lived in as PPR
1.4.2005 - 31.3.2012	- house left empty.

She sells the house on 31 March 2012 for £300,000. The cost was £40,000.

Required

Calculate the CGT payable by Gilly on the disposal in 2011/12. Assume Gilly has no other taxable income.

Loss or destruction of an asset

If an asset is lost or destroyed then this is treated as if the asset has been disposed of. If the asset was insured then the insurance proceeds is treated as being the sale proceeds for the asset. However rollover relief is available if the insurance monies are used to purchase a replacement asset within a period of 12 months.

Where the asset is damaged and insurance proceeds are received, the receipt of proceeds represents a part disposal, unless an election is made to deduct the proceeds from the base cost of the damaged asset. The amount not spent restoring the asset must be small or the capital sum itself must be small (5% of the value of the asset or £3,000) otherwise a part disposal will have deemed to have taken place.

Learning example 15.11

On 25 June 2011 an antique vase owned by Florrie was destroyed in a fire. The antique vase had been purchased on 17 June 2005 for £37,000. Florrie received insurance proceeds of £59,000 on 20 September 2011 and on 22 September 2011 she paid £60,000 for a replacement antique vase. Florrie has made a claim to defer the gain arising from the receipt of the insurance proceeds.

Required

Compute the chargeable gain assessable on Florrie in 2011/12 and the new cost of the replacement vase.

Learning summary

- Roll-over relief is available where an individual disposes of a qualifying asset used in their trade and reinvests the proceeds in another qualifying asset within a permitted time limit. Roll-over relief defers the gain by reducing the base cost of the replacement asset.

- Roll-over relief is restricted where all the proceeds are not reinvested. The gain chargeable is the amount of proceeds not reinvested, if these are less than the actual gain.

- Where roll-over relief is claimed against depreciating assets, the gain becomes chargeable on the earlier of disposal of the asset, date the asset stops being used in the trade or 10 years after the acquisition of the replacement asset.

- Gift relief is available on gifts which give rise to an immediate charge to IHT, and sales at undervalue of business assets. The gain is deferred, through a joint election, against the base cost of the asset.

- Entrepreneurs' relief (lifetime limit of £10m) is available to individuals disposing of a business asset. This relief reduces the amount of the gain that is chargeable to CGT.

- Gains qualifying for Entrepreneurs' relief are taxed at 10%.

- Any capital losses or annual exemption should be used against assets not qualifying for Entrepreneurs' relief as this saves tax at either 18% or 28%.

- Where a sole trader or partner incorporates their business, relief is available against any gains arising on the disposal to the company. The amount of relief is unrestricted where all the proceeds are received as shares in the new company. The gain is deferred against the base cost of the shares. An election can be made to not claim incorporation relief, which is beneficial if entrepreneurs' relief is to be claimed.

- PPR relief is available where a person's main home is sold and there have been periods where the owner has not occupied the house as a main home.

Exam standard question

(a) Katsu has made disposals of the following assets during the year 2011/12:

(1) On 5 July 2011 Katsu made a gift of his entire holding of 5,000 ordinary shares (a 100% holding) in Nobu Ltd, an unquoted trading company, to his son. The market value of the shares on that date was £600,000. The shares had been purchased on 9 September 2008 for £480,000. On 5 July 2011 the market value of Nobu Ltd's chargeable assets was £800,000 of which £750,000 was in respect of chargeable business assets. Katsu and his son have elected to hold over the gain on this gift of a business asset. Katsu has never worked for Nobu Ltd.

(2) On 1 November 2011 Katsu sold UK Government securities (Gilts) for £4,100. The securities had been purchased on 5 November 2009 for £3,800.

(3) On 6 December 2011 Katsu gifted an antique vase to his mother for her birthday. The value of the vase at the date of the gift was £8,900 and the vase had been purchased on 19 May 2006 for £5,000.

(4) On 1 April 2012 Katsu sold a house for £760,000. The house had been purchased on 31 March 1996 for £410,000.

Katsu had occupied the house for the first five years of ownership. He then let the property out for ten years while he travelled around the world, until returning to the property to live in until he sold the property in April 2012.

Katsu has taxable income of £75,000 for the tax year 2011/12. He has unused capital losses of £14,000 brought forward from the tax year 2010/11.

(a) Calculate Katsu's capital gains tax liability for the tax year 2011/12 and state by when this should be paid

London
School of Business
& Finance

shaping success in business and finance

Hiro

On 28 February 2012 Hiro incorporated a business. He had run the business as a sole trader since 1 March 1998. The market value of the business assets on 28 February 2012 was £620,000. This figure, along with the respective cost of each asset, is made up as follows:

	Market value £	Cost £
Goodwill	150,000	Nil
Freehold office	449,500	281,000
Net current assets	20,500	20,500
	620,000	

The freehold office has always been used by Hiro for business purposes and all of the business assets were transferred to the new limited company. Hiro received consideration of 550,000 £1 ordinary new shares and £70,000 cash for the business.

Calculate Hiro's capital gains tax, if any, for the tax year 2011/12 and the base cost of his shares in the new company.

Learning solution 15.1

	Option 1 £	Option 2 £	Option 3 £
Sale proceeds	257,000	257,000	257,000
Less: Cost (Jan 1993)	(124,000)	(124,000)	(124,000)
Gain	133,000	133,000	133,000
Less: Full ROR (all proceeds reinvested)	(133,000)	-	-
Less: Partial ROR (Note 1)	-	(106,000)	-
No rollover relief (Note 2)	-	-	-
Chargeable gain	-	27,000	133,000

Note 1: ROR limited to £106,000 as £27,000 of proceeds not reinvested
Note 2: No ROR available as proceeds not reinvested > gain

Base Cost of the replacement office

	Option 1 £	Option 2 £	Option 3 £
Cost of new office	270,000	230,000	112,000
Less: Roll-over relief	(133,000)	(106,000)	-
Revised cost of new office	137,000	124,000	112,000

Learning solution 15.2

Freehold factory gain 2011/12

	£
Disposal proceeds	250,000
Less: Cost	(102,000)
Gain	148,000
Less: Rollover relief (80% x 148,000)	(118,400)
Chargeable gain	29,600
Less: Annual Exemption	(10,600)
Taxable gain	19,000
CGT (18%)	3,420

Base Cost of the replacement factory

	£
Cost of new factory	260,000
Less: Gain rolled over	(118,400)
Base Cost	141,600

Tutorial notes:

- The proportion of the gain relating to non-business use is £29,600 (148,000 × 20%), and this amount does not qualify for rollover relief.

- The business proportion of the sale proceeds is fully reinvested, and so the balance of the gain can be rolled over

Learning solution 15.3

Capital gains qualifying for Entrepreneurs' relief

	£
Goodwill	350,000
Shares in qualifying company	380,000
	730,000

Other capital gains

	£
Painting	45,000
Capital losses brought forward	(15,000)
	30,000
Annual exemption	(10,600)
	19,400

Capital gains tax:

	£
730,000 x 10%	73,000
19,400 x 28%	5,432
	78,432

Note:

Although Mr Brown does not have any taxable income, his basic rate band of £35.000 is set against the gains qualifying for Entrepreneurs' relief (£730,000).

(b) Entrepreneurs' relief of £9,270,000 (£10,000,000 - £730,000) is available for use in future years

Learning solution 15.4

Gain for Warren

	£
Proceeds (market value at time of gift)	350,000
Less: Cost (July 2001)	(150,000)
Gain	200,000
Less: Gift relief	(200,000)
Gain remaining	-

Base Cost of the asset for Calvin	
Market value at date of gift	350,000
Less: Gift relief	(200,000)
Base cost of asset	150,000

Learning solution 15.5

2011/12	(a) £	(b) £	(c) £	
Deemed proceeds (1 October 2011)	200,000	200,000	200,000	Actual proceeds are ignored. Must still use market value as proceeds figure
Less: Cost	(90,000)	(90,000)	(90,000)	
Gain	110,000	110,000	110,000	
Less: Gift relief	-	(110,000)	(101,000)	Gain is excess of consideration over original cost. £99,000 – £90,000 = £9,000 chargeable
Chargeable gain	110,000	-	9,000	
Less: Annual Exemption	(10,600)	-	(10,600)	
Taxable gain	99,400	-	-	gift relief is a balancing figure

Base cost for Richenda

	£	£	£
Deemed cost	200,000	200,000	200,000
Less: Gift relief	-	(110,000)	(101,000)
Base cost for future CGT disposal	200,000	90,000	99,000

Learning solution 15.6

Disposal of ordinary shares in Chequers Ltd 2011/12

	£
Deemed sale proceeds	210,000
Less: Cost (January 2007)	(120,000)
Gain	90,000
Less: Partial gift relief 90,000 x 100,000/150,000	(60,000)
	30,000
Less: Capital loss brought forward	(4,000)
Chargeable gains	26,000
Less: Annual exemption	(10,600)
Taxable gain	15,400
CGT (18%)	£2,772
Due date	31.1.13

Learning solution 15.7

Gains arising on incorporation:

	£
Goodwill	150,000
Office	170,000
Property	80,000
Total gain on incorporation	400,000
Less: Incorporation relief (W1)	(333,333)
Gain remaining	66,667

W1 incorporation relief

Incorporation relief

Gains on x market value of consideration in shares
incorporation   market value of total consideration

$$\frac{£400,000 \times £500,000}{£600,000} = £333,333$$

Learning solution 15.8

Capital gains computation 2011/12

Incorporation of existing business	£
Goodwill	
Proceeds	120,000
Less: Acquisition cost	-
Potential gain	120,000
Less: Incorporation relief	
$\frac{£210,000^*}{£280,000} \times £120,000$	(90,000)
Chargeable gains	30,000
Gain	
Less: Annual Exemption	(10,600)
Taxable gain	19,400
CGT (10% x 19,400)	1,990

The gain is taxed at 10% as it qualifies for Entrepreneurs' relief.

Base Cost of the shares	£
Cost of the shares	210,000
Less: Incorporation relief	(90,000)
New Cost of the shares	120,000

London
School of Business
& Finance
shaping success in business and finance

Learning solution 15.9

	£
Gain before relief	100,000
Less: PPR relief (W1)	(80,000)
Remaining gain	20,000

W1 PPR relief:

Gain × $\dfrac{\text{exempt periods}}{\text{total period of ownership}}$

£100,000 × $\dfrac{96 \text{ months}}{120 \text{ months}}$ = £80,000

	Exempt months	Chargeable months	Total months
28.2.2002 – 28.2.2007	60	-	60
1.3.2007 – 28.2.2009		24	24
1.3.2009 – 28.2.2012 (last 3 years of ownership)	36	-	36
	96	24	120

Learning solution 15.10

2011/12

	£
Sale proceeds	300,000
Less: Cost	(40,000)
Gain	260,000
Less: PPR relief (W1) £260,000 × 234/336	(181,071)
	78,929
Less: Letting relief (W2)	(40,000)
Chargeable gain	38,929
Less: Annual Exemption	(10,600)
Taxable gain	28,329
CGT (18% × 28,329)	5,099

Tax is payable at 18% as the basic rate band of £35,000 is unused

(1) Compute and analyse total period of ownership 1.4.1984 - 31.3.2012 = 28 years (or 336 months)

	Exempt months	Chargeable months	Total months
1.4.1984 – 31.3.1986	24	-	24
1.4.1986 – 30.9.1993 (3 years any reason)	36	54	90
1.10.1993 – 31.3.2005	138		138
1.4.2005 – 31.3.2009 (Balance)	-	48	48
1.4.2009 – 31.3.2012 (last 3 years of ownership)	36	-	36
	234	102	336

(2) Letting relief:

The house was let for 90 months, from 1.4.1986 to 30.9.1993, but 36 months of that was exempted under the PPR rules as deemed occupation (3 years any reason). Therefore only 54 months is considered.

Letting relief is therefore the lower of:

(1) £40,000

(2) PPR = £181,071

(3) Gain on letting = £260,000 x 54/336 = £41,785

Learning solution 15.11

The insurance proceeds of £59,000 received by Florrie have been fully reinvested in a replacement vase.

The disposal is, therefore, on a no gain/no loss basis, with the capital gain of £22,000 (insurance proceeds of £59,000 less original cost of £37,000) being set against the cost of the replacement antique vase.

	£
Cost of vase (2)	60,000
Less	
Gain rolled over	(22,000)
New cost of vase (2)	38,000

Solution to exam standard question

(a) Katsu – Capital gains tax liability 2011/12

	£
Ordinary shares in Nobu Ltd	
Disposal proceeds	600,000
Cost	(480,000)
	120,000
Less gift relief (W1)	(112,500)
Chargeable gain	7,500

W1
The proportion of gain eligible for gift relief is the proportion of chargeable business assets to chargeable assets, as follows

(120,000 x 750,000/800,000 = £112,500)

No entrepreneurs relief as not an employee of the business

Government securities

These are exempt from capital gains tax and therefore there is no chargeable gain.

Antique vase

The antique vase is a non-wasting chattel:

	£
Proceeds	8,900
Less cost	(5,000)
Chargeable gain	3,900

The maximum gain is 5/3 x (£8,900 -£6,000) = £4,833, therefore the gain is not restricted.

House

	£
Disposal proceeds	760,000
Cost	(410,000)
	350,000
Less principal private residence (W2) 11 /16 yrs	(240,625)
Less letting relief (W3)	(40,000)
	69,375

(W2)

Total period of ownership = 31.3.96 to 1.4. 2012 = 16 years

The first five years qualify for PPR relief

Three years qualify as the owner was absent for any reason but actually occupied the property before and afterthe period of absence.

The last three years qualify for PPR if the owner has lived in the property during ownership.

Qualifying period = 5 + 3 + 3 = 11

During the remaining 5 years (16 – 11) the property was let so will qualify for letting relief

(W3) Letting relief

Lower of :

£40,000

PPR relief = £240,625

Gain for the letting period not covered by PPR = 5/16 x £350,000 = £109,375

	£
Gain on shares	7,500
Govt securities	Nil
Antique vase	3,900
House	69,375
	80,775
Less losses brought forward	(14,000)
Annual exemption	(10,600)
Chargeable gains	56,175
Capital gains tax at 28% x £56,175	15,729

Katsu's capital gains tax liability will be due on 31 January 2013.

(b)   Hiro

Hiro has chargeable gains as follows:

	£
Goodwill (£150,000 – Nil)	150,000
Freehold office (449,500 – 281,000)	168,500
Net current assets (not chargeable)	Nil
Gains	318,500
Incorporation relief	
£318,500 x MV Shares / MV Consideration	
£318,500 x £550,000 / £620,000	(282,540)
Gain after relief	35,960
Less Annual Examption	(10,600)
Chargeable gain	25,360

Capital gains tax @ 10% x £25,360 = £2,536

The base cost of the company shares will become:

	£
Market Value of shares	550,000
Less incorporation relief	(282,540)
Base cost	267,460

16

Self Assessment
for Individuals

Context

Many individuals in the UK are required to fill in a tax return for each tax year, showing their liability for both income tax and capital gains tax. The tax return must be submitted to HMRC. This is known as 'self assessment'. There are dates that the individual must file their tax return by, and if these deadlines are missed there are penalties in place.

Exam hints

Income tax administration is unlikely to be a stand alone question in its own right. It is likely to form a small part of another question on the paper.

Key learning points

- Certain individuals are required to complete a tax return for HMRC. This enables the calculation of their tax liability for the year.
- There are filing dates for the tax return and penalties arise if the return is filed late.
- Payment of the tax due by self assessment is via a system of payments on account.
- Interest is charged if the payments on account are made late.

Notification of liability under self assessment

Where an individual, who have previously not completed a tax return, has a new source of income (trading income, capital gains tax), they must notify HMRC within six months from the end of the year in which the charge occurred. For 2011/12, this is 5 October 2012.

Where the charge to tax does not involve chargeable gains, no notification is required where their income:

- is taken into account under PAYE
- Has had income tax deducted at source
- The taxpayer is not subject to higher rate tax
- The income is a dividend from a UK resident company

The penalty for not providing a notice of chargeability to HMRC is 100% of the tax assessed (on that income), which is not paid prior to 31 January following the tax year.

Tax return

Under self assessment, the taxpayer is responsible for the completion of a tax return. The tax return is a common document (Tax Form) along with a number of supplementary pages for particular forms of income (Employment, Non-Resident, etc). Where the taxpayer has simple affairs, HMRC may issue a Short Tax Return.

A tax return is either issued in electronic or paper format. The filing deadlines are distinct for each type.

Time limit for submission of tax returns

The taxpayer must submit a completed (electronic) tax return by 31 January following the end of the tax year to which the return relates. For example, 2011/12 returns must be filed by 31 January 2013. Where the taxpayer is submitting a paper tax return, this must be done by 31 October following the end of the tax year to which the return relates.

If the taxpayer receives a notice to file a tax return after 31 July but before 31 October, the filing deadlines become:

- 3 months after the notice to file was issued for paper returns
- 31 January following the end of the tax year to which the return relates for electronic returns

If the taxpayer receives a notice to file a tax return after 31 October, the filing deadline becomes 3 months after the notice to file was issued, irrespective of whether it is a paper or electronic return.

Learning example 16.1

You have several clients who have been issued tax returns for 2011/12 and would like advice on the latest dates of filing, either in electronic or paper format

Paul   Notice to file issued by HMRC on 12 May 2012

Roger   Notice to file issued by HMRC on 12 September 2012

James   Notice to file issued by HMRC on 31 October 2012

Simone   Notice to file issued by HMRC on 3 December 2012

Required

Advise each client of the date of submission for their returns for 2011/12.

Penalties

The filing penalties are determined by the lateness of the filing of the tax return.

- If the return is filed late an automatic penalty of £100 arises.
- If the return is more than three months late, there is a daily penalty of £10 per day (for a maximum of 90 days).
- If the return is more than six months late, a penalty of 5% of the tax due will be charged (minimum charge is £300)
- If the return is more than 12 months late, a further penalty of 5% of the tax due will be charged

Learning example 16.2

Simon filed his electronic tax return for the tax year 2011/12 on 31 October 2013. His tax liability for 2011/12 was £1,750.

Required

Calculate the filing penalties which can be imposed on Simon

London School of Business & Finance
shaping success in business and finance

Calculation of tax liability

Under self assessment, it is the responsibility of the taxpayer to calculate their tax liability. However, if the taxpayer wishes HMRC to calculate the tax liability and they are filing a paper return, the taxpayer must file their return by:

*   31 October

*   If the notice to file a return is issued after 31 August, by 31 October

Where the taxpayer is filing their return electronically, their tax liability is automatically calculated as part of the online submission.

Checking the return

HMRC will not make any judgement on the accuracy of the figures submitted but will just calculate the tax liability based on the information submitted. However, any arithmetical error or errors of principle will automatically be corrected within 9 months of the date on which the return is filed.

The taxpayer may make amendments to the return until one year after the due filing date.

Compliance checks into self-assessment returns

HMRC has 12 months from the date the tax return is filed in which to notify an individual that they intend to perform a compliance check into the self-assessment tax return. If the return is filed late, the deadline extends to the quarter day (31 January, 30 April, 31 July or 31 October) following the anniversary of the date the return was filed.

Only one compliance check may be made in respect of any one return.

HMRC can request documents for inspection, and has statutory powers to demand information, although the taxpayer may appeal to the Tribunal. Failure to comply with such a request may incur an initial penalty of £300, with a daily penalty for each day of failure of up to £60 per day.

HMRC may amend the self assessment during a compliance check period if they believe there would otherwise be a loss of tax. The individual may make an amendment to the self assessment return during a compliance check period but this does not cause the compliance check period to close.

When HMRC are satisfied that they have all necessary information they will issue a closure notice. This notice must either state that no amendments to the tax return are needed, or make the necessary amendments. The individual has 30 days after the closure to appeal against the amendments.

Whilst the compliance check is ongoing the taxpayer may apply to the Tribunal for a direction that a closure notice should be issued within a specified period.

Claims

Claims should, wherever possible, be made on a tax return or on an amendment to a tax return, and must be quantified when made.

Unless stated otherwise the time limit for making a claim is four years after the end of the year of assessment to which it relates.

Claims may therefore still be made where the time limit for filing a return or amendment has expired. The rules for record keeping, compliance checks etc. that apply to tax returns also apply to such claims.

Retention of records

Taxpayers who have a business must retain their records until five years after the filing date. Other taxpayers must retain until the latest of:

(a) 12 months after filing date.

(b) date of completion of enquiry into return.

Penalties of up to £3,000 may be charged for failure to keep or retain adequate records.

Adequate records are those required to enable a complete and correct return to be made. This includes:

- details of employment income, eg P60, P45, P11D, P9D, details of deductible expenses

- details of pensions received

- details of any taxable state benefits received

- details of bank interest received, dividend vouchers and details of other investment income

- details of all amounts received and paid in the course of any trade or business

- details of all amounts received and paid in the course of any property business

- details of the acquisitions and disposals of any chargeable assets.

The records can be kept in electronic form.

Worked example

The filing date for the tax year 2011/12 is 31 January 2013.

This means that a sole trader would be required to keep their business records until 31 January 2018.

Payments on account (POA)

Payments on account (POA) are required if the taxpayer had to pay some income tax in the previous tax year. The due dates for payments on account are in two equal instalments 31 January in the tax year and 31 July following the tax year, with a balancing payment made on 31 January in the tax year following.

For 2011/12 the payment on account due dates are as follows:

The first payment on account is due on 31 January 2012
The second payment on account is due on 31 July 2012
The balancing payment is due on 31 January 2013

Each payment on account is equal to 50% of the taxpayer's liability to income tax (less tax deducted at source) and class 4 NIC for the previous tax year. This is also known as the 'Relevant amount'.

From 6 April 2011 Class 2 NICs are paid in two equal instalments on 31 January in the tax year and 31 July following the tax year (i.e. 31 January 2012 and 31 July 2012 for 2011/12). All Class 2 NICs will be paid by way of the two instalments so no balancing payment for Class 2 NICs will arise.

No payments on account are required for 2011/12 where the tax liability for 2010/11 was less than £1,000 or more than 80% of the total tax liability was deducted at source.

A payment on account may be reduced to nil or another stated amount. However, the taxpayer must state a reason for the reduction in payments on account. However, if the taxpayer's liability turns out to be higher than anticipated, interest will be charged from the late payment.

No payments on account are required in respect of CGT.

Balancing payments

After the actual tax liability for the tax year has been determined a balancing payment is due on 31 January following the tax year.

If the taxpayer has overpaid any tax HMRC will refund the excess amount. If the tax due changes as a result of an amendment, any extra tax is payable within 30 days of the amendment date if it is later than the normal due date.

Late payment of tax

Where tax is paid more than one month late, then a penalty of 5% is charged on the amount of tax unpaid.

Additional penalties of 5% will be charged where tax remains unpaid after six months, and again after 12 months.

The penalties only apply to the balancing payments and not the payments on account.

Learning example 16.3

Rob is a self-employed builder, who pays his tax by self assessment. He has provided you with the following information:

Information for 2010/11

	£
Income tax	10,000
Less tax deducted at source	2,500
Class 4 NICs	1,700

Information for 2011/12

	£
Income tax	16,000
Less tax deducted at source	3,100
Class 4 NICs	2,200
Class 2 NICs	130

Required

Calculate Rob's payments on account for 2011/12 and his final balancing payment. State the due date for each payment.

Late payment interest

Late payment interest is automatically charged on tax paid late at 3%. It runs from 31 January in the tax year even if the tax was not actually due until a later date.

Late payment interest is also charged when an excessive claim is made to reduce payments on account.

Penalties for incorrect return

A single new penalty regime has been introduced for incorrect returns.

The amount of penalty is based on the amount of the tax understated, but the actual penalty payable is linked to the taxpayer's behavior as follows:-

Reason for the error	Consequences
The taxpayer simply makes a mistake	No penalty
Careless mistake	30% of the understated lost revenue.
The mistake is made deliberately but does not conceal the error	70% of the understated lost revenue.
The mistake is made deliberately and the taxpayer conceals the error	100% of the understated lost revenue.

However the penalty will be substantially reduced where a taxpayer makes disclosure, especially when this is unprompted by HMRC.

Error	Disclosed	HMRC discovered
Careless mistake	Reduced to 0%	15% of understated lost revenue
The mistake is made deliberately but does not conceal the error	20% of understated tax	35% of understated lost revenue.
The mistake is made deliberately and the taxpayer conceals the error	30% of understated tax	50% of understated lost revenue.

Time limits for assessments

The time limits by which HMRC can make an assessment of income tax, or CGT have been amended to four years. However, this can be increased to six years where tax is lost due to careless behaviour and to 20 years where tax is lost due to deliberate behaviour.

Appeals

A taxpayer can appeal against decisions made by HMRC, such as assessments, amendments to a self assessment or refusal of a claim. The time limit for making an appeal is 30 days from the decision.

The notice of appeal is sent to HMRC. Most appeals are settled by agreement, but where an appeal cannot be settled HMRC may offer, or the taxpayer may request, a review by an officer of HMRC who has not previously been involved.

If the review does not resolve the issue, or no review is made, the appeal can be taken to the First Tier Tribunal. The appeal will then be categorised:

1.   Default paper cases are not normally dealt with in writing without a hearing,

2.   Basic cases are dealt with though an informal hearing,

3.   Standard and complex cases are dealt with through a more formal hearing process, and complex cases may be heard by the Upper Tribunal rather than the First Tier Tribunal.

The Tribunal will make a decision. Further appeals may then be made to the Upper Tribunal, the Court of Appeal and the Supreme Court.

London
School of Business
& Finance
shaping success in business and finance

Learning summary

- It is the individual's responsibility to notify HMRC when they have a new source of income.

- Tax returns must be filed by 31 October (paper) or 31 January (electronic) following the end of the tax year.

- For returns filed non-electronically, a request can be made to HMRC to calculate the tax due. Where a return is filed electronically, the tax is calculated automatically.

- Payments on account are due on 31 January and 31 July each tax year. Each payment is 50% of the income tax and class 4 NIC liability of the previous tax year.

- Class 2 NICs for a tax year are paid in two instalments on 31 January in the tax year and 31 July following the tax year.

- Balancing payments are due on 31 January following the end of the tax year.

- Penalties exist where an error has found to be made. This penalty can be reduced where the error is discovered by the trader and was not deliberately misleading. Where HMRC discovers the error, the penalties are higher.

Exam standard question

Sue Sills has been a self employed seamstress since 1990, making up her accounts to 30 June. Sue's tax liabilities for the tax years 2009/10, 2010/11 and 2011/12 are as follows:

	2009/10	2010/11	2011/12
	£	£	£
Income tax liability	5,720	6,200	4,540
Class 2 National insurance contributions	114	120	130
Class 4 National insurance contributions	1,340	1,580	1,200

No income tax has been deducted at source

(a) Prepare a schedule showing the payments on account and balancing payments that Sue will have made or will have to make during the period 1 July 2011 to 31 March 2013, assuming Sue makes any appropriate claims to reduce her payments on account.

(b) State the implications if Sue had made a claim to reduce her payments on account for the tax year 2011/12 to nil.

(c) Advise Sue of the latest date by which her self assessment tax return for 2011/12 should be submitted if she wants HMRC to prepare the self-assessment tax computation on her behalf.

(d) State the date by which HMRC will have to notify Sue if they intend to perform a compliance check into her self-assessment tax return for the tax year 2011/12 and the possible reasons why such a compliance check would be made.

Learning solution 16.1

	Latest date for filing	
	Electronic	**Paper**
Paul	31 January 2013	31 October 2012
Roger	31 January 2013	11 December 2012
James	31 January 2013	31 January 2013
Simone	2 March 2013	2 March 2013

Learning solution 16.2

As the return was filed on 31 October 2013, Simon would have incurred the automatic late filing penalties of £100 on 31 January 2013.

A daily penalty of £10 would have been charged for the next 90 days. This amounts to £900.

The return is filed 9 months late, so a charge of 5% of the tax due is charged. This amounts to:

£1,750 x 5% = £87.50 but the minimum of £300 is charged

The total filing penalty is therefore, £1,300 (100 + 900 + 300)

Learning solution 16.3

Payments on account 2011/12

		£
31 January 2012	(50% x 9,200)	4,600
Class 2 NICs		65
31 July 2012	(50% x 9,200)	4,600
Class 2 NICs		65
31 January 2013	balancing payment (β)	5,900
		15,230

Tax liability for 2010/11

Income tax	10,000
Less deducted at source	(2,500)
Income tax payable under self assessment	7,500
Class 4 NICs	1,700
	9,200

Tax liability for 2011/12

Income tax	16,000
Less deducted at source	(3,100)
Income tax payable under self assessment	12,900
Class 4 NICs	2,200
Class 2 NICs	130
	15,230

Solution to exam standard question

(a)   Schedule of payments

Payment Date	31.7.11	31.1.12	31.7.12	31.1.13
	£	£	£	£
Payment on Account 2- 2010/11				
½ x (5,720 + 1,340)	3,530			
Balancing payment - 2010/11				
(6,200 + 1,580) – 7,060		720		
Payment on account 1 – 2011/12				
½ x (4,540 + 1,200)		2,870		
Class 2 NIC first instalment		65		
Payment on account 2 – 2011/12			2,870	
Class 2 NIC second instalment			65	
Balancing payment – 2011/12				Nil
Payment on account 1 – 2012/13				2,870
Class 2 NIC first instalment				65

(b)   If Sue reduced her payments on account for 2011/12 to nil then she will be charged interest on overdue tax.

Due Date	Date Paid	Amount Due	Months Late	Penalty
31.1.12	31.1.13	£2,935	12 months	£88
31.7.12	31.1.13	£2,935	6 months	£44

(c)   The due date for submitting the self assessment tax return for 2011/12 is 31 January 2013.

If the taxpayer wants to submit a paper return or wishes HMRC to compute the tax liability on behalf of the taxpayer the return must be submitted by 31 October 2012.

(d)   HMRC must notify Sue within 12 months from the date they receive her return. The reason for making a compliance check is either that the taxpayer has been selected randomly or HMRC have discovered an error or omission in the return.

17

Inheritance Tax

Context

Inheritance tax (IHT) is often mistaken be a tax which is payable only when a person dies. However, if it was only payable on gifts made on death, in accordance with the will, it would be possible to avoid IHT by making gifts of assets just prior to death. For this reason, there are IHT implications on certain gifts made during lifetime. These are known as lifetime transfers and this particular area is covered in this chapter.

Exam focus

Inheritance tax has only recently been incorporated into the F6 syllabus. Questions are likely to cover the basic elements as well as some more tricky parts of cumulation. There will be between 5 and 15 marks on inheritance tax in each F6 exam.

Key learning points

- IHT applies to where a transfer of value takes place. The transfer of value is the diminution in value of the donor's estate.

- To be liable to IHT, the taxpayer must be domiciled in the UK, or transfer UK based assets if non-domiciled.

- Transfers of value can be classified as Chargeable Lifetime Transfers (CLTs) or Potentially Exempt Transfers (PETs). A CLT is chargeable to IHT immediately, with additional IHT becoming due if the donor dies within seven years. A PET is not liable to IHT unless the donor dies within seven years.

- Transfers to a spouse/civil partner are exempt from IHT.

- Various exemptions are available to the donor including marriage exemption, small gifts exemption and the annual exemption.

- A nil rate band, at which if transfers in the past seven years do not exceed the nil rate band, can be deducted from the valuation (after exemptions) of the asset.

- IHT is charged at 20% of lifetime CLTs, with additional IHT being chargeable upon death, subject to taper relief.

- IHT is paid to HMRC Inheritance Tax, with the payment date dependent on the type of transfer.

Introduction

IHT is a tax on chargeable transfers by a chargeable person. A chargeable person can be:

1. An individual; or

2. A trustee of settled property

A UK domiciled individual is liable to IHT on the transfer of their worldwide assets. A non-domiciled individual is only liable to IHT on the transfer of their UK based assets.

With capital gains tax (CGT), death is not considered a chargeable event i.e. it does not trigger a charge to CGT. However, IHT applies to both transfers which take place during an individual's lifetime, and those which take place on their death.

Domicile

The general rule is that an individual is domiciled in the country considered to be their permanent home. There are three different types of domicile: domicile of origin, domicile of dependence and domicile of choice. In addition, there is also a 'deemed domicile' rule for IHT purposes.

For IHT purposes, there are four types of domicile to be aware of:

1. Domicile of origin - A person's domicile of origin is acquired at birth, normally that of the child's father. This remains the person's domicile until it is replaced by a domicile of dependence or a domicile of choice.

2. Domicile of dependency - This applies where the individual's father changes domicile before the individual reaches the age of 16. In these cases, the individual's domicile changes with their fathers.

3. Domicile of choice - An individual can change domicile from one country to another, by choice, where they show a permanent intention to change the country of permanent home (i.e. to sever all ties with their country of origin) such as, not retaining property, moving burial arrangements, changing nationality or citizenship. In practical terms, the individual is required to prove that all ties with their present domicile have been severed.

4. Deemed domicile - For IHT purposes only, where actual UK domicile ceases, the individual is considered to be deemed UK domicile for three years afterwards. Deemed domicile rules also apply to an individual who is not UK domiciled but has been UK resident for at least 17 of the previous 20 tax years ending with the tax year in which the chargeable transfer is made.

Transfers of value

During a person's lifetime, IHT can only arise if transfers of value take place. A transfer of value is defined as 'any gratuitous disposition made by a person which results in a diminution of value of that person's estate'

Diminution in value

Normally there will be no difference between the diminution in value of the donor's estate and the increase in value of the donee's estate. However, in some cases, it may be necessary to compare the value of the donor's estate before the transfer, and the value after the transfer in order to compute the diminution in value. This is covered later in more detail.

Where the transfer of value takes place within the lifetime of the donor, these are known as 'lifetime transfers'. Lifetime transfers fall into two separate categories:

1. Chargeable lifetime transfer (CLT)

2. Potentially exempt transfer (PET)

Where the transfer of value takes place on the death of the donor, these are dealt with from the death estate.

Rates of IHT

The rate of IHT payable as a result of a person's death is 40%. This is the rate that is charged on a person's estate at death, on PETs that become chargeable as a result of death within seven years, and is also the rate used to see if any additional tax is payable on CLTs made within seven years of death.

The rate of IHT payable on CLTs at the time they are made is 20% (half the death rate). This is the lifetime rate. The tax rates information that will be given in the tax rates and allowances section of the June and December 2012 exam papers is as follows:

£1 – £325,000	Nil (Nil rate band)
Excess – Death rate	40%
- Lifetime rate	20%

Nil rate band (NRB)

All individuals are entitled to a NRB. This determines the maximum value of lifetime and death transfers which can be made without incurring any IHT liability.

The NRB changes each tax year. The NRB for 2011/12 is £325,000.

Learning example 17.1

Audrey is 91 years of age and in poor health. Audrey's estate is £600,000 and she intends to leave it all to her grandson who has visited her every week since she was entered a care home.

Required

a) Compute the IHT payable when Audrey dies on 1 August 2011.

Potentially exempt transfers

A PET is a lifetime transfer from an individual to another individual. If the transfer is made by an individual to a trust or vice versa, this is a CLT.

A PET is treated as exempt whilst the donor is alive, and in the seven year period following the transfer. If the individual dies within seven years of making the transfer, it becomes a chargeable transfer.

Learning example 17.2

Continuing with example 17.1

Required

b)   Explain the tax implications if instead, Audrey makes a lifetime gift of the £600,000 on 31 July 2011.

c)   Explain the tax implications if Audrey makes the lifetime gift on 31 July 2011 and continues to live for more than 7 years after 1 August 2011.

Chargeable lifetime transfers

A CLT arises where a transfer of value is made and there is not a specific exemption for the transfer, or it is not a PET. IHT is calculated, on the CLT, using a lifetime rate (computation 1).

If the donor survives seven years after the CLT has been made, there is no additional IHT on the CLT. Where the donor dies within seven years of the CLT, additional tax will be due at the rate of IHT due on the death estate (computation 2).

Exempt transfers

These transfers are exempt from IHT both during lifetime and on death.

A transfer of property between spouses/civil partners is exempt from IHT provided the donee is domiciled in the UK.

Husband and wife and civil partners get a nil rate band

Husband and wife get a nil rate band each. If a person has any unused nil rate band left at the time of their death, the unused amount can be transferred to the spouse or civil partner if the necessary election is made within two years from the end of the month of the second death.

Learning example 17.3

Terry dies on 30 June 2011 and leaves £610,000 to Susie his wife and nothing to his son.

(a)   Explain the IHT implications on Terry's death, your answer should evaluate the amount of Terry's unused nil rate band.

(b)   Explain the IHT implications on the subsequent death of Susie, assuming she dies on 15 December 2011 and leaves everything to her son. State the due date for making any necessary elections.

Summary of lifetime versus death gifts

Lifetime Gifts	Definition	IHT Payable During Donor's Lifetime	IHT Payable When Donor Dies
Potentially Exempt Transfer (PET)	Lifetime gifts from one individual to another	No IHT is payable during donor's lifetime	If Donor dies in ≤7 years then IHT may be payable by the donee.
Chargeable Lifetime Transfers (CLTs)	Lifetime gifts into a discretionary trust	IHT maybe payable during the donor's lifetime using lifetime rates.	Additional IHT may be payable if the donor dies in ≤ 7 years by the donee.
Exempt Transfers	Transfers which are exempt from IHT	No IHT is payable during the donor's lifetime	No IHT is payable when the donor dies.

Exemptions and reliefs

Introduction

A number of exemptions exist to reduce or take out of the charge of IHT any transfers made during an individual's lifetime. As these exemptions apply equally to CLTs and PETs, it is advised, where possible, to make CLTs first in any tax year so as to use any available exemption.

Small gifts

This applies to lifetime transfers of no more than £250 per person per tax year. Where the gift is valued at > £250, the exemption does not apply. Also, the exemption does not apply to transfers made into trusts.

Marriage exemption

Lifetime transfers made in the event of marriage are exempt up to the following limits:

1.   £5,000 where made by a parent

2.   £2,500 where made by remoter ancestor (grandparent)

3.   £1,000 where made by anyone else

Qualifying political party

Transfers of value to a qualifying political party are exempt if the party, at the last general election, had two MP's, or one MP and at least 150,000 votes.

Annual exemption

The first £3,000 of value transferred each year is exempt from IHT. It is taken into account after all other exemptions have been used. Where several transfers are made in any year, the annual exemption is applied to the earlier gifts first.

Where an annual exemption has not been used or is not fully used in one tax year, any unused exemption can be carried forward for one tax year only, with the current year exemption being used first to the carry forward exemption.

Normal expenditure out of income

IHT is not intended to apply to gifts of income. Therefore a gift is exempt if it is made as part of a person's normal expenditure out of income, provided the gift does not affect that person's standard of living. To count as normal, gifts must be habitual. Therefore, regular annual gifts of £2,500 made by a person with an annual income of £100,000 would probably be exempt. A one-off gift of £70,000 made by the same person would probably not be, and would instead be a PET or a CLT.

Learning example 17.4

Steve Francis made the following gifts in date order during 2011/12. He previously had not made any lifetime gifts.

£8,900 to his son on his marriage

£30,000 to his favourite charity

£200 to other 20 members of his rugby team

£1,600 to his friend Larry West

£7,000 each year to his nephew to pay for his school fees

Required

Explain the exemption position on each of the above. Assume Steve has income in excess of £100,000 each year.

Learning example 17.5

Lucas made the following gifts in date order during 2011/12. He previously had not made any lifetime gifts.

£5,000 to his grandson on his marriage

£60,000 to the Labour Party

£20,000 to his wife

£350 to his business partner

Required

Explain the exemption position on each of the above.

Computing IHT on Lifetime Transfers – Computation 1

Introduction

The exact nature of the computation for IHT depends on whether:

1. the transfer is on a lifetime transfer where the donee pays the IHT

2. the transfer is on a lifetime transfer where the donor pays the IHT

The principle of cumulation

Chargeable transfers within the seven-year period ending with the date of the latest chargeable transfer are cumulated, for the purposes of determining the IHT rate. Where chargeable lifetime transfers do not exceed the NRB, there is no IHT liability.

Where the chargeable lifetime transfers exceed the NRB, IHT is charged at the lifetime rate, which is currently 20%, or half the death rate

Cumulation calculation:

Step 1   £
Consider the NRB   325,000

Step 2

Add (cumulate) the CLTs that have occurred within the 7 years
prior to the date of the current CLT   (X)
NRB left   X

Step 3

The gross value of the transfer should be calculated. Deduct any exemptions which are available (Marriage, Small Gifts, Annual exemption). It is only possible to take an exemption against a CLT if it is available for that tax year. Where a PET has been made in the tax year, at an earlier date than the CLT, the exemptions must be applied against the PET first.

Step 4

Deduct the remaining NRB from the current CLT being considered in computing the IHT payable. If the CLT is covered by the remaining NRB, no IHT is charged. Where the CLT is greater than the remaining NRB, IHT is due at 20%

Lifetime tax – donee pays tax

IHT is payable on CLTs made during the donor's lifetime on a CLT. The only lifetime gifts which give rise to IHT while the donor is still alive are gifts into a discretionary trust.

Lifetime tax – donor pays tax

The donor is primarily responsible for ensuring the lifetime tax (IHT) which arises on a CLT is paid. In this case, the loss to the donor's estate is both the amount of the gift and the related tax liability.

To correctly calculate the amount of IHT payable, it is, therefore, necessary to gross up the net gift, by multiplying the net amount by 25%.

Grossing up is not necessary if the donee pays the IHT on the lifetime transfer.

Learning example 17.6

Elanor set up a discretionary trust for the benefit of her two children.

On 1 August 2001 she put £268,000 into the trust

On 1 May 2006 she transferred a property to her sister, valued at £155,000

On 1 May 2008 she transferred a property valued at £137,000 into the same trust (Elanor pays tax)

Required

Compute the IHT payable on the lifetime gifts. Use the 2011/12 NRB in all cases.

Learning example 17.7

Mr Brain set up a discretionary trust for the benefit of his two children.

1 February 2005 he put £410,000 into the trust (Mr Brain is going to pay the IHT).

1 June 2007 he put another £87,000 into the same trust (the trustee is paying the IHT).

Required

Compute the IHT payable on the lifetime gifts.

Nil rate bands

2004/05   £263,000

2007/08   £300,000

Learning example 17.8

Mr Plank set up a discretionary trust for the benefit of his two children.

1 February 2005 he put £270,000 into the trust (the trustee pays the IHT).

1 June 2007 he put another £87,000 into the same trust (Mr Plank pays the IHT).

Required

Compute the IHT payable on the lifetime gifts.

Learning example 17.9

Mr Jones set up a discretionary trust for the benefit of his two children. In all cases, Mr Jones will pay the tax

1 January 2001 he put £50,000 into the trust

1 May 2003 he put another £197,000 into the same trust

1 July 2007 he put another £155,000 into the same trust

Required

Compute the IHT payable on the lifetime gifts. Use the 2011/12 NRB in all cases.

Additional IHT on Lifetime Transfers – Computation 2

Introduction

Where a donor survives seven years after he has made a transfer of value, in the case of a PET there will be no IHT arising, or, in the case of a CLT no additional IHT upon death. Where the donor dies within seven years of making a CLT, additional IHT will be chargeable at the death rate of 40% on chargeable transfers.

Taper relief

IHT on all lifetime transfers made within seven years before death is subject to a potential reduction for taper relief, if the lifetime transfer was made more than three years before death. The longer a donor survives after a PET or CLT; any additional IHT due on death, is reduced by available taper relief.

Taper relief reduces the IHT payable on the transfer and not the value of the transfer itself.

Time between transfer and death	Reduction in IHT on death (%)
3 years or less	0
> 3 but < 4 years	20
> 4 but < 5 years	40
> 5 but < 6 years	60
> 6 but < 7 years	80

The IHT is payable by the donee and the amount payable is determined using the principle of cumulation. No grossing up is necessary.

Chargeable lifetime transfers – calculation on death

The steps required for the calculation of death tax on lifetime transfers is the same regardless of whether or not the lifetime transfer was a CLT or a PET.

Step 1

Look back seven years prior to the date of the CLT/PET to see if any chargeable transfers were made. If so, use up the NRB (as per year of transfer) and calculate any remaining NRB.

Step 2

Take the gross value of the CLT/PET as calculated whilst working out the lifetime tax. Remember, where the transfer is a PET and this was dated prior to a CLT made in the same year, any annual exemptions should be given against the PET.

Step 3

Deduct the NRB from the gross transfer value. Where the CLT is greater than the remaining NRB, IHT at 40% is charged. Taper relief is applied according to the taper relief rules.

Step 4

Deduct any IHT paid on the CLT.

This is an area where students often struggle. The computations in themselves are not difficult but the steps involved in remembering the above rules, often get mistaken.

Learning example 17.10

Don Napier made the following lifetime gifts:

4 May 2003 – £239,000 cash gift to a discretionary trust

4 December 2004 – £15,000 cash as a birthday present to his son John

4 February 2006 – 20% of the shares in DN plc to his daughter Janet as a wedding present. At that time they were valued at £200,000.

4 August 2008 – A further £200,000 cash gift to the discretionary trust created on the 4 May 2003.

Required

(a) Compute the IHT payable on the lifetime gifts assuming Don agreed to pay the IHT.

(b) Assuming Don dies on 14 January 2012 compute the IHT payable by the daughter and by the trustee.

(c) Compute the remaining nil rate band available to use in the death estate.

The nil rate bands are:

2003/04   £255,000

2008/09   £312,000

London
School of Business
& Finance
shaping success in business and finance

Learning example 17.11

Continuing with example 17.6, Elanor dies on 28 December 2011.

Required

(a) Compute the IHT payable by the daughter and by the trustee on Elanor's death

(b) Compute the remaining NRB available to use in the death estate.

Lifetime Versus Death Gifts to Individuals but Excluding Gifts Between Husband and Wife

Tax implications for lifetime gifts	Tax implications for lifetime gifts	Tax implications for death gifts
CGT Capital gains tax may be assessable on the donor in the tax year in which the gift is made. No CGT on the gift of any assets which are defined as exempt assets for CGT or if the donor and donee make a joint election to defer the donor's gain by claiming gifts holdover relief. The CGT is computed as if the donor is making a disposal of a chargeable asset and the donor is treated as receiving market value at the date of disposal.	**IHT** No IHT is payable when the gift is made as this is called a PET. IHT may be payable by the donee if the donor dies within the next 7 years. The amount of IHT payable by the donee is computed by including the PET in computation 2 at the market value at the date of the gift.	**IHT** IHT is payable when the donor dies based on the market value at the date of death or more commonly this is called the probate value. In order to compute the IHT payable the probate value of the gift is included in the death estate (computation 3). The detailed rules for computing IHT in computation 3 are covered later in the chapter. In the death estate IHT is normally payable by the executors or administrators of the estate.

Advantages of Lifetime Transfers

Lifetime transfers are the easiest way for a person to reduce their potential IHT liability.

- A PET is completely exempt from IHT after seven years

- A CLT will not incur any additional IHT liability after seven years.

- Even if the donor does not survive for seven years, taper relief will reduce the amount of IHT payable after three years.

- The value of the PETS and CLTs is fixed at the time they are made, so it can be beneficial to make gifts of assets that are expected to increase in value such as property or shares.

IHT Death Estate Computation

Composition of death estate

Valuation Rules for IHT

Sometimes exam questions will give you the value of the death estate but often you will be required to determine its value using the valuation rules that apply to IHT, particularly important at F6 is the diminution in value principal. The rules relating to the death estate, including the diminution in value principal will be illustrated using the next example Henry Harbottle.

A death estate consists of all the property owned immediately prior to his death. Excluded property is not included in the death estate.

	£	£
Freehold property	x	
Less: Repayment mortgage and accrued interest	(x)	
	---	x
Foreign property	x	
Less: Expenses restricted to 5% of property value	(x)	
	---	x
Business owned by sole trader/ partnership		x
Farm		x
Stocks and shares (including Maxi ISA)		x
Government securities		x
Insurance policy proceeds		x
Death in service policy		x
Leasehold property		x
Motor cars		x
Personal chattels		x
Debts due to the deceased		x
Interest and rent due to the deceased		x
Cash and bank and on deposit (including Mini Cash ISA)		x
		---
		x
Less: Debts due by the deceased	(x)	
Outstanding taxes (e.g. IT, CGT due)	(x)	
Funeral expenses	(x)	
	---	(x)
		---
		x
Less: **Exempt legacies**		
(e.g. legacy to wife, charity, national heritage body, political party)		
		(x)
CHARGEABLE ESTATE		---
		x

Debts and funeral expenses

The following expenses will be allowed to be deducted in the death estate

- Taxes to the date of death
- Debts incurred by the deceased bona fide
- Debts which have accrued up to the date of death (rents) but payable after death
- Cost of a tombstone
- Reasonable costs of mourning for the family

Death Estate Exam technique – Computation 3

Step 1	Put all the assets owned at date of death into the death estate at their probate value (PV),
Step 2	Reduce the value of the death estate by any outstanding liabilities owed by the deceased. E.g. funeral expenses, income tax/CGT owed by the deceased, outstanding repayment mortgages and any other outstanding loans.
Step 3	Reduce the value of the death estate by the value of any legacies which are exempt from IHT e.g. to spouse, to charity, to a political party, to a national heritage body.
Step 4	Compute the IHT on the chargeable estate by deducting the remaining NRB from the chargeable estate and multiplying any balance by the death rate (40%). Any PETs or CLTs made in the seven years prior to death are now chargeable and must reduce the NRB (Chargeable Estate – Remaining NRB) x 40% = X

Learning example 17.12

Herbert, aged 79, died on 5 October 2011 survived by his wife, Sarah, also aged 79, and two children, Cyril and Irene.

At the date of Herbert's death he owned the following assets

1   60% of the shares in Cedar Ltd an investment company.

2   A house valued on 5 October 2011 at £370,000. The property had an outstanding repayment mortgage of £80,000 at the date of Herbert's death. This property was his and Sarah's family home but was owned outright by Herbert.

At the time of Herbert's death he owed £2,500 of income tax to HMRC and £1,800 for his funeral expenses. Herbert left the house to his wife and everything else to Cyril and Irene.

The only gift made by Herbert during his lifetime was on 1 January 2008 when he made a gift of 20% of the shares in Cedar Ltd to his daughter Irene.

Cedar Ltd shares were valued as follows:

Shareholding	Value at 1 January 2008	Value at 5 October 2011
20%	120,000	150,000
60%	500,000	650,000
80%	720,000	900,000
100%	900,000	1,100,000

Herbert had agreed to pay any inheritance tax arising on these lifetime gifts.

Required

(a)   Calculate the value of the lifetime gift to Irene on 1 January 2008 and state how much IHT will be payable at the time of making this gift.

(b)   Calculate the IHT payable by Irene when Herbert dies.

(c)   Calculate the IHT payable by the executors on Herbert's death.

Learning example 17.13

Bill aged 80, died on 5 October 2011 survived by his wife Betty, also aged 80 and his two children Ben and Barbie. Bill owned the following assets:

	£
House	370,000
Quoted shares	120,000
Villa	150,000
Bank account	90,000
Car	10,000

Bill owed income tax of £2,500 and funeral expenses of £2,000. Under the terms of his will Bill left the house and shares to Betty. The villa to his daughter and the son inherits everything else. Bill made a lifetime gift of £180,000 to his son on the occasion of his marriage in June 2010.

Required

Compute the IHT payable on Bill's death by the executors of Bill's estate.

London
School of Business
& Finance
shaping success in business and finance

Transfer of unused nil rate band (nrb)

If:

- An individual (A) dies; and

- They had a spouse or civil partner (B) immediately before the death of B; and

- B had unused NRB on death

then a claim can be made to increase the NRB of A by the unused NRB of B.

The increased NRB of A will be used in the calculation of additional IHT on CLTs made by A, PETs made by A becoming chargeable, and the death estate of A.

If the NRB increases between the death of B and A, the amount of B's unused NRB is scaled up so that it represents the same proportion of the NRB at A's death as it did at B's death.

Any increase in the NRB maximum cannot exceed the NRB maximum at the date of A's death.

Learning example 17.14

Jenna and Nick were married for many years. Nick died on 1 December 2006, leaving a death estate valued at £400,000. This was left to Jenna and his sister equally. The nil band at Nick's death in 2006/07 was £285,000.

Jenna died on 21 February 2012, leaving a death estate valued at £600,000 (this included the assets passed to Jenna on the death of Nick). In 2007 Jenna made one lifetime gift of £80,000 after deducting the relevant annual exemptions and left the entire estate to her brother.

Required

Calculate the maximum nil rate band and the available nil rate band for use in Jenna's death estate.

IHT administration

Introduction

IHT is administered by HMRC Inheritance Tax. There is no system of regular returns (like self-assessment) for IHT. The taxpayer is expected to deliver a return when a relevant transfer is made.

Where the transfer is on death, the Personal Representative (PR) is required to deliver an account showing full details of the death estate.

Payment of IHT

Chargeable lifetime transfers

The donor is primarily responsible for any IHT that has to be paid in respect of a CLT. However, a question may state that the donee is to instead pay the IHT. Remember that grossing up is only necessary where the donor pays the tax.

The due date is the later of:

- 30 April following the end of the tax year in which the gift is made.

- Six months from the end of the month in which the gift is made.

Therefore, if a CLT is made between 6 April and 30 September in a tax year then any IHT will be due on the following 30 April. If a CLT is made between 1 October and 5 April in a tax year then any IHT will be due six months from the end of the month in which the gift is made.

The donee is always responsible for any additional IHT that becomes payable as a result of the death of the donor within seven years of making a CLT. The due date is six months after the end of the month in which the donor died.

Potentially exempt transfers

The donee is always responsible for any additional IHT that becomes payable as a result of the death of the donor within seven years of making a PET. The due date is six months after the end of the month in which the donor died.

Death estate

The personal representatives of the deceased's estate are responsible for any IHT that is payable. The due date is six months after the end of the month in which death occurred. However, the personal representatives are required to pay the IHT when they deliver their account of the estate assets to HM Revenue & Customs, and this may be earlier than the due date.

Where part of the estate is left to a spouse then this part will be exempt and will not bear any of the IHT liability. Where a specific gift is left to a beneficiary then this gift will not normally bear any IHT. The IHT is therefore usually paid out of the non-exempt residue of the estate.

Instalment option

IHT in respect of certain assets can be paid in instalments. Qualifying assets are:

(i)   Land and buildings wherever situated

(ii)   A business or an interest in a business

(iii)   A shareholding in a company controlled by the deceased

(iv)   Unquoted shares that represents 10% or more of the company's shares with a value in excess of £20,000

10 equal annual instalments are made with the first instalment being due 6 months after the end of the month of death.

Interest is due from the normal due date on IHT on land and buildings and investment company shares, however interest on IHT due on other assets is only charged if the instalment is paid late.

N.B The instalment option is only available provided the instalment asset is still owned by the donee, and if it is sold the whole of the outstanding IHT on that asset becomes payable immediately.

Learning summary

- IHT applies to where a transfer of value takes place. The transfer of value is the diminution in value of the donor's estate.

- To be liable to IHT, the taxpayer must be domiciled in the UK, or transfer UK based assets if non-domiciled.

- Transfers of value can be classified as Chargeable Lifetime Transfers (CLTs) or Potentially Exempt Transfers (PETs). A CLT is chargeable to IHT immediately, with additional IHT becoming due if the donor dies within seven years. A PET is not liable to IHT unless the donor dies within seven years.

- Transfers to a spouse/civil partner are exempt from IHT.

- Various exemptions are available to the donor including marriage exemption, small gifts exemption and the annual exemption.

- A nil rate band, at which if transfers in the past seven years do not exceed the nil rate band, can be deducted from the valuation (after exemptions) of the asset.

- IHT is charged at 20% of lifetime CLTs, with additional IHT being chargeable upon death, subject to taper relief.

- IHT is paid to HMRC Inheritance Tax, with the payment date dependent on the type of transfer.

Exam standard question

Patsy was widowed in August 2006. Her husband Paddy left £110,000 to their eldest son Shaun and the remainder to Patsy. Patsy died on 30 May 2011. She lived with her partner John, who is wealthy in his own right, and so she left her estate to her three adult children, Shaun, Penny and Ireland.

On the date of Patsy's death, she owned the following assets and owed the following liabilities:

Assets:	£
Home	600,000
Holiday apartment	350,000
Shares in a quoted company	43,700
Bank and cash in ISA accounts	5,700
Chattels and jewellery	3,000
Liabilities	
Funeral expenses	5,090
Outstanding tax bill	600

During Patsy's lifetime, she made the following gifts:

1 May 2006	Gift to charity	£30,000
3 April 2008	Gift into a discretionary trust of	£360,000
5 November 2009	Gift to her god-daughter on her marriage	£15,000

The trustees paid any IHT due on the 3 April 2008 gift

The nil rate band for earlier years are as follows:

2006/07	£285,000
2007/08	£300,000
2008/09	£312,000
2009/10	£325,000

Required

(a) Calculate the inheritance tax payable during Patsy's lifetime and as a result of her death.

(b) State the due date for paying the inheritance tax on her death estate

Learning solution 17.1

(a)   IHT payable if Audrey makes the gifts on her death

	£
Chargeable Estate	600,000
IHT (600,000 - 325,000) x 40%	110,000
The amount inherited by the son will be	490,000
(600,000 - 110,000)	

Learning solution 17.2

(b)   IHT payable by her grandson on Audrey's death if she makes the gift during her lifetime.

	£	£
PET	600,000	
AE 11/12	(3,000)	
AE 10/11	(3,000)	
Chargeable PET	594,000	
IHT (594,000 - 325,000) x 40%		107,600
IHT saving by making the gift during her lifetime		2,400
(110,000 - 107,600)		

(c)   If Audrey lives for more than 7 years after making the lifetime gift to her grandson, this is defined as an exempt PET and the grandson will not pay any IHT when his grandmother dies.

Learning solution 17.3

(a)   No IHT is payable on Terry's death as the legacy to Susie is exempt from IHT. Terry's unused nil rate band is 100% (£325,000) which can then be transferred to Susie and used when she dies provided the necessary election is made two years from the end of the month of her death.

(b)   On Susie's death she has a total nil rate band of £650,000, made up of her own nil rate band (NRB) of £325,000 and also her husband's unused NRB, which can be transferred to Susie provided an election is made by 31 December 2013.

Learning solution 17.4

Gift	Amount of the gift	Type of gift	Available IHT Reliefs
Gift to Steve's son	£8,900	PET	ME = £5,000 AE 11/12 = £3,000 AE 10/11 = £900
Gift to charity	£30,000	Exempt transfer	
Gifts to team members	£200 each	PET	The small gift relief aplies to all gifts
Gift to Larry West	£1,600	PET	AE 10/11 = £1,600
Gift each year to his nephew	£7,000	Exempt	Normal expenditure out of income

London
School of Business
& Finance

shaping success in business and finance

Learning solution 17.5

Gift	Amount of the gift	Type of gift	Available IHT Reliefs
Gift to grandson	£5,000	PET	ME = £2,500 AE 11/12 = £2,500
Gift to Labour Party	£60,000	Exempt transfer	
Gifts to wife	£20,000	Exempt transfer	
Gift to business partner	£350	PET	Small gift relief not available as gift > £250. AE 11/12 = £350

Learning solution 17.6

	£	Gross £	IHT £	Net £	Due date
1.8.01					
CLT 1	268,000				
AE 01/02	(3,000)				
AE 00/01	(3,000)				
	262,000	262,000	Nil	262,000	
1.5.06	155,000				
PET 1					
AE 06/07	(3,000)				
AE 05/06	(3,000)				
	149,000	149,000	-	149,000	
				PET, therefore, no immediate charge to IHT	
1.05.08					
CLT 2	137,000				
AE 08/09	(3,000)				
AE 07/08	(3,000)				
	131,000	148,000	17,000	131,000	Elanor pays £17,000; Nil band 325,000
					Used (262,000)
(131,000 – 63,000) x 25%					NRB left 63,000

Learning solution 17.7

	£	Gross £	IHT £	Net £	Due date
1.2.05					
CLT 1	410,000				
AE 04/05	(3,000)				
AE 03/04	(3,000)				
	404,000	439,250	35,250	404,000	Donor pays £35,250 by 31.8.05
IHT					
(404,000 - 263,000) x 25%					
Remaining NRB 2007/08 is £Nil					
1.6.07					
CLT 2	87,000				
AE 07/08	(3,000)				
AE 06/07	(3,000)				
IHT	81,000	81,000	16,200	64,800	Trustee pays £16,200 by 30.4.08

(81,000 x 20%) £16,200

Learning solution 17.8

	£	Gross £	IHT £	Net £	Due date
1.2.05					
CLT 1	270,000				
AE 04/05	(3,000)				
AE 03/04	(3,000)				
	264,000	264,000	200	263,800	The trustees pay £200 by 31.8.05

(264,000 - 263,000) x 20% - £200

Remaining NRB 2007/08

£36,000 (300,000 - 264,000)

	£	Gross £	IHT £	Net £	Due date
1.6.07					
CLT 2	87,000				
AE 07/08	(3,000)				
AE 06/07	(3,000)				
	81,000	92,200	11,250	81,000	Mr Plank pays £11,250 by 30.4.08

IHT £11,250 (81,000 - 36,000) x 25%

Learning solution 17.9

		£	Gross £	IHT £	Net £
1.1.01	CLT 1	50,000			
	AE 00/01	(3,000)			
	AE 99/00	(3,000)			
		44,000	Covered by NRB		
1.5.03	CLT 2	197,000			
	AE 03/04	(3,000)			
	AE 02/03	(3,000)			
IHT		191,000	Covered by NRB		
1.7.07	CLT 3	155,000	Nil rate band 325,000 Used (235,000) Remaining 90,000		
	AE 07/08	(3,000)	IHT (149,000 − 90,000) x 25% = £14,750		
	AE 06/07	(3,000)			
	IHT	149,000	163,750	14,750	149,000

Learning solution 17.10

(a) IHT payable during Don's lifetime (Computation 1)

	£	Gross £	IHT £	Net £	Due date
4.5.03					
CLT 1	239,000				
AE 03/04	(3,000)				
AE 02/03	(3,000)				
	233,000	233,000	Nil	233,000	

The NRB in 03/04 is £255,000
Remaining NRB to use in 2008/09
is £79,000
(312,000 - 233,000)

4.8.08					
CLT 2	200,000				
AE 08/09	(3,000)				
AE 07/08	(3,000)				
	194,000	222,750	28,750	194,000	Donor pays £28,750 by 30.4.09

(194,000 - 79,000) x 25%

IHT payable on Lifetime Gifts as a result of the donor's death

	£	Gross £	IHT £	Taper relief £	Tax paid £	Tax payable £	Due date
4.5.03 Gift - CLT 1		233,000	Nil	Nil	Nil	Nil	
4.12.04 Gift - PET (exempt)		Nil					
4.2.06 Gift - PET 2	200,000						
ME	(5,000)						
AE 05/06	(3,000)			60%			
Remaining NRB is £92,000 (325,000-233,000) IHT (192,000-92,000) x 40%	192,000 425,000	192,000	40,000	(24,000)	(Nil)	16,000	31.7.12 by daughter
4.8.07 Gift - CLT 2 222,750 x 40% = £89,100		222,750 647,750	89,100	20% (17,820)	(28,750)	42,530	31.7.12 by trustee
Remove Gift on 4.6.03		(233,000) 414,750					

(b) **The IHT payable by the daughter on the gift of the shares in DN plc is £16,000. This should be paid by 31 July 2012. The IHT payable by the trustees is £42,530 by 31 July 2012.**

(c) **The is no remaining nil rate band to use in the death estate.**

Learning solution 17.11

(a) **IHT payable during Elanor's lifetime (Computation 1)**

The CLT made on 1.8.01 is made more than seven years before death. No further IHT arises on this CLT

The PET made on 1.5.06 is within seven years of death and therefore, becomes chargeable on death. The annual exemptions for 06/07 and 05/06 are available, making the PET chargeable at a value of £149,000 (155,000 – 3,000- 3,000)

The PET is cumulated with the CLT made on 1.8.01 for the purposes of calculating the NRB

Nil rate band	325,000
CLT	(262,000)
NRB	63,000

IHT (149,000-63,000) x 40% = £34,400

Taper relief is available as the transfer was made more than three years before death

Taper relief % = 60% leaving 40% chargeable

IHT x 40% = £13,760

The CLT on 1.5.08 was made within seven years of death and so additional IHT is payable at 40%. All the NRB has been used up in cumulating prior transfers. IHT at 40% x £148,000 = £59,200

Taper relief is available as the transfer was made more than three years before death.

Taper relief % = 20% leaving 80% chargeable less tax paid of £17,000 = £30,360 (£59,200 x 80% = £47,360 - 17,000)

London School of Business & Finance
shaping success in business and finance

IHT Payable on Lifetime Gifts as a Result of the Donor's Death

			Gross	IHT	Taper relief	Tax paid	Tax payable
		£	£	£	£	£	£
1.8.01	Gift – CLT (1)		262,000	Nil	Nil	Nil	Nil
1.5.06	Gift – PET (1)	155,000					
	AE 06/07	(3,000)					
	AE 05/06	(3,000)			60%		
IHT		149,000	149,000	34,400	(20,640)	(Nil)	13,760
(149,000-63,000) × 40%							
			411,000				
					20%		
1.5.08	Gift – CLT (2)		148,000	59,200	(11,840)	(17,000)	30,360
(148,000) × 40% = £59,200			559,000				
Death							
Remove							
Gift on 1.8.01			(262,000)				
			297,000				

(b) **The remaining NRB to use in the death estate is £28,000 (325,000 – 297,000).**

Learning solution 17.12

(i) Lifetime gift of the shares to the daughter is called a PET for the purposes of IHT. This means that no IHT is payable at the time of giving.

The value of the PET which is frozen at the time of given is evaluated using the diminution in value principal.

Before Herbert gives his daughter the shares he has 80% which are valued at £720,000, and after making the gift, Herbert is left with 60% of the shares which according to the table are worth £500,000. The fall in value of Herbert's shares is £220,000, and this is the value of the PET.

(ii) The IHT payable by Irene on her lifetime gift is £nil when Henry dies.

		Gross	IHT	Taper relief	Tax paid	Tax payable
	£	£	£	£	£	£
1.1.08						
Gift - PET 1	220,000					
AE 07/08	(3,000)					
AE 06/07	(3,000)					
	214,000	214,000	Nil	Nil	Nil	Nil
		214,000				

Remaining NRB = £111,000
(325,000 - 214,000)

(iii) The IHT payable by the executors when Herbert dies is £213,880 which is evaluated using the rules of the death estate shown below.

Computation 3 - Death estate

Step 1

Include all assets owned at death in the estate at probate value.	**£**
House	370,000
Less: Repayment mortgage	(80,000)
60% of shares in Cedar Ltd	650,000

Step 2

Reduce the value by any outstanding liabilities	
Income tax owed to HMRC	(2,500)
Funeral expenses	(1,800)
	935,700

Step 3

Reduce the value of the estate by any legacies which are exempt from IHT	
Legacies to Sarah	(290,000)
Chargeable estate	645,700

Step 4

IHT (645,700 - 111,000) x 40%	213,880

London
School of Business
& Finance
shaping success in business and finance

Learning solution 17.13

IHT payable on Bill's lifetime gift as a result of his death.

Computation 2

		£
30.6.10	PET	180,000
	ME	(5,000)
	AE 10/11	(3,000)
	AE 09/10	(3,000)
		169,000

The remaining nil rate band is £156,000 (325,000 – 169,000). This can be used to reduce the value of the chargeable estate (computation 3).

Step 1

Include all the assets owned at the date of death in the death estate at probate value.

Step 2

The value of the estate is then reduced by any outstanding liabilities owed by Bill at the date of death.

Computation 3

	£
House	370,000
Quoted shares	120,000
Villa	150,000
Bank account	90,000
Car	10,000
Less	
Allowable expenses	
Funeral expense and tax liabilities owed to HMRC	(4,500)

Step 3

Less legacies which are exempt from IHT	
To spouse	(490,000)
Chargeable Estate	245,500

Step 4

Compute the IHT payable on the chargeable estate £89,500 (245,500 – 156,000) x 40% = £35,800.

Learning solution 17.14

Consider any unused nil band

Lifetime transfer made by Jenna of £80,000 in seven years before her death

Nil rate band at death was £325,000. Nil rate band is increased by claim to transfer Nick's unused nil rate band at death (285,000 – (400,000/2) = 85,000). The unused proportion is £85,000/285,000 = 29.8%.

The adjusted unused proportion is £325,000 x 29.8% = £96,850. The maximum nil rate band at Jenna's death is £421,850 (325,000 + 96,850), with the available nil rate band being £341,850 (421,850 – 80,000).

Solution to exam standard question

Step 1, Calculation 1 – Lifetime IHT on lifetime gifts

	£	£
1 May 2006		
Gift to charity		30,000
Less, charity exemption:		(30,000)
PET		Nil
3 April 2008		
Gift to discretionary trust		360,000
Less, annual exemptions:		
2007/08		(3,000)
2006/07		(3,000)
CLT		354,000
Less, Nil Band for 2007/08	300,000	
Reduced by any chargeable gifts in the previous 7 years	(Nil)	(300,000)
Chargeable lifetime transfer (CLT)		54,000
Lifetime tax due on the CLT at 20%		
(trustees are paying the tax)		10,800
5 November 2009		
Gift to god-daughter		15,000
Less marriage exemptions		(1,000)
		14,000
Less annual exemptions:		
2009/10		(3,000)
2008/09		(3,000)
PET		8,000

Step 2, Calculation 2 – Additional IHT on the lifetime gifts due to death within 7 years of the gifts

Now that the calculations have been done for the lifetime IHT, we need to work through the method to ascertain the change in liability when death has occurred within 7 years of the lifetime gifts. There may be *additional IHT* due as a result of the death.

	£m	£m
1 May 2006		
Gift to charity		Still exempt
3 April 2008		
Gift to discretionary trust		
CLT revised transfer value		354,000
Nil Band 2011/12 (year of death)	325,000	
CLTs in the previous 7 years	(Nil)	
		(325,000)
Chargeable		£29,000
Tax due at 40%		11,600
Less taper relief (3 to 4 years) 20%		(2,320)
Tax due		9,280
Less lifetime tax paid		(10,800)
		No repayment due

5 November 2009		£	£
Gift to god-daughter	After marriage exemption		8,000
	And annual exemptions		
Nil Band for 2011/12 (year of death)		325,000	
Reduced by any chargeable gifts in			
the previous 7 years		(354,000)	(Nil)
Chargeable at death			8,000
Death rate of tax due at 40%			3,200
Less taper relief			Nil
IHT due			3,200

Step 3, Calculation 3 – IHT on the death estate

Finally, the death estate calculation can be done, including any balance of the Nil band that we have established.

Assets held at death – 30 May 2011	£	£
Home		600,000
Holiday apartment		350,000
Shares in the quoted company		43,700
ISA accounts – taxable		5,700
Personal possessions and jewellery		3,000
Less liabilities	Funeral	(5,090)
	Tax bill	(600)
Total taxable estate		996,710
Nil Band for 2011/12	325,000	
Reduced by any chargeable gifts in		
the previous 7 years	(354,000 + 8,000)	(Nil)
Chargeable estate		996,710
Tax due at the death rate 40%		398,684

(b)   Inheritance tax due on the death estate is payable six months after the end of the month of death

18

Corporation Tax

Context

This chapter is concerned with the tax payable by a company. A company is intangible but it is a legal person and as such has the right to own a business and to own business assets.

The people responsible for running a company are called employees or staff. In this chapter the tax implications for companies will be considered, focusing on the similarities and differences between a person owning a business (a sole trader) and a company owning a business.

Companies only pay one tax on their income and gains and this is corporation tax.

Exam hints

This particular topic will always be tested as question 2 on the paper for between 20 and 30 marks. It could also come up as part of another question, so clearly it is an important tax to understand.

Key learning points

- UK resident companies pay corporation tax on their Taxable total profits.

- Taxable total profits includes worldwide income and gains, such as trading income, interest income and rental income.

- The calculation of these types of income is based on the same basic principles as a sole trader but a few differences.

- The rate of corporation tax is based on a company's 'Augmented profits', which are computed by adding together Taxable total profits and franked investment income (FII).

- The 'Augmented profits' are compared to the upper and lower limits to determine the rate of corporation tax. The upper and lower limits must be prorated for a short accounting period or for associated companies.

- The rate of corporation tax will vary depending on the Financial Year. The Financial Year 2011 runs from 1 April 2011 – 31 March 2012.

- There are dates and deadlines concerning both the filing of a corporation tax return and the payment of corporation tax due.

Scope of corporation tax (CT)

Payable by UK resident companies on their Total taxable profits for an accounting period (AP).

Definitions for corporation tax:

UK resident:	company incorporated in the UK or centrally managed and controlled in the UK
Taxable total profits:	worldwide income and gains
AP:	An AP is the period for which a charge to corporation tax is made and is usually a company's period of account.

Accounting period (AP)

An AP begins when:

- A company starts to trade; or

- The profits of a company first become liable to corporation tax; or

- The previous chargeable accounting period ends

The company must notify HMRC within 3 months of the start of its first AP

An AP ends on the earlier of the following:

- 12 months after the period of account started (i.e. an AP cannot exceed 12 months); or

- Any of the following:

    - The end of the period of account

    - Company ceases to trade

    - Company ceases to be UK resident

    - Company ceases to be liable to corporation tax

    - Company commences/ceases winding up

A period of account is the period for which the company prepares its statutory accounts.

Proforma corporation tax computation

Corporation tax computation - for the AP

	£
Profits from trading (adjusted profits less capital allowances)	X
Overseas income (gross of overseas tax suffered)	X
Rental income	X
Interest income (from non trading)	X
Chargeable gains (chargeable gains less capital losses)	X
Total profits	X
Gift aid donations to charity	(X)
Taxable total profits	X
Corporation tax (CT) at relevant rate	X
Less Marginal relief (if any)	(X)
Corporation tax liability	X
Less	
Double tax relief (DTR)	(X)
Corporation tax (CT) payable	X/Nil

Due date 9 months and one day after the end of the AP
          (unless a large company which pays in quarterly instalments)
File date 12 months after the end of the period of account

(a)   In general income and expenses are included in a corporation tax computation on a gross accruals basis.

(b)   A company cannot be an employee and so cannot have employment income.

(c)   A company is not a "person" and is not entitled to claim personal allowances.

(d)   A company does not pay corporation tax on UK and overseas dividends received.

Calculation of Taxable total profits

	£
Trading income	X
Overseas income (see chapter 21)	X
Rental income	X
Interest income	X
Chargeable gains	X
Total Profits	X
Gift aid donations to charity	(X)
Taxable total profits	X

Trading income

The calculation of profits from trading uses the financial statements of the company as a starting point. The company must calculate the profit from each trade it carries on separately.

It is necessary to adjust the reported accounting profits as per the pro-forma below. Over the past few years, changes in legislation have brought taxable profits closer in line with accounting profits, which have been calculated with reference to generally accepted accounting principles.

Adjustment of profit proforma

Many tax computations start with 'Profits per accounts' and are then adjusted for items specifically not allowed (for tax deduction) in legislation.

Accounts should be prepared on an accruals basis, rather than a receipts basis. The complexity of the accounts depends on the nature of the business.

Adjustment of Accounting Profit to Give Tax Adjusted Accounting Profit

	£	£
Net profit per accounts		X
Add:		
Expenditure charged in the accounts not allowed for tax purposes (disallowed items)	X	
Income taxable as trade profits but not credited to the accounts	X	
		X
Less:		
Profits included in the accounts not taxable as trade profits (e.g. bank interest receivable, dividends)	(X)	
Expenditure deductible for tax purposes but has not been charged in the accounts (e.g. capital allowances)	(X)	
		(X)
Trade profits adjusted for tax purposes		X

Disallowable expenses

Certain expenditure is disallowed through legislation and case law, although it is acceptable to include the expense in calculating the accounting profits of the business. In these circumstances, the deduction is required to be 'added back' into the accounting profit.

Capital expenditure

The acquisition of a capital asset is not a cost that can be deducted in arriving at the profits for tax purposes. The definition of assets extends beyond that of tangible fixed assets and includes the acquisition of goodwill, and payments to secure the release of the trader from an onerous liability (lease or fixed rate loan).

Most difficulties have arisen in the definition of repairs and improvements. Repairs are generally revenue in nature (tax deductible), whereas improvements are generally capital in nature (not tax deductible).

Entertaining

Where the expenditure is in relation to entertaining customers or suppliers, this is a disallowable expense. Staff entertaining is an allowable expense but depending upon the annual value and nature, it may lead to an assessable benefit-in-kind on the employee.

Gifts to customers/charities

Costs for gifts are disallowed unless:

- they advertise the business, and
- are not food or drink or tobacco, or
- a voucher which is capable of being converted into such goods, and
- is an item which costs less than £50 per recipient per year.

A donation to a local charity is allowable, although a donation to a national charity and political party is disallowed. Gift aid donations will reduce a company's corporation tax by reducing its total profits.

Lease rentals on expensive cars

Where the lease contract commenced after 1 April 2009, the amount disallowed is a flat 15% for cars with CO_2 emissions exceeding 160g/km hired for a period exceeding 45 days. The lease costs should exclude any maintenance charges but include the 50% VAT charge where the company is VAT registered. The restriction will not apply to the hire of low CO_2 emission cars or electric cars.

Impaired debts and trade debt recoveries

Impaired debts are allowable if they are trade related. If an impaired debt is not trade related it is a disallowable expense. The recovery of a previously written off trader debt is an allowable credit.

Remuneration not paid within nine months of the year-end

Bonus payments to employees may be made after the year end. If they clearly relate to a period of account, it is normal for a company to include the bonus as a provision. This provision is only allowable if the remuneration is paid within 9 months of the year end.

Pension contributions

Payments to a pension scheme are a revenue expense and deductible from profits in the year in which the premium is paid.

Expenditure not wholly and exclusively for trade purposes

Expenditure must be for the purposes of the trade and incurred wholly and exclusively for the trade. Company expenditure must be viewed from this perspective.

Reverse premiums

Relief is available where a builder or property developer pays a reverse premium to induce a tenant to take a lease.

Legal fees

Legal costs in relation with the acquisition of capital assets, issuing shares, drawing up a partnership agreement or in connection with renewing a lease of more than 50 years are not allowable. Legal fees incurred in connection with tax appeals are also not allowable.

Allowable expenses

The following table is a summary of the position of HMRC with regards allowable expenses

Item	Allowable
Employee costs	Wages and salaries, employers NIC, pension contributions on behalf of employees, restrictive covenants (provided employee is taxed on the payment as employment income), costs incurred in setting up an approved share scheme
Finance costs	Interest on loans and overdrafts used solely for business purposes, cost of arranging such finance
Professional	Accountancy fees, debt recovery, renewing leases of < 50 years, defending business rights
Travel	Travel on business to meet customers, travel between business premises, accommodation and reasonable overnight expenses, vehicle running expenses (business use part only where vehicle belongs to owner)
Subscriptions	Payments to certain professional bodies
Rents	Normal rents, lease premiums on short leases (spread over the course of the lease)
Entertaining	Costs of entertaining staff, gifts (not food or drink or vouchers able to be turned into food or drink) up to £50 per person per year
VAT	VAT not recoverable because the business is exempt or partially exempt but not VAT on capital items (this should be added to the capital cost for capital allowances purposes)
Other	Personal security costs, counselling and retraining expenses of employees made redundant.

Pre-trading expenditure

Pre-trading expenditure, ie expenditure incurred in the seven years before the trade started, is treated as incurred on the day trade commenced. It is therefore treated as an allowable expense provided it would qualify as deductible under the normal rules for expenses.

Capital allowances

The calculation of capital allowances for a company is very similar to the calculation of capital allowances for a sole trader. The key difference is that there no private use adjustment in a company's capital allowances working.

The following provides a recap of the key capital allowances issues.

Allowances on plant and machinery

Main pool

Capital expenditure on plant and machinery is generally placed in a main pool of expenditure and an annual writing down allowance claimed. The annual writing down allowance (WDA) on the pool is 20% per year on a reducing balance basis. The WDA is calculated after taking into account any of the current year's additions and disposals.

The WDA must be reduced if the chargeable accounting period is less than 12 months.

Some items are not included in the main pool. These are:

*   Cars already owned at 1 April 2009 and costing > £12,000.

*   Short-life assets (if the election is made).

On disposal of assets from the main pool, proceeds are used as the disposal value. However, the disposal value cannot exceed the original purchase price.

Expenditure on medium emission motor cars

A motor car will be classified as a medium emission motor if:

*   it has medium CO_2 emissions $\leq$ 160g/km but > 110g/km

The expenditure will be allocated to the main pool and will qualify for WDA at 20%.

Special rate pool

The special rate pool has a rate of WDA of 10%. This special rate pool is for expenditure on long life assets and on plant and machinery integral to a building. A number of items of plant and machinery are treated as integral to a building, particularly: electrical and lighting systems, cold water systems, space or water heating systems, powered systems of ventilation, cooling, or air purification, lifts and escalators.

From 1 April 2009, the special rate pool also includes expenditure on a high emission car. A high emission car is one with an emission rating > 160g/km.

Annual investment allowance

The first £100,000 per annum of expenditure on plant and machinery (other than cars) qualifies for the annual investment allowance (AIA). In effect, the AIA provides a 100% allowance for the first £100,000 invested in plant and machinery each year.

A company is free to allocate the AIA between different types of expenditure in any way that it sees fit. For example, a business which invests £80,000 in general plant and machinery and £40,000 in "integral features" in a 12-month chargeable accounting period might allocate £60,000 of the AIA to general plant and machinery and the remaining £40,000 to the special rate pool. This would maximise allowances for the period, since general plant and machinery attracts the WDA at 20%, whereas the special rate pool attracts a WDA at only 10%.

The £100,000 allowance is for qualifying expenditure in a 12 month chargeable accounting period. If the chargeable accounting period is < 12 months then the £100,000 allowance is reduced accordingly.

If a business spends more than £100,000 then the expenditure beyond the £100,000 enters the main pool or special rate pool and is eligible for the WDA.

First-year allowances

Certain expenditure qualifies for a 100% first year allowance. The main 100% FYAs are as follows:

(a)   Expenditure on low emission motor car is eligible for a 100% FYA so long as the expenditure is incurred on or before 31 March 2013. The definition of a low emission car for the purposes of the 100% FYA is one with an emission rating not exceeding 110 g/km. An exam question will state the emissions of the car.

(b)   Expenditure by businesses on energy-saving or environmentally beneficial plant and machinery qualifies for enhanced capital allowances (ECA) of 100%.

The FYA for low emission cars is available to all businesses whether they are small, medium or large. Low emission cars should be included in the main pool.

Expensive cars

Prior to 1 April 2009 for companies an expensive car, one costing £12,000 or more, would be allocated to a separate expensive car pool and a writing down allowance of 20% , up to a maximum of £3,000 per 12 month chargeable accounting period, would be given.

Where a motor car is already owned at 1 April 2009, the tax treatment, as described above, is to continue for five tax years. CO_2 emissions will not be relevant.

From 1 April 2009 for companies the writing down allowances on cars will depend upon its CO_2 emissions:

*   Motor cars with CO_2 emissions of between 111 – 160g/km qualify for WDA of 20% on the full purchase price.

*   Motor cars with CO_2 emissions of more than 160g/km qualify for WDA of 10% on the full purchase price

*   Motor cars with CO_2 emissions of 110g/km and less qualify for FYA of 100% on the full purchase price

Short-life assets

A short-life asset is an asset which is expected to be sold within an eight year period for less than its tax written down value. Once an election is made to treat an asset as a short-life asset this is irrevocable.

A balancing charge or allowance will arise on the disposal of the asset if it is made within eight years. This can greatly enhance the speed at which the asset allowance is matched against its useful life.

For example, where an asset costing £100,000 is added to the pool, it will qualify for WDA and be pooled with other assets. If in year four, it is sold for say £5,000, the proceeds of £5,000 will be deducted from the main pool. The tax written down value of the asset would have been £52,000 (approximately).

Had the asset been included in the short-life pool, the WDA would have been the same. However, in year four, no WDAs would have been given and instead, the proceeds would have been deducted from the tax written down value of the asset, leaving a balancing allowance of £47,000.

If a short-life election is made, the balancing allowance is obtained when the asset is sold. Under the main pool, the allowance would only be received if the business ceases.

An asset which has a short-life election and is still used in the trade after eight years is transferred into the main pool in year nine.

Small pool balance relief on plant and machinery

If the TWDV brought forward at the beginning of the chargeable accounting period on the main pool or the special rate pool is £1,000 or less, the business may claim small balance relief equivalent to the amount of the balance brought forward.

Assets are included in the capital allowances computation at their VAT exclusive price if the input VAT is recoverable, however VAT on cars is irrecoverable, and therefore cars are generally included at their VAT inclusive price.

Proforma capital allowances on plant and machinery – for each accounting period

	AIA/FYA £	Main pool £	Short life asset £	Special Rate Pool £	Expensive cars 1 £	Expensive cars 2 £	Total Capital allowances £
Tax WDV b/f (at beginning of AP)		X	X		X	X	
Add: Additions							
AIA in SRP and MP	X						
Less: AIA (UL = £100,000 for 12m AP)	(X)	X/Nil					X
Add: High CO$_2$ cars				X			
Add: Medium CO$_2$ cars		X					
Less:							
Disposal proceeds (lower of SP and cost)		(X)	(X)	—	(X)	—	
		X		X	X	X	
Balancing allowance					X		X
Balancing charge			(X)				(X)
Small balance relief if the balance on the main pool or special rate pool is < £1,000							
Writing down allowance (WDA)							
@ 20%		(X)					X
@ 10%				(X)			X
@ 20% restricted to (max of £3,000 per 12m AP)		—	—	—	—	(X)	X
		X	Nil	X	Nil	X	
Add: Motor cars (low CO$_2$)	X						
Less: FYA @ 100%	(X)						X
		X/Nil					
Tax WDV c/f		X	Nil	X	Nil	X	—
Allowances to be claimed							X

Property income

In general a company's income from UK property is calculated in much the same way as an individual's income from property with some differences such as:

- the property income is based on the rent receivable during the chargeable accounting period and

- any interest payable on a loan to buy an investment property is disallowable when computing the property income

- If a property income loss is made during the period, the property income is entered as NIL in the corporation tax computation. The property income loss is then relieved against total profits of the loss making AP with any remaining loss being carried forward against total profits of future chargeable accounting periods or surrendered by way of group relief.

Learning example 18.1

A company has the following results for the year ended 31 March 2012:

	£
Trading profits	95,000
Interest income	7,000
Rental income	?
Capital gains	11,000

The rental income for the period has not yet been calculated. The information is as follows:

Property	1	2	3
	£	£	£
Rent	7,000	7,000	9,000
Less: expenses	(4,000)	(10,000)	(11,000)

Required

Calculate the Taxable total profits for the company for the year ended 31 March 2012, showing the use of the rental income loss.

Interest income

Interest income and expense treatment is determined by the 'loan relationship rules'. The loan relationship rules state:

- If the interest income or expense relates to trade, then it is included in TRADING PROFITS

- If the interest income or expense does not relate to trade, then it is included in INTEREST INCOME

Trading profits or interest income?

	Trade related	**Non trade related**
Interest income	Unlikely	• Bank interest
		• Building society interest
		• Debenture interest
		• Interest on overpaid tax
Interest expense	• Overdraft interest	• Interest on loans to buy investment property
	• Interest paid on trade related loans. E.g. loans to acquire plant and machinery	• Interest on loan to buy shares
	• Loans used to raise finance used for trading purposes	• Interest on overdue tax

Included in trading income   Included in interest income

Once you have decided which interest should be included in interest income, the interest income and expense is netted off in a working as follows:

Interest income working:

	£
Bank and building society interest receivable	X
Debenture interest receivable	X
Interest on overpaid tax	X
Less:	
Interest on loan to buy investment property	(X)
Interest payable on loan to buy shares	(X)
Insert payable on overdue tax	(X)
Loan to employee/customers/supplier written off	(X)
Interest income into tax computation	X

NB companies receive interest GROSS, so there is no need to you to gross up the interest figure before including it in your working

Chargeable gains for company

Companies are not liable to CGT on chargeable gains but instead, these chargeable gains are subject to corporation tax at the company's effective marginal rate.

Chargeable gains are computed in broadly the same way as for individuals. However, a company will be allowed to claim an indexation allowance but not an annual exemption or taper relief. Chargeable gains arising on the disposal of an intangible asset are taxed under the intangible assets rules.

The chargeable gains for an AP are offset against any chargeable losses for the same AP.

However, a company cannot use chargeable losses against total profits; they can be relieved against capital gains arising in a future AP (carry forward) or surrendered to another group company for it to offset against its chargeable gains (of the same AP).

This is the gain calculation for a company:

	£	£
Proceeds		X
Less: Incidental costs of sale		(X)
Net sale proceeds		X
Less: Allowable expenditure:		
- Acquisition cost	X	
- Incidental costs of acquisition	X	
		(X)
- Enhancement expenditure		(X)
Unindexed gain/loss		X/(X)
Less: Indexation allowance		
$\frac{\text{RPI disposal} - \text{RPI acquisition}}{\text{RPI acquisition}} = 0.XXX$ (round to 3dp)		
= 0.XXX x Cost/Enhancement expenditure		(IA)
Indexed gain into corporation tax computation		X/Nil

Indexation allowance

Indexation allowance provides relief for the inflation element of a capital gain. It is given from the date of acquisition to the date of disposal of the asset and is based on the Retail Price Index (RPI).

Indexation allowance is given on the original cost of the asset. Where an enhancement or improvement of the asset takes place, indexation allowance is given separately on this expenditure.

The indexation allowance is calculated, to three decimal places, as follows:

$$\frac{\text{RPI disposal} - \text{RPI acquisition}}{\text{RPI acquisition}} = 0.XXX \text{ (round to 3dp)}$$

$0.XXX \times \text{cost} = IA$

In the examination, a table of RPIs for each month will be provided.

Three important points to note about an Indexation allowance are:

- it reduces an unindexed gain;

- it cannot be used to increase an unindexed loss

- it cannot be used to turn an unindexed gain into a loss.

Matching rules for shares for companies

When a company disposes of shares, the share disposal is matched with shares in the following order:

1. Acquisitions made on the same day. (no indexation allowance available and not examinable)

2. Acquisitions made in the previous 9 days on FIFO basis (first in, first out) (no indexation and not examinable)

3. Any shares in the 1985 pool (also known as s104 pool)

Exam technique for calculating gain on disposal of shares by a company

Step one: **set up a gain calculation**

	£
Net sale Proceeds	X
Less: Cost (W)	(X)
Unindexed gain	X
Less: IA (W)	(X)
Indexed gain	X

Step two: **set up the 1985 pool working to calculate cost and IA for the gain calculation**

Description	Number of shares	Cost	Indexed Cost (Cost+Indexation)
Purchase	X	X	X
Index to 1st operative event			X
Purchase	X	X	X
	X	X	X
Index to 2nd operative event			X
	X	X	X
Disposal	(X)	(X)	(X)
		(W)	(W)
Pool carried forward	X	X	X

Points to note:

- An operative event will be the acquisition or disposal of shares from the s104 pool.

- The IA in the pool is NOT rounded to 3 decimal places when calculating indexation

Learning example 18.2

On 12 November 2011 First Ltd sold 10,000 £1 ordinary shares in Last plc, a quoted company for £125,000.

First Ltd had originally purchased 15,000 shares in Last plc on 30 June 1987 for £35,000 and purchased a further 2,000 shares on 1 October 2005 for £15,000.

The retail price index for June 1987 was 101.8, for October 2005 was 193.3 and for November 2011 was 226.8

Required

Compute the chargeable gain on the disposal of the shares in Last plc.

Bonus and rights issues

Bonus issue

This is an issue of FREE shares to existing shareholders in proportion to the number of shares owned at the date of the bonus issue.

These shares are deemed to be acquired on the same date as the original shares to which the bonus issue shares relate.

Shares acquired through a bonus issue should be added to the 1985 pool as an acquisition but it does not constitute an operative event. This means that the shares already in the 1985 pool do not need to be indexed before the bonus issue is added.

As a bonus issue is free shares, only the number of shares in the 1985 pool needs to be adjusted. The cost and indexed cost remain unchanged.

Rights issue

A rights issue occurs where a company offers its shareholders the right to buy extra shares, usually at a preferential price (i.e. below market value). Rights issues are similar to bonus issues in that the number of shares offered to each shareholder is generally in proportion to his or her existing shareholding.

Shares acquired through a rights issue should be added to the 1985 pool as an acquisition and it does constitute an operative event. This means that the shares already in the 1985 pool must be indexed before the new shares can be added. Remember, we do not round to 3 decimal places when calculating indexation allowance in the 1985 pool.

Once the indexation has taken place, the shares acquired through the rights issue can be added to the pool. As the company pays for the shares, the addition will impact all columns of the 1985 pool working.

Learning example 18.3

Sunny Ltd sold 300 shares in Cloudy Ltd, an unquoted trading company, on 10 November 2011 for £36,000. Sunny Ltd acquired 500 shares in Cloudy Ltd on 21 May 1997 for £6,000.

On 8 August 2001 there was a 1:5 rights issue for £14 per share.

Sunny Ltd purchased all of the shares it was entitled to under the rights issue.

The relevant RPI's are:

May 1997	156.9
August 2001	174.0
November 2011	217.7

Required

Calculate the chargeable gain arising on Sunny Ltd on the sale of the shares.

Roll-over relief

Where the proceeds on the disposal of a qualifying asset are reinvested in further qualifying assets, roll-over relief is available. It operates as a deferral of the corporation tax liability arising on the chargeable gain if the proceeds are fully reinvested in qualifying assets within 12 months before and three years after the date of disposal.

Where the proceeds are only partly reinvested, some of the gain will be chargeable i.e. the proceeds not reinvested. The proportion of the gain, deferred or rolled over, will be deducted from the new asset's base cost for capital gains tax purposes.

To qualify, the assets must be used in the trade of the business upon its acquisition and must be broadly fall into either:

- land and buildings; or

- fixed plant and machinery.

If the asset is a depreciating asset, the chargeable gain is not deducted from the base cost of the new asset but is held over and becomes chargeable at the earliest of the following events:

- the new asset is disposed of;

- the asset is no longer used for the purposes of the trade;

- 10 years have elapsed since the acquisition of the new asset

A depreciating asset is any asset which will become a wasting asset within 10 years of acquisition. A wasting asset is defined as having a useful life of 50 years or less. Therefore, a lease with 55 years left to run when entered into will be a wasting asset.

Learning example 18.4

Greenwood Ltd disposed of an investment property on 31 December 2011 legal costs and estate agents fees of £7,000 were incurred in relation to the disposal.

Greenwood Ltd had purchased the property originally on 12 March 1986 for £27,000 and incurred acquisition costs of £2,000. Greenwood spent £35,000 on an extension to property on 31 July 2003.

Required

Assuming the sale proceeds were:

(a) £130,000

(b) £55,000

(c) £80,000

compute the indexed gain assessable on Greenwood Ltd in the chargeable accounting period to 31 March 2012. Retail price indices are as follows:

March 1986	96.73
July 2003	181.3
December 2011	228.4

Gift aid donations

If a company makes a gift aid donation to charity, they are deducted from the face of the corporation tax computation. Companies pay gift aid gross and they are deducted from the corporation tax computation in the period which the donation is made

Learning example 18.5

Aztec Ltd sold a factory on 1 February 2012 for £480,000. The factory was purchased on 1 November 1995 for £205,000, and was extended at a cost of £52,000 during April 1998. During July 2001 the roof of the factory was replaced at a cost of £24,000 following storm damage.

Aztec Ltd incurred legal fees of £5,200 in connection with the purchase of the factory, and legal fees of £7,500 in connection with the disposal. Retail price indices (RPIs) are as follows:

November 1995	149.8
April 1998	162.6
July 2001	173.3
February 2012	231.3

Required

(a)   Compute Aztec Ltd's chargeable gain on the disposal of the factory.

(b)   Assuming Aztec Ltd prepares accounts to 31 March each year state the chargeable accounting period in which the chargeable gain will be subject to tax.

(c)   If Aztec Ltd purchased a replacement factory on 1 April 2012 compute Aztec Ltd's chargeable gain on the disposal of the factory on 1 February 2012 assuming that the cost of the replacement factory was:

(i)   £520,000

(ii)   £450,000

(iii)   £350,000

Learning example 18.6

Hot Chip Ltd has the following results for the year end 31 March 2012:

	£
Tax adjusted profits before capital allowances	750,000
Capital allowances	(35,000)
Non trade related interest	15,000
Chargeable gains	19,000
Rental income	2,000
Gift aid donation	(1,000)
Dividend from UK companies	8,000

Required

Calculate the Taxable total profits of Hot Chip Ltd for the year ended 31 March 2012.

Corporation tax liability

Financial years

Corporation tax is payable on the profits of a particular AP. Corporation tax rates and limits are set for financial years, which run from 1 April to 31 March.

The rates of corporation tax, along with marginal relief fractions, will be provided in the examination.

Profits

A company pays tax on its Taxable total profits. However, this figure is not the final figure used in calculating the rate of corporation tax which the company will be liable. Where the company received any dividends from a UK resident or overseas entity (other than group members) in the AP, this dividend must be grossed up by 100/90 and added to Taxable total profits. The grossed up dividend is often referred to as Franked Investment Income (FII).

Rates of corporation tax

A company will either be taxed at:

*   the main rate (26% for FY 2011) if 'augmented profits' are > £1,500,000

*   small profits rate (20% for FY 2011) if 'augmented profits' are < £300,000

Where the 'augmented profits' fall between £300,000 and £1,500,000, the corporation tax liability is calculated at the main rate, with a deduction for a marginal relief fraction.

$$ £$$

Taxable total profits x main rate   X
Less: Marginal relief

$(\frac{3}{200})$ Taper fraction x (Upper limit - 'Augmented profits') x $\dfrac{\text{Taxable total profits}}{\text{'Augmented profits'}}$ (X)

CT   X

The effective tax rate on profits earned between the small profits rate and main rate is 27.5%. A corporation tax rate of 27.5% does not exist; it is an important rate to consider when considering any loss relief and group relief.

Learning example 18.7

Daniels Ltd had the following results for the year ending 31 March 2012.

	£
Trading income	50,000
Rental income	12,000
Bank interest	17,000
Capital gains	25,000
Dividends received (net) from unconnected company	45,000

Required

Calculate the corporation tax liability.

London
School of Business
& Finance
shaping success in business and finance

Learning example 18.8

McGee Ltd had the following results for the year ending 31 March 2012.

	£
Trading income	1,405,000
Dividends received (net) from unconnected company	90,000

Required

Calculate the corporation tax liability.

Learning example 18.9

Beauty Ltd had the following results for the year ending 31 March 2012.

	£
Trading income	400,000
Bank interest	2,000
Capital gains	5,000
Donation to charity under gift aid	(2,000)
Dividends received (net) from unconnected company	45,000

Required

Calculate the corporation tax liability.

Points affecting upper and lower limits

(a) For short accounting periods the limits must be pro-rated.

(b) A company is associated with another if one company is controlled by the other or both are under the control of the same person/company.

Control means possession of > 50% of the issued share capital or voting rights. The significance of associated companies is that the limits are divided by the total number of associated companies.

Learning example 18.10

Soporific Ltd had the following results for the 10 months ending 31 March 2012.

	£
Trading income	200,000
Rental income	24,000
Bank interest	5,000
Capital gains	15,000
Donation to charity under gift aid	2,000
Dividends received (net) from unconnected company	9,000

Required

Calculate the corporation tax liability.

Long periods of account

For accounting purposes the company's accounting period can be up to 18 months in length. If a company prepares accounts for more than 12 months it will be necessary to divide the period of account into two taxable accounting periods. This is because an accounting period for tax purposes cannot exceed 12 months.

The two taxable accounting periods (APs) will be as follows:

(1)   First 12 months

(2)   Remainder of account.

When computing capital allowances and allocating income and charges use the following procedure:

Capital allowances	Two separate computations for each AP
Trading profits	Time apportion
Rental income	Receivable basis
Interest income	Receivable basis
Capital gain/loss	Date of realisation
Franked investment income	Date the UK dividend is received

Prepare separate corporation tax computations for each accounting period.

Learning example 18.11

Parvenue Ltd is a United Kingdom resident company that installs solar panels. The company commenced trading on 1 April 2011 and its results for the fifteen month period ended 30 June 2012 are summarised as follows:

The trading profit as adjusted for tax purposes is £360,000. This figure is before taking account of capital allowances.

Parvenue Ltd purchased equipment for £25,000 on 1 April 2011.

On 1 October 2011 Parvenue Ltd disposed of some investments and this resulted in a capital loss of £7,000. On 12 June 2012 the company made a further disposal and this resulted in a chargeable gain of £43,000.

Franked investment income of £20,000 was received on 11 April 2012.

Parvenue Ltd has two associated companies.

Required

Calculate Parvenue Ltd's corporation tax liabilities in respect of the fifteen month period ended 30 June 2012 and advise the company by when these should be paid. You should assume that the rates in FY2011 are the same as FY2012.

Accounting periods straddling more than one Financial Year

The rates and marginal relief fractions may be different for each year:

	FY2011	FY2010	FY2009
Main rate	26%	28%	28%
Small profits rate	20%	21%	21%
Marginal relief fraction	3/200	7/400	7/400
Upper limit	1,500,000	1,500,000	1,500,000
Lower limit	300,000	300,000	300,000
Effective marginal tax rate	27.5%	29.75%	29.75%

A company may produce a set of accounts that fall into more than one Financial Year. For example:

Company A has a year end 31 December 2011. This 12 month set of accounts spans two different Financial Years. The Financial Year 2011 runs from 1 April 2011 to 31 March 2012. So for Company A:

*   3 months fall into the Financial Year 2010 (1 January 2011 – 31 March 2011)

*   9 months fall into the Financial Year 2011 (1 April 2011 – 31 December 2011)

If this is the case, the company's Taxable total profits, Augmented profits and corporation tax limits need to be time apportioned between the two different financial years.

Learning example 18.12

Illusion plc has the following results for the 12 month AP ended 31 December 2011.

	£
Trading profits	510,000
Loan interest paid (non trade)	(7,000)
Bank interest received	20,000
Capital gains	35,000
UK dividends received (net) from unconnected company	22,500
Donation to charity under the gift aid scheme	(5,000)
The following balances were brought forward:	
Capital loss	7,000
Trading loss	14,000

Required

Compute the corporation tax for Illusion plc.

Corporation tax administration

Self-assessment basis

Companies fall under a self-assessment basis of taxation. The rules are similar (but not identical) to that which applies to individuals.

Notification

A company must notify HMRC of the beginning of its first accounting period within three months of the relevant date.

The penalty for not notifying HMRC is the same as penalties for incorrect returns (see below).

Returns

A company makes a return of its corporation tax online. The return is due for filing on its filing date. This is the later of:

- 12 months after the period to which it relates

- Where the relevant period is < 18 months long, 12 months from the end of the period of account

- If the period is > 18 months long, 30 months from the start of the relevant period

- Three months from the date on which the notice was made

The company may make amendments to the return until one year after the due filing date.

Along with the tax return, companies must also submit supporting tax computations and a copy of their accounts. These must be submitted online using inline eXtensible Business Reporting Language (iXBRL). This is a standard for reporting business informaton in an electronic format using tags that can be read by computers.

Small companies with simple accounts can use the software provided by HMRC and this will automatically produce accounts and tax computations in the correct format.

Other companies can use:

- Other software that automatically produces iXBRL accounts and computations

- A tagging service which will apply the appropriate tags to accounts and computations.

- Software that enables the appropriate tags to be added to accounts and computations.

These rules apply where a return is filed after 1 April 2011 in respect of an accounting period ending after 31 March 2010. Prior to this a paper return (CT600) could be made.

Filing penalties

Where a return is submitted late, there is a £100 penalty, which rises to £200 when the return is not submitted within three months of the filing date. If the returns of the prior two accounting periods were also late, the filing penalties are £500 and £1,000 respectively.

Where the return is over six months late, a tax geared penalty is also levied. Where the return is filed up to 12 months late, this is 10% of the total unpaid tax, and where the return is filed more than 12 months late, this rises to 20% of the unpaid tax.

Claims

Claims should, wherever possible, be made on a tax return or on an amendment to a tax return, and must be quantified when made.

Unless stated otherwise the time limit for making a claim is four years after the end of the year of assessment to which it relates.

Claims may therefore still be made where the time limit for filing a return or amendment has expired. The rules for record keeping, enquiries etc. that apply to tax returns also apply to such claims.

Tax due dates

From1 April 2011 and for returns for accounting periods ending after 31 March 2010, all companies must pay corporation tax by electronic transfer.

The due date for corporation tax is dependent upon whether the company qualifies as a small/medium company or a large company.

Small/medium companies must pay their corporation tax liabilities nine months and one day after the end of the AP.

Large companies must pay their corporation tax in quarterly instalments. A large company is any company which pays corporation tax at the main rate. For companies within a large group, this could well be at a low value of profits.

Quarterly instalments

Where a company is a liable to pay corporation tax by quarterly instalments, it does so on the following dates:

*   14th day of the month starting in the seventh month;
*   14th day of the tenth month;
*   14th day of the first month (after the end of the AP);
*   14th day of the fourth month (after the end of the AP)

For example, if the AP ends on 31 December 2011, quarterly instalments are due on 14 July 2011, 14 October 2011, 14 January 2012 and 14 April 2012.

If the AP is less than 12 months in length, the final payment is due in the fourth month of the next AP.

For example, where the AP ends on 31 December 2010, and the company changes its AP to the nine months ended 30 September 2011, quarterly instalments are due on 14 July 2011, 14 October 2011 and 14 January 2012.

Where the company fails to estimate its quarterly instalments effectively, it will be liable to late payment interest on any under declared tax.

Learning example 18.13

Quebec plc is a single company with no associates. On 1 October 2011 Quebec plc estimates that its Taxable total profits will be £1.9 million for the year ended 31 March 2012. Their Taxable total profits for the year ended 31 March 2011 was £1.7 million and for the year ended 31 March 2010 was £1.2 million. Quebec plc does not receive any dividends.

Required

(a)   Calculate Quebec plc's corporation tax liabilities for the year ended 31 March 2011 and 31 March 2012 and explain how they will be paid.

(b)   In December 2011 the company revises its forecast profit figure to £2.1 million. State the difference, if any, this will make to their corporation tax payments.

Late payment interest

Late payment interest is charged on tax not paid by the due date. Where the company is required to pay by quarterly instalments interest is charged on underpaid and late paid instalments. The amount of the instalments due is calculated once the corporation tax liability for the year is agreed.

In practice the rate of tax on underpaid instalments is lower than tax not paid on the normal due date of nine months and one day from the end of the accounting period, but the exam convention is to use the same interest rate.

Learning example 18.14

Himalaya plc paid instalments of its corporation tax liability for the year ended 31 March 2012 as follows:

14 October 2011	£50,000
14 February 2012	£60,000
14 April 2012	£60,000
14 August 2012	£80,000

The agreed corporation tax liability for the year was £280,000 and Himalaya plc paid the balance of £30,000 on 14 September 2012

Required

State the amounts and periods for which interest will be due.

Compliance checks into self-assessment corporation tax returns

Previously, HMRC normally had 12 months after the tax return filing deadline in which to notify a limited company that they intended to perform a compliance check on its self-assessment corporation tax return. This window has now changed to 12 months from the date that a corporation tax return is received by HMRC.

Only one compliance check may be made in respect of any one return.

Where a compliance check is made, HMRC can demand documents for inspection. Failure to comply with such a request will incur a penalty of £50, with a daily penalty, which may be imposed by HMRC, of £30 per day.

If an amendment is made during a compliance check, the company has 30 days to appeal against the amendment. A company may make an amendment to its self-assessment return during a compliance check period but this does not cause the compliance check period to close. A compliance check will be closed by HMRC when they are satisfied that the correct amount of tax has been charged. The company has 30 days after the date of closure of a compliance check to amend its self-assessment return.

Penalties for incorrect returns

A single new penalty regime has been introduced for incorrect returns. The amount of penalty is based on the amount of tax understated, but the actual penalty payable is linked to the company's behaviour, as follows:

- There will be no penalty where a taxpayer simply makes a mistake.

- There will be a moderate penalty (up to 30% of the understated tax) where a taxpayer fails to take reasonable care.

- There will be a higher penalty (up to 70% of the understated tax) if the error is deliberate, and even higher penalty (up to 100% of the understated tax) where there is also concealment of the error.

However the penalty will be substantially reduced where the company makes disclosure, especially when this is unprompted by HMRC.

A company has six years from the end of the AP to make a claim for an error in a return (incorrect figures). Where tax legislation specifies a particular time limit for a claim, this must be adhered to (elections for certain reliefs).

Records

A company which fails to keep and preserve adequate records is liable to a penalty of up to £3,000.

A company must keep records until the latest of:

- Six years from the end of the AP; or

- The date any enquiries are completed; or

The date after enquiries can no longer be commenced

Adequate records are those required to enable a complete and correct return to be made. This includes details of all amounts received and paid in the course of the company's activities. The duty to keep accounting records is also imposed on companies by the Companies Act 2006.

The records can be kept in electronic form.

Appeals

A taxpayer can appeal against decisions made by HMRC, such as assessments, amendments to a self assessment or refusal of a claim. The time limit for making an appeal is 30 days from the decision.

The notice of appeal is sent to HMRC. Most appeals are settled by agreement, but where an appeal cannot be settled HMRC may offer, or the taxpayer may request, a review by an officer of HMRC who has not previously been involved.

If the review does not resolve the issue, or no review is made, the appeal can be taken to the First Tier Tribunal. The appeal will then be categorised:

1. Default paper cases are not normally dealt with in writing without a hearing,

2. Basic cases are dealt with though an informal hearing,

3. Standard and complex cases are dealt with through a more formal hearing process, and complex cases may be heard by the Upper Tribunal rather than the First Tier Tribunal.

The Tribunal will make a decision. Further appeals may then be made to the Upper Tribunal, the Court of Appeal and the Supreme Court.

Learning summary

After studying this chapter, you should have an understanding of:

- Companies pay corporation tax on their profits for an accounting period (AP). An AP can be a maximum of 12 months in length.

- A company will pay corporation tax on its profits if it is resident in the UK. A company can be resident through incorporation or through its central management and control being in the UK.

- Capital allowances are available for expenditure on capital equipment used in the trade of the business. The rate of capital allowances depends on the type of asset.

- Writing down allowances (WDA) of 20% are available for main pool assets, 10% for special rate pool assets.

- First year allowances are available for low emission cars.

- Cars owned at 1 April 2009 and valued at over £12,000 are kept separately and are restricted to WDA of £3,000 per 12 months AP.

- A loan relationship will exist whenever a company lends or borrows money. If the loan relationship exists as part of the trade of the company, gains and losses are dealt with as trading income. Non-trading loan relationships are treated as interest income.

- A company pays corporation tax on its chargeable gains.

- Generally the same rules applying to the calculation of capital gains in companies as individuals. However, companies are still able to claim an indexation allowance on cost.

- Roll-over relief is available where a company disposes of a qualifying asset and reinvests the proceeds, in another qualifying asset.

- Companies are taxed at the main rate (26%), small profits rate (20%) or marginal rate depending on their profits.

- 'Augmented profits', for the purposes on determining rates, includes dividends received from UK and overseas companies, grossed up by 100/90.

- The number of associated companies will impact the rate of tax paid. The upper and lower limits of £1,500,000 and £300,000 respectively are divided by the number of associated companies in the AP.

- A company must file its tax return online within 12 months of the end of its AP.

- A company must pay corporation tax by electronic transfer.

- Corporation tax is paid 9 months and 1 day after the end of an AP for non-large companies.

- A large company, which is a company which pays tax at the higher rate of 26%, pays its corporation tax by quarterly instalments.

Exam standard question

(a) Fusilli Ltd is a UK resident company that runs a chain of restaurants.

The company's summarised income statement for the year ended 30 June 2011 is as follows:

	Note	£	£
Gross profit			800,000
Depreciation		51,000	
Amortisation of leasehold property	1	13,890	
Gifts and donations	2	3,100	
Professional fees	3	18,400	
Other expenses	4	67,930	
			(154,320)
Operating profit			645,680
Income from investments			
Loan interest received	5	47,800	
Dividends	6	5,500	
Rental income	7	30,200	
			83,500
Profit before taxation			729,180

Note 1 – Leasehold property

On 1 July 2010 Fusilli Ltd acquired a leasehold unit which the company then used as an additional restaurant throughout the year. The company paid a premium of £160,000 for the grant of the fifteen year lease.

Note 2 – Gifts and donations

The expense for the gifts and donations is made up as follows:

	£
• Gifts of wine to customers at Christmas (each bottle costing £5)	750
• Gifts of calendars to customers at Christmas, each calendar advertising restaurants in the chain (each calendar costing £7.50 each)	1,350
• Donation to a national charity (under gift aid scheme)	1,000
	3,100

Note 3 – Professional fees

The professional fees include an amount of £5,000 in relation to the issue of debentures which was issued to finance the company's trading activities. Also included in the expense for professional fees is an amount of £2,500 in relation to the sale of an asset that was sold in the last accounting period.

Note 4 – Other expenses

The figure for other expenses includes £6,500 for staff parties, £4,700 for staff training and £3,800 for entertaining suppliers.

Note 5 – Loan interest received

The loan interest received is the accrued amount for the accounting period and is in relation to an non-trading loan.

Note 6 – Dividends received

Fusilli Ltd received the following dividends during the year ended 30 June 2011:

Fettuccine Ltd	£3,000
Other UK companies (minority holdings)	£2,500

Note 7 – Rental income

Fusilli Ltd receives income from the letting of a freehold office building that is surplus to requirements. The office building was let for the whole of the accounting period at £2,100 per month, payable in advance.

Note 8 - Plant and machinery

On 1 July 2010 the tax written down values of Fusilli Ltd's plant and machinery were as follows:

	£
Main pool	40,900
Special rate pool	16,000

The company purchased the following assets during the year ended 30 June 2011:

		£
19 March 2011	Motor car [1]	11,000
30 March 2011	Motor car [2]	30,250
21 April 2011	Motor car [3]	9,500
1 May 2011	Ventilation system	70,000
1 June 2011	Equipment	110,000

Motor car [1] has a CO_2 emission rate of 165 grams per kilometre. Motor car [2] purchased on 30 March 2011 has a CO_2 emission rate of 140 grams per kilometre. Motor car [3] purchased on 21 April 2011 has a CO_2 emission rate of 107 grams per kilometre.

The ventilation system purchased for £70,000 is integral to one of the restaurants in which it was installed.

Note 9 – Subsidiary companies

Fusilli Ltd has investments in other companies as follows:

- Fusilli Ltd owns 100% of the ordinary share capital of Gnocchi Ltd and has done so for the last ten years.

- Fusilli Ltd acquired 100% of the ordinary share capital in Linguine Ltd on 1 April 2011

- Fusilli Ltd owns 60% of the ordinary share capital of Fettuccine Ltd.

- Fusilli Ltd owns 80% of the ordinary share capital of Fiori Inc, an overseas company

Required

(i) **State, giving reasons, which companies will be treated as being associated with Fusilli Ltd for corporation tax purposes and state the effect of the companies being associated.**

(ii) **Calculate Fusilli Ltd's corporation tax liability for the year ended 30 June 2011.**

Note: you should assume that the whole of the annual investment allowance is available to Fusilli Ltd, and that the company wishes to maximise its capital allowances claim.

London
School of Business
& Finance
shaping success in business and finance

Learning solution 18.1

Year end 31 March 2012

	£
Trading profits	95,000
Interest income	7,000
Rental income	Nil
Capital gains	11,000
Total Profits	113,000
Less: Property income loss	(3,000)
Revised total profits	110,000
Less	
Donations under the gift aid scheme	Nil
Taxable total profits	110,000

Property income working	1	2	3	Total
	£	£	£	£
Rent	7,000	6,000	9,000	22,000
Less: Expenses	(4,000)	(10,000)	(11,000)	(25,000)

Rental Income = NIL
The loss available for relief = (3,000)

Learning solution 18.2

Ordinary Shares in Last plc: the disposal is matched against shares in the 1985 pool:

	£
Disposal proceeds	125,000
Cost (W)	(29,412)
Unindexed gain	95,588
Indexation (56,221 – 29,412) (W)	(26,809)
Chargeable gain	68,779

Working: 1985 Pool

	Number	Cost	Indexed cost
	£	£	£
Purchase June 1987	15,000	35,000	35,000
Indexation to October 2005			
35,000 x (193.3 – 101.8)/101.8			31,459
			66,459
Addition October 2005	2,000	15,000	15,000
	17,000	50,000	81,459
Indexation to November 2011			
81,459 x (226.8 – 193.3)/193.3			14,117
	17,000	50,000	95,576
Disposal			
Cost x 10,000/17,000	(10,000)	(29,412)	(56,221)
Balance carried forward	7,000	20,588	39,355

Learning solution 18.3

Step 1: set up gain calculation

	£
Proceeds	36,000
Cost	
Unindexed gain	
Less IA	
Indexed gain	

Step 2: set up 1985 pool working to find cost and IA

	Number of shares	Cost	Indexed cost
21 May 1997 acquisition	500	6,000	6,000
Index to 8 August 2001			
$\frac{174.0 - 156.9}{156.9} \times 6,000$			
			654
	500	6,000	6,654
8 August 2001 rights issue	100	1,400	1,400
	600	7,400	8,054
Index to 10 November 2011			
$\frac{217.7 - 174.0}{174.0} \times 8,054$			
			2,023
	600	7,400	10,077
10 November 2011 disposal (300/600)	(300)	(3,700)	(5,039)
c/f	300	3,700	5,038

Now complete gain calculation:

	£
Proceeds	36,000
Cost	(3,700)
Unindexed gain	32,300
Less IA (5,039 – 3,700)	(1,339)
Indexed gain	30,961

Learning solution 18.4

(a) Sale proceeds £130,000

	£	£
Gross sale proceeds		130,000
Less: Costs of sale		(7,000)
Net sale proceeds		123,000
Less: Cost	27,000	
Incidental acquisition costs	2,000	(29,000)
Enhancement expenditure		(35,000)
Unindexed gain		59,000
Less: Indexation allowance		
Cost (Dec 2011 – March 1986)		

$$\frac{228.4 - 96.73}{96.73} = (1.361 \times £29,000) \qquad 39,469$$

Enhancement (Dec 2011 – July 2003)

$$\frac{228.4 - 181.3}{181.3} = (0.260 \times £35,000) \qquad 9,100$$

	9,100	(48,569)
Indexed gain		10,431

(b) Sale proceeds £55,000

	£	£
Gross sale proceeds		55,000
Less: Costs of sale		(7,000)
Net sale proceeds		48,000
Less: Cost	29,000	
Enhancement expenditure	35,000	(64,000)
Allowable loss		(16,000)

(c) Sale proceeds £80,000

	£	£
Gross sale proceeds		80,000
Less: costs of sale		(7,000)
Net sale proceeds		73,000
Less: Cost	29,000	
Enhancement expenditure	35,000	
		(64,000)
Unindexed gain		9,000
Less: Indexation allowance		
Cost (Dec 2011 – March 1986)		
1.361 × £29,000	39,469	
Enhancement (Dec 2011 – July 2003)		
0.260 × £35,000	9,100	
Restricted as indexation cannot create a loss		(9,000)
Indexed gain		Nil

Learning solution 18.5

Chargeable gain – disposal of factory

	£	£
Disposal proceeds (February 2012)		480,000
Incidental costs of disposal		(7,500)
Net sale proceeds		472,500
Cost (November 1995)	205,000	
Incidental costs of acquisition	5,200	
		(210,200)
Enhancement expenditure (April 1998)		(52,000)
Unindexed gain		210,300
Indexation – Cost		
210,200 x .544		
(231.3 – 149.8)/149.8 = .544		(114,349)
Indexation – Enhancement		
52,000 x .423		
(231.3 – 162.6)/162.6 = .423		(21,996)
Chargeable gain		73,955

(1) The factory extension is enhancement expenditure as it has added to the value of the factory.

(2) The replacement of the roof is not enhancement expenditure, being in the   nature of a repair.

(b) The gain is chargeable in year ended 31.3.2012.

(c)

	Option 1 £	Option 2 £	Option 3 £
Indexed gain (from a)	73,955	73,955	73,955
Less full ROR (all proceeds reinvested	(73,955)		
Less partial ROR (Note 1)		(43,955)	
No ROR (Note 2)			
Chargeable gain	-	30,000	73,955

Note 1: ROR is limited to £43,955 as £30,000 (480,000 - 450,000) of proceeds were not reinvested.

Note 2: No ROR is available as proceeds not reinvested > original gain.

Learning solution 18.6

	£
Trading income	715,000
Interest income	15,000
Rental income	2,000
Chargeable gains	19,000
Gift aid donation	(1,000)
Taxable total profits	750,000

NB Dividends received from UK companies are not taxable as part of Taxable total profits

London
School of Business
& Finance

shaping success in business and finance

Learning solution 18.7

Daniels Ltd

AP y/e 31 March 2012

	£
Trading profits	50,000
Rental income	12,000
Interest income	17,000
Chargeable gains	25,000
Total profits	104,000
Less: Donation to charity under gift aid	(Nil)
Taxable total profits	104,000
Add: FII	
Net div x 100/90	
45,000 x 100/90	50,000
'Augmented profits'	154,000

Lower limit	£300,000
Upper limit	£1,500,000

Small company

	£
£104,000 x 20%	20,800

Learning solution 18.8

AP y/e 31 March 2012

	£
Taxable total profits	1,405,000
Add: FII £90,000 x 100/90	100,000
'Augmented profits'	1,505,000

Lower limit	£300,000
Upper limit	£1,500,000

Large company

	£
Corporation tax: £1,405,000 x 26%	365,300

Learning solution 18.9

AP y/e 31 March 2012

	£
Profits from trading	400,000
Interest income	2,000
Capital gain	5,000
Total profits	407,000
Less: Donation under gift aid	(2,000)
Taxable total profits	405,000
Add: FII £45,000 × 100/90	50,000
'Augmented profits'	455,000

Lower limit   £300,000
Upper limit   £1,500,000

Medium company

	£
Corporation tax: £405,000 × 26%	105,300
Less: Marginal relief 3/200 [(1,500,000 – 455,000) × 405,000]	(13,952)
455,000]	
Corporation tax	91,348

Learning solution 18.10

AP 10 months ending 31 March 2012

	£
Trading profit	200,000
Rental income	24,000
Interest income	5,000
Capital gain	15,000
Total profits	244,000
Less: Donation under gift aid	(2,000)
Taxable total profits	242,000
Add: FII £9,000 × 100/90	10,000
'Augmented profits'	252,000

Limits need to be pro-rated as 10 month accounting period:
Lower limit: £300,000 × 10/12 = £250,000
Upper limit: £1,500,000 × 10/12 = £1,250,000
The company is medium size

	£
Corporation tax: £242,000 × 26%	62,920
Less: Marginal relief	
3/200 × [(1,250,000 - 252,000) × 242,000]	(14,376)
252,000	
Corporation tax	48,544

Learning solution 18.11

	1.4.11– 31.3.12 £	1.4.12 – 30.6.12 £
Trading profits		
12/15 x 360,000	288,000	72,000
Capital allowances	(25,000)	(Nil)
(AIA 25,000x 100% = 25,000)		
Profits from trading	263,000	72,000
Chargeable gain 43,000		
Capital loss (7,000)		
36,000	Nil	36,000
Total Profits	263,000	108,000
Less:		
Donations under gift aid	(Nil)	(Nil)
Taxable total profits	263,000	108,000
Add:FII	Nil	20,000
'Augmented profits'	263,000	128,000
	12 Months	3 Months
Upper Limit / 3	500,000	125,000
Lower Limit / 3	100,000	25,000
	Medium company	Large company
Corporation tax		
FY11		
263,000 x 26%	68,380	
Less Marginal relief		
3/200 (500,000 – 263,000) x 263,000	(3,555)	
263,000	64,825	
FY12		
108,000 x 26%	64,825	28,080
Due date for payment	1.1.13	1.4.13

Remember that as there are 3 associated companies, the corporation tax limits are divided by the number of associates

Learning solution 18.12

AP 12 months ended 31 December 2011

	£	£
Trading profits (510,000 - 14,000)		496,000
Interest income (20,000 - 7,000)		13,000
Capital gains	35,000	
Less: Capital losses b/f	(7,000)	
		28,000
Total profits		537,000
Less: gift aid donation to charity		(5,000)
Taxable total profits		532,000
Add: FII £22,500 x 100/90		25,000
'Augmented profits'		557,000

Lower limit	£300,000
Upper limit	£1,500,000

Medium company – straddling period

FY10

	£
£532,000 x 28% x 3/12	37,240
Less: Marginal relief	
7/400 x (1,500,000 – 557,000) x $\dfrac{532,000}{557,000}$ x 3/12	(3,940)

FY11

£532,000 x 26% x 9/12	103,740
Less: Marginal relief	
3/200 x (1,500,000 – 557,000) x $\dfrac{532,000}{557,000}$ x 9/12	(10,133)
	126,907

Learning solution 18.13

The company was a main rate company in the year ended 31 March 2011 but would not have had to make quarterly instalments in that year. This is because a company does not have to make instalment payments in the first year that they start paying at the main rate provided the profits of that year do not exceed £10million. The liability for the year ended 31 March 2011 of £476,000 (1,700,000 x 28%) will be due on 1 January 2012.

With an expected Taxable total profits of £1.9million in the year ended 31 March 2012, the company will be liable to tax at the full rate of 26%, which gives a forecast liability of £494,000. As the company is expecting to pay at the main rate of corporation tax for the second year running for profits arising in 31 March 2012, they will have to pay in quarterly instalments as follows.

	£
14 October 2011	123,500
14 January 2012	123,500
14 April 2012	123,500
14 July 2012	123,500
	494,000

Interest will be charged from the due date until the date of payment for any instalment paid late.

(b)   If the profit forecast is revised upwards the company will have to revise its forecast tax payments. The corporation tax liability will increase by £52,000 (200,000 x 26%). Therefore an extra £13,000 will be due for each instalment from October 2011. As the instalment for October 2011 has already been paid, the additional £13,000 will attract interest from 14 October 2011 until it is paid.

Learning solution 18.14

Instalments of £280,000 x ¼ = £70,000 were due on each of 14 October 2011, 14 January 2012, 14 April 2012 and 14 July 2012.

Date	Total due £	Total paid £	Underpayment £	Period for which interest charged
14 October 2011	70,000	50,000	20,000	14.10.11 – 14.01.12
14 January 2012	140,000	50,000	90,000	14.01.12 – 14.02.12
14 February 2012	140,000	110,000	30,000	14.02.12 – 14.04.12
14 April 2012	210,000	170,000	40,000	14.04.12 – 14.07.12
14 July 2012	280,000	170,000	110,000	14.07.12 – 14.08.12
14 August 2012	280,000	250,000	30,000	14.08.12 – 14.09.12
14 September 2012	280,000	280,000	Nil	

Solution to exam standard question

(a) (i)

- Gnocchi Ltd is associated as the shareholding is over 50%

- Linguine Ltd is associated as the shareholding is over 50%, even though the company was acquired during the accounting period.

- Fettuccine Ltd is associated as the shareholding is over 50%

- Fiori Ltd is associated as the shareholding is over 50%, even though the company is overseas.

- Therefore, there are five companies associated with each other.

The effect is that the tax rates are divided between the associated companies:

£1,500,000 /5 = £300,000
£300,000 / 5 = £60,000

(a) (ii)

Fusilli Ltd – Corporation tax computation for the year ended 30 June 2011

	£
Net profit	729,180
Depreciation	51,000
Amortisation	13,890
Deduction for lease premium (W1)	(7,680)
Gifts and donations	
Gifts of wine – food and drink therefore not allowable	750
Gifts of calendars – allowable	Nil
Donation to national charity – gift aid therefore add back	1,000
Professional fees	
Debentures – allowable	Nil
Capital fees	2,500
Other expenses	
Staff parties	Nil
Staff training	Nil
Entertaining suppliers	3,800
	794,440

	£
Income from investments	
Loan interest received	(47,800)
Dividends	(5,500)
Rental income	(30,200)
Less capital allowances (W2)	(142,430)
Tax adjusted trading profit	568,510

Working 1 – Deduction for lease premium

(1) The amount assessed on the landlord is £115,200 calculated as follows:

	£
Premium received	160,000
Less: 160,000 x 2% x (15 - 1)	(44,800)
	115,200

(2) This is deductible over the life of the lease, so the deduction for the year ended 30 June 2011 is £7,680 (115,200/15).

Working 2 – Capital allowances

		Pool	Special rate pool	Allowances
		£	£	£
WDV brought forward		40,900	16,000	
Additions qualifying for AIA				
Ventilation system	70,000			
AIA – 100%	(70,000)		-	70,000
Equipment	110,000			
AIA (100,000 – 70,000)	(30,000)			30,000
		80,000		
Other additions				
High CO$_2$ car [1]			11,000	
Medium CO$_2$ car [2]		30,250	_____	
		151,150	27,000	
WDA 20%		(30,230)		30,230
WDA 10%			(2,700)	2,700
Adds - FYA				
Motor car [3]		9,500		
100% FYA		(9,500)	_____	9,500
WDV c/f		120,920	24,300	
Total allowances				142,430

Tutorial notes:

(1) The ventilation system is integral to the building and so is included in the special rate pool.

(2) Motor car [1] has CO$_2$ emissions over 160 grams per kilometre and therefore only qualifies for writing down allowances at the rate of 10%.

(3) Motor car [2] has CO$_2$ emissions of between 111 and 160 grams per kilometre and therefore goes into the general pool.

(4) Motor car [3] has CO$_2$ emissions of under 160 grams per kilometre and therefore qualifies for a FYA of 100% as a low emission car.

Corporation tax computation – year ended 30 June 2011

	£	£
Tax adjusted trading profit		568,510
Interest		47,800
Rental income £2,100 × 12		25,200
Gift aid		(1,000)
Total taxable profits		640,510
Corporation tax (W3)		
FY 2010 £640,510 × 28% × 9/12	134,507	
FY 2011 £640,510 × 26% × 3/12	41,633	
Total CT liability	176,140	

Working 3

Fusilli Ltd has five associated companies, so the upper limit is reduced to £300,000 (1,500,000/5).

Working 4

The dividends taken into account for the augmented profits, to determine the rate of tax will only include the other UK dividends of £2,500 x 100/90 = £2,778. The dividends received from Fettuccine Ltd are not taken into account as this is a connected company

Augmented profit = £640,510 + 2,778 = £643,288

As this exceeds the adjusted upper limit of £300,000, it means that the company is a main rate company.

19

Corporation Tax
Losses

Context

This chapter is concerned with the tax payable by a company and is building on what was learned in the previous chapter. A company can make profits but similarly it can make trading losses.

The focus in this chapter is to consider how a company can use its trading losses in order to reduce its corporation tax in

- the current accounting period
- the previous accounting period or
- in future accounting periods.

This chapter is going to consider a number of different types of losses and consider the uses of each type of loss.

Exam hints

The use of corporation tax trading losses is very important in the F6 paper. The rules covered in this chapter will frequently be examined and can appear in question 2, question 4 or 5.

Key learning points

- The trading loss can be carried forward against first available future trading profits.
- The trading loss can be used in the current AP and/or the prior AP against the company's total profits.
- Additional loss relief is available for companies that have ceased to trade. This is known as terminal loss relief.

If a company has a trading loss for the period, the trading income in the corporation tax computation is entered as NIL.

We then need to consider the different loss relief options available to the company. The different loss relief options are as follows:

Loss reliefs available where trade is continuing

A corporation tax loss is calculated in exactly the same manner as a profit. It is reported on the tax return as chargeable profits of nil. Where a company makes a loss for corporation tax purposes in an AP, legislation allows the company to claim relief for the loss in a number of ways. Where the company is a member of a corporation tax group, it may also surrender losses to fellow group companies. This is covered in Chapter 20.

The two main methods available to companies which are not members of a corporation tax group are:

Trading losses carried forward

A trading loss may be carried forward and offset against the first available future trading profits of the same trade s45 CTA 2010. The loss can only be used if there are available profits and once used, cannot be used again.

s45 CTA 2010 provides relief against future profits and so there is no certainty that the losses will be relieved.

Trading losses set against profits of same AP

A trading loss may be offset against total profits of the loss making AP under s37 CTA 2010. The profits which are eligible are the total profits of the same AP.

It is also possible to make a second claim to carry back any remaining loss for 12 months on a LIFO basis and offset the loss against total profits of the previous 12 months provided that the same trade was being carried on in that period.

The relief must be taken in that order and it is not possible to restrict a claim in the current AP in order to carry back more losses to the previous AP. Only after full relief of current AP profits can the balance of the loss be set against the total profits of the previous AP.

It is not compulsory to take s37 CTA 2010 relief. The relief can be ignored and the loss will be carried forward under s45 CTA 2010.

If a s37 CTA 2010 claim is made to carry back the trading loss this will result in a repayment of corporation tax previously paid, which offers a cash flow advantage to the company.

The time limit for claims under s37 CTA 2010 is two years from the end of the loss making AP. The claim is made through the company's tax return. Where a claim is made against a previous AP, the CT600 for the earlier AP will need amending to reflect the claim for losses.

Gift aid donations

Gift aid donations are deducted from total profits. Relief for trading losses given by set off against total profits is given before deducting gift aid donations. Excess gift aid donations are wasted as they cannot be carried back or forward.

Proforma – corporation tax losses (without extended carry back relief)

	PY	CY	CY +1
	£	£	£
Trading profits	X	-	X
s45 CTA 2010 c/f	-	-	(X)
Property business profits	X	X	X
Interest income	X	X	X
Capital gains	X	X	X
Total profits	X	X	X
s37 CTA 2010 c/y	-	(X1)	-
s37 CTA 2010 p/y	(X2)	-	-
	X	-	X
Less:			
Charges on income	(X)	(X)	(X)
Taxable total profits	X	-	X

Loss memo

	£
Trading loss	X
s 37 CTA 2010	(X1)
	x
s37 CTA 2010	(X2)
	X
s45 CTA 2010 (loss carry forward)	(X)
	-

Terminal loss relief

Where a company has decided to cease trading, any loss which arises in the final 12 months of trading is known as the terminal loss (s39 CTA 2010). A terminal loss relief is more generous than loss relief under s37 CTA 2010, as the loss can be carried back 36 months.

Proforma – Corporation tax terminal losses

	CY -3	CY -2	CY -1	CY
	£	£	£	£
Trading profits	X	X	X	Nil
Property business profits	X	X	X	X
Interest income	X	X	X	X
Capital gains	X	X	X	X
Total profits	X	X	X	X
s37 curent CTA 2010	-	-	-	(XI)
s39 carry back CTA 2010	(X4)	(X3)	(X2)	-
	-	-	-	-
Less: Gift aid donation to charity	(a)	(a)	(a)	(a)
		Unrelieved payments		
Taxable total profits	-	-	-	-

Working – Loss memo

	£
Trading loss	X
s37 current	(XI)
	X
s39 carry back	(X2)
	X
s39 carry back	(X3)
	X
s39 carry back	(X4)
	X

Learning example 19.1

Cerne Ltd commenced trading on 1 July 2008 and ceased trading on 31 December 2012. The company's results for all its periods of trading are as follows:

	Year ended 30 June 2009	6 months 31 Dec 2009	Year ended 31 Dec 2010	Year ended 31 Dec 2011	Year ended 31 Dec 2012
	£	£	£	£	£
Total adjusted profit/(loss)	250,000	70,000	40,000	(60,000)	(240,000)
Property business profits	9,000	13,000	4,500	5,000	–
Chargeable gains	–	–	5,500	–	20,500
Gift aid donation to charity	(1,000)	(1,000)	–	–	(500)

Cerne Ltd does not have any associated companies.

Required

(a) Assuming that Cerne Ltd claims the maximum possible relief for its trading losses, calculate the company's Taxable total profits for the year ended 30 June 2009, six months to 31 December 2009, years ended 2010, 2011 and 2012.

Your answer should clearly identify the amounts of losses which are unrelieved.

(b) State the dates by which Cerne Ltd must make the loss relief claims in part (a).

(c) Calculate the amount of corporation tax that will be repaid to Cerne Ltd as a result of making the loss relief claims in part (a).

London
School of Business
& Finance

shaping success in business and finance

Choice of loss relief

If a company makes a trading loss there are three basic ways of obtaining tax relief:

1.   carry the whole loss forward against future trading profits, or

2.   set the loss against total profits of the same AP and carry any unused balance forward against future trading profits, or

3.   set the loss against total profits of the same AP, then against the total profits of the previous 12 months and carry any unused balance forward against future trading profits.

The factors that will affect the choice of loss relief include:

•   The rate of tax relief; relief should be taken in the accounting period with the highest marginal tax relief.

•   The timing of tax relief; relief should be taken in the earliest possible accounting period.

•   The wastage of gift aid donations should be avoided where possible.

The factors must be weighed against each other; it may be preferable to take relief against total profits at the small profits rate rather than carry the loss forward if relief, albeit at the main rate, will not be obtained for several years.

Exam standard question

Samurai Ltd is a company that has been trading as a retailer of martial arts products for many years.

The company prepares accounts to 30 June and its results have been as follows:

	Year ended 30 June 2009	Year ended 30 June 2010
	£	£
Trading profit	100,000	310,000
Property business profit	23,400	34,500
Gift aid donations	(11,000)	(1,200)

The following information is available in respect of the year ended 30 June 2011:

Trading loss

Draft company financial statements suggest that Samurai Ltd made a trading loss of £261,934.

Business property income

Samurai Ltd lets out three properties that are surplus to requirements.

The first, an investment property, is owned freehold and is let out furnished. The property was let throughout the year ended 30 June 2011 at a monthly rent of £2,000, payable in arrears. Samurai Ltd paid water rates of £400 and insurance of £1,600 in respect of this property for the year ended 30 June 2011. The company claims the wear and tear allowance for this property.

The second, a retail unit is owned leasehold, and is let out unfurnished. Samurai Ltd pays an annual rent of £21,000 for this property, but did not pay a premium when the lease was acquired. On 1 July 2010 the property was sub-let to a tenant, and Samurai Ltd received a premium of £72,000 for the grant of this fifteen year lease. Samurai Ltd also receives a monthly rent of £3,010 for this unit which is payable annually in advance. Samurai Ltd paid business rates of £2,000 in respect of this property for the year ended 30 June 2011.

The third, an office building, is also let out unfurnished. Samurai Ltd purchased the freehold of this building on 1 August 2010, and it was empty until 1 June 2011. The new tenants will pay a rent of £5,000 per quarter, in arrears and so no rent has been received during the year ended 30 June 2011. On 1 August 2010 Samurai Ltd paid insurance of £800 in respect of this property for the year ended 31 July 2011, and during September 2010 spent £490 on advertising for tenants. Samurai Ltd also paid £760 for a repair to the plumbing system in June 2011.

Loan interest received

On 1 October 2010 Samurai Ltd made a loan for non-trading purposes. Loan interest of £10,500 was received on 31 March 2011, and £1,600 will be accrued at 30 June 2011.

Dividends

On 19 May 2011 Samurai Ltd received a dividend of 24,000 (net) from a 3% shareholding in Martial Ltd.

Chargeable gain

On 21 April 2011 Samurai Ltd sold 4,000 ordinary shares in Sword Ltd for £49,120. Samurai had originally purchased 20,000 shares in Sword Ltd on 19 March 2005 for £18,000. A further 4,000 shares were purchased on 19 March 2009 for £7,800. The shareholding never represented more than a 1% interest in Sword Ltd.

RPI factors are: March 2005   184.6, March 2009   212.10 and April 2011   222.80.

Other information

Samurai Ltd has one associated company, Kwondo Ltd.

Required

(a) Calculate Samurai Ltd's property business profit for the year ended 30 June 2011.

(b) Assuming that Samurai Ltd's relief for its trading loss as early as possible, calculate the company's corporation tax liabilities for the years ended 30 June 2009, 30 June 2010 and 30 June 2011.

Learning solution 19.1

(a) Taxable total profits

	Year ended 30 June 2009	6 months 31 Dec 2009	Year ended 31 Dec 2010	Year ended 31 Dec 2011	Year ended 31 Dec 2012
	£	£	£	£	£
Trading profit	250,000	70,000	40,000	–	–
Property business income	9,000	13,000	4,500	5,000	–
Capital gains	–	–	5,500	–	20,500
	259,000	83,000	50,000	5,000	20,500
s37 current				(5,000)	
s37 carry back			(50,000)		
s37 current					(20,500)
s39 carry back		(83,000)	–	–	
(6/12 x 259,000)	(129,500)				
	129,500	–	–	–	–
Gift aid donation	(1,000)	unrelieved	–	–	unrelieved
Taxable total profits	128,500	–	–	–	–
Revised corporation tax					
FY08 128,500 x 9/12 x 21%}	26,985	–	–		
FY09 128,500 x 3/12 x 21%}					

				£	£
Loss for the year ended 31 December 2011				60,000	–
Loss for the year ended 31 December 2012				–	240,000
Losses utilised	– Year ended 31 December 2011			(5,000)	–
	– Year ended 31 December 2010			(50,000)	–
	– Year ended 31 December 2012			–	(20,500)
	– 6 months 31 December 2009			–	(83,000)
	– Year ended 30 June 2009			–	(129,500)
Losses unrelieved				5,000	7,000

Tutorial notes:

(1) Gift aid donations of £1,000 and £500 for respectively the 6 months ended 31 December 2009 and the year ended 31 December 2012 are unrelieved.

(2) The trading loss for the period ended 31 December 2011 can be relieved against total profits of the current period and the previous 12 months under s37.

(3) The trading loss for the year ended 31 December 2012 can be relieved against total profits of the current year and the previous 36 months under s39 CTA 2010 because it is a terminal loss.

(4) For the year ended 30 June 2009 loss relief is restricted to £129,500 (259,000 x 6/12).

(b) Due date for loss relief claims

(1) The loss relief claims under s37 CTA 2010 in respect of the loss for the year ended 31 December 2011 must be made by 31 December 2013.

(2) The loss relief claims under s39 CTA 2010 in respect of the loss for the year ended 31 December 2012 must be made by 31 December 2014.

(c) Corporation tax repayments

(1) Corporation tax refund in the year ended 30 June 2009 of £27,195 (54,180 - 26,985).

The corporation tax originally paid £54,180 (FY08 258,000 x 9/12 x 21% + FY09 258,000 x 3/12 x 21%). The revised corporation tax after relieving the losses is £26,985.

(2) The Taxable total profits for the 6 months ended 31 December 2009 were originally £82,000 (83,000 - 1,000), so corporation tax of £17,220 (82,000 at 21%) will be repaid.

(3) The Taxable total profits for the year ended 31 December 2010 were originally £50,000, so corporation tax of £10,500 (£50,000 x 21%) will be repaid.

The total corporation tax repayable is £54,915 (27,195 + 17,220 + 10,500).

Solution to exam standard question

(a) Samurai Ltd - Property business profit for the year ended 30 June 2011

	£	£
Premium received for sub-lease		72,000
Less: 72,000 x 2% x (15 - 1)		(20,160)
		51,840
Rent receivable - Property 1 (2,000 x 12)		24,000
- Property 2 (3,010 x 12)		36,120
- Property 3 (£5,000 x 4 x 1/12)		1,667
		113,627
Water rates	400	
Wear and tear allowance (24,000 – 400) x 10%	2,360	
Rent paid	21,000	
Advertising	490	
Insurance (1,600 + (800 x 11/12))	2,333	
Business rates	2,000	
Repair	760	
		(29,343)
Property business profit		84,284

(b) Samurai Ltd – Corporation tax liabilities for the years ended 30 June 2009, 30 June 2010 and 30 June 2011.

	Year ended 30 June 2009	Year ended 30 June 2010	Year ended 30 June 2011
	£	£	£
Trading profit	100,000	310,000	-
Property business profits	23,400	34,500	84,284
Interest income(10,500 + 1,600)	-	-	12,100
Chargeable gain (WI)	-	-	44,134
	123,400	344,500	140,518
Loss relief (s37)		(121,416)	(140,518)
	123,400	223,084	-
Gift aid donations	(11,000)	(1,200)	-
Taxable total profits	112,400	221,884	Nil

Tax due:

	£	£
Y/e 30 June 2009		
CT liability at 21%	23,604	
Y/e 30 June 2010		
CT liability		
28%		62,128
Less marginal relief		
(750,000 – 221,884) x 221,884/221,884 x 7/400		(9,242)
CT liability		52,886

Y/e 30 June 2011
CT liability = £Nil as no Taxable total profits

Tutorial note:

The trading loss of £261,934 for the year ended 30 June 2011 is relieved as follows:

	£
Loss	261,934
Year ended 30 June 2011	(140,518)
Year ended 30 June 2010	(121,416)
Unrelieved as at 30 June 2011	Nil

There is no restriction to the amount of loss relief that can be claimed for the year ended 30 June 2010 as this is within the normal 12 month carry back period. A current year claim must be made before carrying any loss back 12 months.

Working 1 – Chargeable gain

	£
Proceeds	49,120
Less cost	(4,300)
Unindexed gain	44,820
Less indexation	
(4,986 – 4,300)	(686)
Indexed gain	44,134

Share Pool – Sword Ltd

	No of shares	Cost	Indexed cost
	£	£	£
Purchase (March 2005)	20,000	18,000	18,000
Index to March 2009			
(212.10 – 184.60)/184.60 x £18,000			2,681
	20,000	18,000	20,681
Add purchase	4,000	7,800	7,800
	24,000	25,800	28,481
Index to April 2011			
(222.80 – 212.10)/212.10 x £28,481			1,437
	24,000	25,800	29,918
Disposal	(4,000)	(4,300)	(4,986)
C/f	20,000	21,500	24,932

Upper / lower limits

There are two associated companies so the UL becomes £1,500,000 / 2 = £750,000 and the LL becomes £300,000 / 2 = £150,000

There are no dividends received hence no FII so for the year ended 30 June 2009 Augmented profit = Taxable total profit = £112,400 so the company is a small rate company

For the year ended 30 June 2010 the Augmented profit = £221,884 so the company is a medium / marginal company for this period.

London
School of Business
& Finance
shaping success in business and finance

20

Corporation Tax
Groups

Context

This chapter covers corporation tax groups and is going to build on the earlier chapters we covered on corporation tax.

If a company owns shares in another company, this can have implications for corporation tax purposes. Each company is a separate legal entity in its own right, with its own corporation tax computation but there are certain complications that arise if a company is part of a group.

You need to be able to identify what type of group the companies in the question are in and then understand and apply the tax consequences of the group.

Exam hints

The contents of this chapter could form part of question 2 or question 4 or 5

Key learning points

- Companies are associated with one another if one company controls the other. If companies are associated, the corporation tax limits are divided by the number of associates.

- Companies in a group can also form a 75% loss group. For a loss group to be formed, there needs to be a 75% direct and indirect holding.

- If two companies are in a 75% loss group together, losses can be surrendered in the group, to minimise the group's corporation tax liability.

- Companies in a group can also form a 75% gains group. For a loss group to be formed, there needs to be a 75% direct holding and an indirect holding > 50%.

- If two companies are in a 75% gains group together, assets can be moved between the companies at no gain, no loss. Group rollover relief can also be claimed.

A group of companies is like a family, the overall objective is to minimise the total tax liability of the group as a whole. Different tax implications arise depending on the degree of control that exists between the companies. There are three different group relationships that must be studied for the F6 exam:

- Associated companies

- 75% loss groups

- 75% gains groups

Associated companies

Definition of associated

A company is associated with another in either of the following situations:

(i)   One company **controls** the other(s)

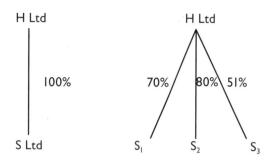

(ii)   OR both are **controlled** by the same 'person' (company or individual).

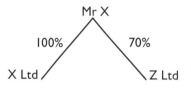

X Ltd and Z Ltd are associates. Mr X is the controlling link, although as an individual he does not impact upon the number of associated companies.

Definition of control

*   owns more than 50 per cent of the issued share capital of another company (the subsidiary) or

*   controls more than 50 per cent of the votes or

*   has the right to receive more than 50 per cent of distributable profits or

*   has the right to receive more than 50 per cent of the net assets in the event of a winding up.

Control can be exercised directly or indirectly:

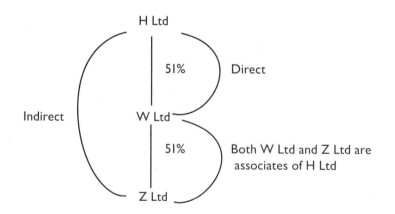

Both W Ltd and Z Ltd are associates of H Ltd. It is not necessary to have effective interest for associates therefore it does not matter that H Ltd's effective interest in Z Ltd is only 26.01% (0.51 x 0.51).

The definition of associated companies specifically includes:

- overseas resident companies
- subsidiaries joining/leaving during the accounting period

but excludes:

- dormant companies
- non-trading holding companies.

Tax implications of associates

The upper and lower limits are divided by the total number of associates, so potentially increasing the effective rate of tax each company pays.

Dividends received from associated companies are excluded from FII in the calculation of 'augmented profits'.

Learning example 20.1

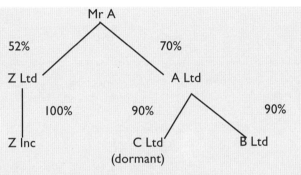

All companies except Z Inc are UK resident and prepare accounts to 31 March 2012.

Required

How many associates does A Ltd have for corporation tax purposes?

What will the corporation tax limits be for the associated companies?

75% loss group

Definition of 75% loss group

A 75% loss group exists where a parent company:

- owns at least 75 per cent of the ordinary shares of another company (the subsidiary) and

- has the right to receive at least 75 per cent of distributable profits and

- has the right to receive at least 75 per cent of the net assets in the event of a winding up.

Two (or more) companies are members of a 75% loss group where:

- one is a 75% subsidiary of another, or

- both are 75% subsidiaries of a third company.

A company can belong to more than one 75% loss group.

For a 75% loss group to exist, the direct and indirect holding must be ≥ 75%. For example:

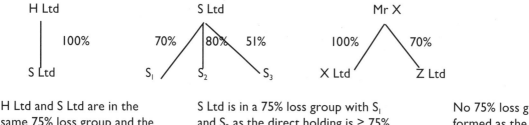

H Ltd and S Ltd are in the same 75% loss group and the direct holding is ≥ 75%.

S Ltd is in a 75% loss group with S_1 and S_2 as the direct holding is ≥ 75%. S_3 is not in the loss group as the direct holding is only 51%.

No 75% loss group is formed as the group is headed by an individual, not a company

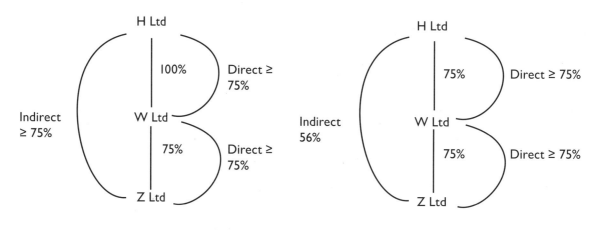

H Ltd, W Ltd and Z Ltd are all in a 75% loss group together as the direct and indirect holding is ≥ 75%.

H Ltd and W Ltd are in a 75% loss group together as the direct holding is ≥ 75%. W Ltd and Z Ltd are in 75% loss group together as the direct holding is ≥ 75%.

H Ltd, W Ltd and Z Ltd are not all in the same 75% loss group as the indirect holding is only 56% from H Ltd to Z Ltd. This means that two separate 75% loss groups are formed in this case.

London
School of Business
& Finance
shaping success in business and finance

Implications of a 75% loss group

UK resident members of a 75% group can surrender losses to other UK resident group members. This form of loss relief is called 'group relief'. Group relief is normally only available between UK resident companies within the 75% group.

Group relief

A Ltd   Company with loss (surrendering company)

75%

B Ltd   Company with profit (claimant company)

Surrendering company

The surrendering company can surrender all the following types of **current period** losses:

*   Trading losses

*   Excess unrelieved donations under the gift aid scheme

*   Excess unrelieved property losses

The surrendering company can surrender to whichever UK group company it wants to, provided the receiving company is in the 75% loss group. The surrendering company can surrender any amount of the loss, and it can surrender to more than one other group company if it wants to.

There is no requirement for the surrendering company to use any of the loss against its own profits first. It can surrender all of its losses if it wants to. However there may be a restriction on the amount of loss the claimant company can receive.

Claimant company

The maximum amount of loss that the claimant company can claim is the amount which will reduce its Taxable total profits down to nil.

Learning example 20.2

A Ltd and B are members of a 75% loss group. Their results for the year ended 31 March 2012 are as follows:

	A Ltd	B Ltd
Trading profit/(loss)	115,000	(80,000)
Interest income	12,000	3,000
Chargeable gain	5,000	6,000
Gift aid donation	-	(10,000)

Required

Calculate the maximum possible group relief available.

Corresponding accounting periods

Group relief can only be claimed in the 'corresponding accounting period'. The corresponding accounting period is the period common to both the surrendering company and the claimant company's accounting periods.

If the accounting periods are not coterminous, profits and losses must be time apportioned:

- The surrendering company can only surrender the time-apportioned loss of the AP.

- The claimant company can only relieve against time apportioned Taxable total profits for the AP.

Learning example 20.3

Gold Ltd owns 100% of the ordinary share capital of Silver Ltd. Gold Ltd has an accounting date of 31 December, whilst Silver Ltd has an accounting date of 30 June.

The results of Gold Ltd are as follows:

	Year ended 31 December 2010 £	Year ended 31 December 2011 £
Trading profit	177,000	90,000
Property income	5,000	–
Chargeable gain	–	12,000
Gift aid donation	(2,000)	(2,000)

For the year ended 30 June 2010 Silver Ltd had Taxable total profits of £260,000. The company made a trading loss of £140,000 for the year ended 30 June 2011. No information is available regarding the year ended 30 June 2012.

Gold Ltd has no other associated companies.

Required

Assuming that the maximum possible claim for group relief is made in respect of Silver Ltd's trading loss of £140,000, calculate Gold Ltd's Taxable total profits for the year ended 31 December 2010 and the year ended 31 December 2011.

Group relief and tax planning

Group relief should ideally be claimed as follows in order to maximise the tax saving i.e. claiming relief at the highest rate of tax first.

Remember that group relief is flexible, so the surrendering company can give away as little or as much as it wants up to the maximum available. It can also choose to give the loss to more than one company in the loss group.

Order of claiming group relief

Which member of losses group should you give loss to? One paying highest rate of tax:

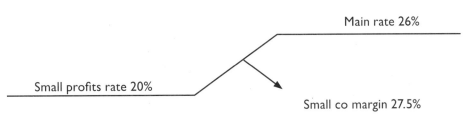

1. To any company paying 27.5%. As group relief is flexible, give them enough to take them out of margin and down to 20%

2. To any company paying 26%. As group relief if flexible, give them enough to take them down to 20%

3. To any company paying 20%

Approach to group loss questions

Step 1   Draw the group structure if it is not drawn in the question.

Step 2   Analyse the group and identify:
Associated companies, Upper/ lower limits, 75% loss groups

Step 3   Set up proforma group losses working and put in the numbers given in the question for each group company.
No losses should appear at this stage but the loss relief sections should be inserted at the correct position in the proforma.

Step 4   Set up the loss memo

Step 5   Write the size of each company at the top of each column, before allocating any losses and then decide how to use each loss in the most tax efficient way.
Remember to consider the number of associated companies when deciding the size of each company.

Step 6   At the bottom of each column record the revised sizes of each company then compute the corporation tax for each group company using the adjusted Taxable total profits.

Proforma losses working

	A Ltd	B Ltd	C Ltd
Trading profit	x	-	x
Interest income	x	x	x
Chargeable gain	x	x	-
Gift aid donation	(x)	(x)	(x)
Taxable total profits	x	x	x
Group relief	–	–	–
Adjusted Taxable total profits	x	x	x

Learning example 20.4

Warren plc owns 100% of the ordinary share capital of Bunny Ltd and Hare Ltd. The results of each company for the year ended 31 March 2012 are as follows:

	Warren plc £	Bunny Ltd £	Hare Ltd £
Tax adjusted trading profit/(loss)	900,000	210,000	(150,000)
Property business income	-	10,000	30,000
Interest income	-	-	80,000

As at 31 March 2011 Bunny Ltd and Hare Ltd have unused trading losses of £15,000 and £20,000 respectively. Warren plc has not other associated companies.

Required

Assuming that reliefs are claimed in the most favourable manner, calculate the corporation tax liabilities of Warren plc, Bunny Ltd and Hare Ltd for the year ended 31 March 2012.

75% gains group

Definition of 75% gains group

- Two companies are in a **75% group** if one company is the 75% subsidiary of the other, or both companies are 75% subsidiaries of a third company.

- The direct holding must be ≥ 75% and indirect >50%

- A company cannot be in more than one gains group

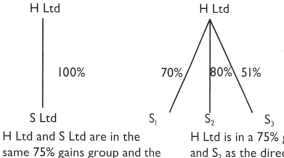

H Ltd and S Ltd are in the same 75% gains group and the direct holding is ≥ 75%.

H Ltd is in a 75% gains group with S_1 and S_2 as the direct holding is ≥ 75%. S_3 is not in the gains group as the direct holding is only 51%.

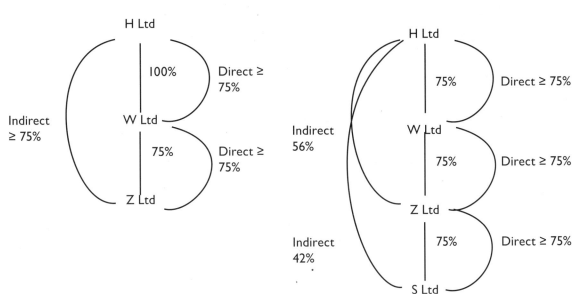

H Ltd, W Ltd and Z Ltd are all in a 75% gains group together as the direct and indirect holding is > 50%.

H Ltd, W Ltd and Z Ltd are all in a 75% gains group together as the direct and indirect holding is > 50%. S Ltd is not in the gains group as the indirect holding is only 42%. As Z Ltd is already in a gains group and cannot be in more than one gains group, S Ltd is not in a gains group with anyone.

Implications of 75% gains group

There are 3 main implications of a 75% gains group. These are:

*   No gain, no loss transfers
*   Transfers of gains and losses
*   Group rollover relief

No gain, no loss transfers (NGNL)

Assets are automatically transferred between companies in the capital gains group at no gain and no loss.

Learning example 20.5

A Ltd and B Ltd are in a gains group together. On 1st March 1997 A Ltd bought land for £537,000. On 25th May 2006, it was transferred to B Ltd. Its market value at the time was £1m. On 7 July 2011, B Ltd sold the land for £1.7m

Ignore indexation allowance

Required

Calculate the gain arising on B Ltd when it sells the land.

Transfers of gains and losses

Capital losses CANNOT be group relieved, but an election allows capital losses and capital gains to be transferred within a 75% gains group thus maximising the use of capital losses.

The election can be made in respect of the whole or part of the gain or loss. This means that gains and losses can be matched in the same company, and any remaining net gains can arise in the company (or companies) with the lowest marginal rate of tax.

Group rollover relief

For rollover relief purposes all the companies within a 75% gains group are treated as carrying on a single trade.

Therefore an asset can be sold by one company realising a chargeable gain and that company's gain can be rolled over by another company in the same 75% gains group which is making a reinvestment in a qualifying asset within 48 months (12 months before the disposal and 36 months after the disposal).

Learning summary

- A 75% loss group will exist where one company is a 75% subsidiary of another.

- In a 75% loss group, trading losses can be surrendered between UK members of the group.

- Consideration has to be given for companies joining and leaving a group or where the group members have different accounting periods. Losses can only be surrendered or claimed for corresponding periods of account.

- Capital gains tax groups are formed where one company is a 75% subsidiary of another and is at least a 50% subsidiary of the parent company.

- Within a gains group, assets are transferred at nil gain nil loss. A degrouping charge arises where the company holding the transferred asset leaves the group within 6 years of acquiring the asset.

- An election can be made to notionally transfer assets between gains group companies.

- Roll-over relief is available in a gains group.

Exam standard question

Animal Ltd is the holding company for a group of companies. The results of each group company for the year ended 31 March 2012 are as follows:

	Trading profit/(loss)	Property income	Franked Investment Income
	£	£	£
Animal Ltd	450,000	5,000	20,000
Bat Ltd	65,000	15,000	–
Cat Ltd	85,000	–	–
Dog Ltd	100,000	–	–
Elk Ltd	–	–	–
Fox Ltd	60,000	–	5,000
Gnu Ltd	(200,000)	–	–

Animal Ltd owned 100% of each subsidiary company's ordinary share capital throughout the year ended 31 March 2012 with the following exceptions:

(1)   Animal Ltd only owned 90% of Bat Ltd's ordinary share capital.

(2)   Animal Ltd's shareholding in Cat Ltd was disposed of on 31 December 2011. The tax adjusted trading profit of £85,000 is for the year ended 31 March 2012.

(3)   Animal Ltd's shareholding in Dog Ltd was acquired on 1 January 2012. The tax adjusted trading profit of £100,000 is for the year ended 31 March 2012.

Elk Ltd was a dormant company throughout the year ended 31 March 2012.

Required

(a)   Explain the group relationship that must exist in order that group relief can be claimed.

(b)   Explain why there are six associated companies in the Animal Ltd group of companies. Your answer should identify the six associated companies.

(c)   Assuming that relief is claimed for Gnu Ltd's trading loss of £200,000 in the most favourable manner; calculate the Taxable total profits of Animal Ltd, Bat Ltd, Cat Ltd, Dog Ltd and Fox Ltd for the year ended 31 March 2012.

Learning solution 20.1

A Ltd has 3 associated companies, so the corporation tax limits will need to be divided by 4.

The associated companies are: A Ltd, B Ltd, Z Ltd and Z Inc

C Ltd is not associated as is a dormant company

The corporation tax limits are:

£
1,500,000/4 = 375,000
300,000/4 = 75,000

Each associated company will use these lower limits when deciding the rate of corporation tax it should pay.

Learning solution 20.2

Surrendering company (B Ltd)

The surrendering company can give away up to:

	£
Trading loss	(80,000)
Excess gift aid donation	(1,000)
	(81,000)

Claimant company (A Ltd)

The claimant company can accept anything up to:

	£
Trading profit	115,000
Interest income	12,000
Chargeable gain	5,000
	132,000

A Ltd has enough profits to accept ALL of B Ltd's loss. Therefore the maximum group relief is £81,000.

B Ltd can surrender anything up to this amount to A Ltd

Points to note:

- B Ltd does not have to use any of the loss against its own interest income and gains. It can choose to surrender it all to A Ltd.

- Only £1,000 of the gift aid donation can be given away by B Ltd. This is because the other £9,000 can be used against B Ltd's interest income and gains. Only £1,000 of the donation is unrelieved. This can be given away to A Ltd.

Learning solution 20.3

Gold Ltd – Taxable total profits

	Year ended 31 December 2010	Year ended 31 December 2011
	£	£
Trading profit	177,000	90,000
Property income	5,000	–
Chargeable gain	–	12,000
	182,000	102,000
Gift Aid donation	(2,000)	(2,000)
Taxable total profits	180,000	100,000
Group relief	(70,000)	(50,000)
Adjusted Taxable total profits	110,000	50,000

Notes:

- The accounting periods are not coterminous, so both Gold Ltd's Taxable total profits and Silver Ltd's trading loss must be apportioned on a time basis.

- For the year ended 31 December 2010 group relief is restricted to the lower of £90,000 (180,000 * 6/12) and £70,000 (140,000 x 6/12).

- For the year ended 31 December 2011 group relief is restricted to the lower of £50,000 (100,000 * 6/12) and £70,000 (140,000 x 6/12).

- Gold Ltd has one associated company so the small company lower limit is £150,000 (300,000/2).

London
School of Business
& Finance

shaping success in business and finance

Learning solution 20.4

Warren Plc

Step 1 Draw the group structure (W1)

Step 2 Analyse the group (W1)

Step 3 Set up the corporation tax computations for all companies required by the question, in columns across the page

	Large Warren plc £	Med Bunny Ltd £	Med Hare Ltd £
Trading profit	900,000	210,000	-
Less loss b/f (s45)		(15,000)	
		195,000	
Property business profit		10,000	30,000
Interest income			80,000
	900,000	205,000	110,000
Current year relief (s37)			(10,000)
Group relief (s402)	(35,000)	(105,000)	
Revised Taxable Total Profits = 'P'	865,000	100,000	100,000
Corporation tax @ 20%		20,000	20,000
@ 26%	224,900		

(W1)

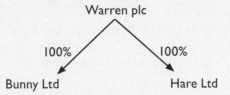

Warren plc

100%   100%

Bunny Ltd   Hare Ltd

There are three associated companies and three 75% group companies

Upper Limit $\dfrac{150,000}{3}$ = 500,000

Lower Limit $\dfrac{300,000}{3}$ = 100,000

(W2)

	£
Hare Ltd trading loss	(150,000)
Group relief to Bunny Ltd (to reduce profits to lower limit)	105,000
	(45,000)
Group relief to Warren plc	35,000
	(10,000)
Current year relief (to reduce profits to lower limit)	10,000
	-

(W3)

Hare Ltd's trading loss brought forward at 31 March 2011 must be carried forward as it is not a current AP loss and cannot be group relieved.

Learning solution 20.5

Gain on disposal by B Ltd

	£
Proceeds	1,700,000
Cost (to A Ltd)	(537,000)
Gain arising in B Ltd	1,163,000

There is no gain arising on the transfer of the asset from A Ltd to B Ltd as they are in a 75% gains group

Solution to exam standard question

(a) Group relief relationship

- One company must be a 75% subsidiary of the other, or both companies must be 75% subsidiaries of a third company.

- The holding company must have an effective interest of at least 75% of the subsidiary's ordinary share capital.

- The holding company must have the right to receive at least 75% of the subsidiary's distributable profits and net assets on a winding up.

(b) Analyse the group

Associates Associated companies in the Animal Ltd group = 6
Bat Ltd, Cat Ltd, Dog Ltd, Fox Ltd and Gnu Ltd are all under the common control (shareholding of over 50%) of Animal Ltd, and are therefore associated companies.

Where a company such as Elk Ltd has been dormant throughout the accounting period, it does not count as an associated company. Companies that are only associated for part of the accounting period, such as Cat Ltd and Dog Ltd, count as associated companies for the whole of the period.

The relevant lower and upper limits for corporation tax purposes are £50,000 (300,000 / 6) and £250,000 (1,500,000/6)

75% loss groups = 1

Members are Animal Ltd, Bat Ltd, Cat Ltd (it leaves on 31.12.11), Dog Ltd (it joins on 1.1.12), Fox Ltd and Gnu Ltd.

(c) Taxable total profits

Step 1 Draw the group structure

Step 2 Analyse the group (part (a) of the answer)

Step 3   Set up the corporation tax computations for all companies required by the question, in columns across the page.

	Large Animal Ltd £	med Bat Ltd £	med Cat Ltd £	med Dog Ltd £	med Fox Ltd £
Trading profit	450,000	65,000	85,000	100,000	60,000
Property income	5,000	15,000	-	-	-
Total profits	455,000	80,000	85,000	100,000	60,000
Less: gift aid donations	-	-	-	-	-
Taxable total profits	455,000	80,000	85,000	100,000	60,000
Group relief	(95,000)	(30,000)	(35,000)	(25,000)	(15,000)
Adjusted Taxable total profits	360,000	50,000	50,000	75,000	45,000
FII	20,000	-	-	-	5,000
'Augmented profits'	380,000	50,000	50,000	75,000	50,000

Step 4   Set up the loss memorandum and record the possible ways of using the loss.

Loss Memorandum

	Gnu Ltd Y/e 31.3.2012
Trading losses	200,000
Group relief with Fox Ltd	(15,000)
	185,000
Group relief with Bat Ltd	(30,000)
	155,000
Group relief with Dog Ltd (W1)	(25,000)
	130,000
Group relief with Cat Ltd (W2)	(35,000)
	95,000
Group relief with Animal Ltd	(95,000)

(W1)

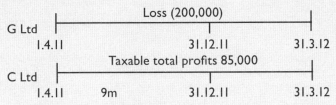

The maximum amount of loss that Gnu Ltd can surrender to Dog Ltd is 3/12 x 100,000 = £25,000

(W2)

The maximum amount of loss that Gnu Ltd can surrender to Cat Ltd is 9/12 x 85,000 = £63,750

It is possible to surrender less than the maximum which is advisable in this case only £35,000 of the loss should be surrendered to Cat Ltd to ensure that maximum relief is given at the marginal rate of 27.5%.

21

Corporation Tax
and Overseas
Aspects

Context

This chapter covers overseas aspects of corporation tax groups and is going to build on the earlier chapters we covered on corporation tax.

If a company is trading overseas, this will have an impact on its corporation tax computation. As we saw in the previous corporation tax chapter, a UK resident company pays UK corporation tax on its worldwide income and gains.

In this chapter, we are going to look at how worldwide income gets included in the corporation tax computation

Exam hints

The contents of this chapter could form part of question 2 or questions 4 or 5.

Key learning points

- A UK resident company will pay UK corporation tax on its worldwide income and gains.

- To be a UK resident, a company must either be incorporated in the UK or centrally managed and controlled from the UK.

- A UK company could expand overseas either by setting up an overseas branch of the UK company or by setting up a new overseas subsidiary company.

- The overseas income received by the UK company may have suffered overseas tax as well as UK tax. As a result, double tax relief may be available.

- Foreign dividends are exempt from corporation tax.

- The overseas income received must be grossed up for the overseas tax suffered and included in the Taxable total profits of the UK company (for branch profits only).

- Double tax relief is the lower of the UK tax paid on the overseas income and the overseas tax suffered.

Scope of corporation tax

Payable by UK resident companies on their Taxable total profits for a chargeable accounting period (AP)

Definitions for corporation tax:

UK resident: company incorporated in the UK or centrally managed and controlled in the UK

Taxable total profits: worldwide income and gains

AP: An AP is the period for which a charge to corporation tax is made and is usually a company's period of account.

Residency

A company is UK resident if either:

- It is incorporated in the UK; or

- It is centrally managed and controlled in UK

> e.g. location of head office, location of board meetings, where directors spend their time

If company is a UK resident company they pay UK CT on worldwide profits

If company is not a UK resident company they pay UK CT on UK income only

Overseas branch v overseas subsidiary

A company may be thinking of expanding overseas in one of two ways. It could be done either by setting up an overseas branch of the UK company, or by setting up a new overseas subsidiary company.

	Overseas branch	Overseas subsidiary
Legal status	Part of the UK company = one single entity	Separate legal entity with its own corporation tax computation overseas
Additional associate?	No	Yes
Income taxed in the UK company	Branch profits are taxed as trading income for the UK company as normal	Overseas dividends received by UK company are exempt from UK corporation tax but may count as FII (not examinable)
Overseas trading losses	Overseas branch losses can be offset against UK company's trading income	Overseas losses cannot be surrendered to a UK company
Capital allowances	UK capital allowances	Overseas capital allowances

Double tax relief (DTR)

Branch profits may be taxed in the country of origin and again in the UK. Double taxation relief (DTR) will occur where an overseas branch's profits are taxed overseas as well as being subject to UK corporation tax. Double taxation relief will be available in respect of the overseas tax up to the amount of the UK tax on the overseas profits.

The gross overseas branch profits are included in the Taxable total profits of the UK company and the UK corporation tax is calculated as normal, before DTR is given via Double Taxation Relief (a deduction from CT liability.

Method for grossing up foreign branch profits

* Gross up branch profits received for withholding tax suffered

	£
Branch profits received	X_A
Add: Withholding tax $\quad \dfrac{X_A \times \% \text{ WT}}{100 - \% \text{ WT}}$	$\underline{X}$
Gross branch profits	X

DTR relief

Once the gross overseas income figure has been calculated and included in the Taxable total profits, UK corporation tax should be calculated as normal. Once the UK corporation tax has been calculated, DTR is available to reduce the corporation tax liability.

The DTR is calculated as follows:

Lower of

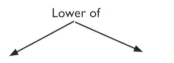

UK tax on overseas income   Overseas tax suffered

Approach to DTR questions

If asked to calculate the Taxable total profits of a UK company with overseas income, you should layout your corporation computation in column format as follows:

A Ltd CT comp

	Total	UK income	Overseas income (Utopia)	Overseas income (Ruritania)
	£	£	£	£
Trading income	x	x	-	-
Interest income	x	x	-	-
Overseas income	x	-	x	x
Taxable total profits	x	x	x	x
CT@26%/20%	x	x	x	x
DTR (WI)	(x)	-	(x)	(x)
UK CT	x	x	x	x

Set up basic corporation tax comp (with a separate column for each source of overseas income) and put in easy numbers e.g. trading income, interest income. Then set up a working to calculate gross overseas income figure

Learning example 21.1

Lancaster Ltd is a UK resident company. The company's UK trading profit for the year ended 31 March 2012 is £400,000. Lancaster Ltd has an overseas branch and an overseas subsidiary.

The overseas branch is controlled from overseas. It has a trading profit of £70,000 for the year ended 31 March 2012. The overseas corporation tax on these profits is £28,000.

Lancaster Ltd has one associated company.

Required

(a) Explain the advantages for taxation purposes of operating overseas through a branch rather than through an overseas subsidiary.

(b) Calculate Lancaster Ltd's UK corporation tax liability for the year ended 31 March 2012.

Transfer Pricing

Where companies are members of the same group or are controlled by the same person they can set their own prices for transactions between themselves. It would be possible, for example, for company A to sell inventories to company B at an artificially low price. This would have the effect of decreasing A's profits and increasing B's profits. If B is an overseas company which pays corporation tax at a lower rate, this reduces the group's total tax bill.

There are special rules in place to ensure that companies cannot reduce the total UK corporation tax by substituting a transfer price which is below an arm's length price. The transfer pricing legislation applies to transactions between companies where one company controls the other or both are controlled by the same person.

The transfer pricing legislation covers not only sales but also lettings/hiring of property and loan interest.

If a company is found to have received a tax advantage through its transfer pricing, the legislation requires the profit be recalculated as if the transactions had been carried out at arm's length. The adjustment must be reflected in the self-assessment tax return.

An arm's length price is one which might have been expected if the parties had been independent persons dealing with each other in a normal commercial manner unaffected by any special relationship between them.

For the purposes of your exam you will only be expected to consider situations where one of the companies is an overseas company.

A company can enter into an advance pricing arrangement (APA) with HMRC whereby a company can agree in advance that the transfer pricing policy it is to adopt is acceptable to HMRC. Once an APA is entered into, the company is required to maintain the pricing policy insofar as it still produces an arm's length price.

Any material changes to the circumstances which may cause an alteration in the arm's length price, should be communicated to HMRC. It may be necessary to draft a new APA or simply amend the existing one.

If a company has an APA with HMRC, it is not required to adjust its self-assessment of its liability to corporation tax under the transfer pricing rules.

Learning summary

- A company is resident in the UK if it was incorporated in the UK or exerts its central management and control from the UK.

- Company residence determines how the profits of a company are taxed.

- DTR will enable a company taxed on overseas profits to reclaim the tax suffered overseas.

- Overseas dividends are not subject to UK corporation tax. They are treated as franked investment income and will impact the corporation tax rate.

- Trading overseas through a branch will mean the profits are taxed as part of the UK company's trading profits, with any losses being relieved against any company profits. Capital allowances are also available where the company trades overseas through a branch.

Learning solution 21.1

(a) Advantages of operating through an overseas branch

- Relief is usually available in the UK for trading losses if incurred by an overseas branch, but no UK relief is available for trading losses incurred by an overseas subsidiary

- UK capital allowances are available in respect of plant and machinery purchased by an overseas branch.

- Unlike an overseas subsidiary, an overseas branch cannot be an associated company. The UK corporation tax limits will therefore not be reduced.

(b) UK Ltd – Corporation Tax computation - Year Ended 31 March 2012

	Total £	UK £	Branch £
Trading profits	470,000	400,000	70,000
Overseas income	-	-	-
	470,000	400,000	70,000
Corporation tax at 26%	122,200		
Marginal relief			
3/200 x (750,000 – 470,000)	(4,200)		
	118,000	100,426	17,574
Double tax relief (W1)	(17,574)	-	(17,574)
Corporation tax liability	100,426	100,426	-

Notes:

- The full profits of the overseas branch are assessed as trading income in the year that they arise.

- Lancaster Ltd has one associated company, so the upper limit for corporation tax purposes is £750,000 (£1,500,000/2) and lower limit is £150,000 (£300,000/2).

Working 1 DTR

The effective rate of tax on Taxable total profits = 25.106% (118,000/470,000).

The UK corporation tax on the branch profits is £17,574 (£70,000 x 25.106%). Overseas corporation tax of £28,000 has been paid in respect of branch profits. Therefore, double taxation relief is restricted to the related UK corporation tax of £17,574.

22

Value Added Tax
(VAT)

Context

Accounting for VAT is relevant to sole traders, partnerships and companies who may be VAT registered. This chapter is dealing with the VAT rules which are very important in the F6 exam.

Exam hints

The examiner has stated that VAT will always be tested in the F6 exam for at least 10 marks and will either be part of questions one or two or it maybe tested in a completely separate question, such as question four or five.

It is not possible to avoid VAT and it is the easiest 10 marks on the paper if you know certain very important rules which are described in this chapter

Key learning points

- VAT is chargeable on a taxable supply by a taxable person.

- VAT charged on sales is known as output VAT and VAT reclaimable on purchases is known as input VAT.

- There are different types of supplies: Taxable supplies, which can be standard or zero rated and exempt supplies.

- VAT registration is compulsory once the registration threshold of £73,000 is reached. There are two tests to determine if the threshold has been reached. These are the historic and future test.

- A person can also register voluntarily if they so choose, as long as they make taxable supplies. If only exempt supplies are made, VAT registration is not possible.

- To determine when output VAT should be included on a VAT return, the basic tax point is used.

- If a discount is offered on the selling price, the VAT is always calculated on the discounted figure, even if the discount is not taken up.

- Input VAT on certain items is irrecoverable. This means that it cannot be reclaimed. This includes items such as cars and UK client entertaining.

- VAT on fuel is reclaimable as input VAT. If the fuel is used partly for private purposes then some output VAT must also be charged, known as the scale charge.

- There are special VAT schemes only available to small businesses. These are the cash accounting scheme, the annual accounting scheme and the flat rate scheme.

- Fines and penalties apply if errors are made. The most important is the default surcharge system caused by a late return or a late payment.

Definitions and terms for VAT

VAT was introduced in Finance Act 1972 as a precondition of the UK's acceptance into the European Economic Community (EEC, now known as the European Union (EU).

VAT is an indirect tax, which is levied on turnover and not profits. VAT is borne by the final user of the goods or services, and this is usually the general public, although certain businesses cannot register for VAT and hence, they bear a VAT cost.

If a trader is VAT registered, then they are entitled to claim relief for VAT on purchases (input VAT) but must account for VAT on their sales (output VAT).

The difference between any output VAT and input VAT is paid over to HMRC on a quarterly basis. A trader may be in a position to reclaim VAT from HMRC (input VAT > output VAT); if the trader is considered a net repayment trader, returns can be submitted monthly to ease cash flows.

Take the example of production of a wooden table:

VAT registered timber felling and processing business	wood →	**VAT registered furniture maker**	table →	**Customer**
Sells wood for £100 plus 20% VAT (£20): • Timber business receives £120 from customer • £100 of this is income for the timber business • Timber business owes HMRC £20 tax which it has collected on their behalf		Buys wood for £100 plus 20% VAT (£20): • Furniture maker pays £120 to timber business • £100 of this is an expense to furniture maker • The other £20 can be recovered from HMRC Makes a table from the wood and sells it for £300 plus 20% VAT(£60): • Furniture maker receives £360 from customer • £300 of this is income for the furniture maker • Furniture maker owes HMRC £60 VAT which it has collected on their behalf.		Buys a table for £300 plus 20% VAT (£60) • Customer pays £360, £60 of which is VAT

VAT payable: £20

	£
VAT payable	60
VAT to reclaim	(20)
Net payable	40

As the example above illustrates, it is the final consumer who bears the cost of sales tax, but the businesses which collect the tax during the production process who are responsible for paying it to the authorities.

Scope of VAT

VAT is chargeable on the supply of any goods or services (for a consideration) in the UK when supplied 'in the course or furtherance of any business' by a taxable person. Any supplies made outside the UK are outside the scope of VAT.

VAT law is predominantly found in the Value Added Tax Act 1994 (VATA 1994, and is administered by HMRC. All VAT law has its roots in the EC Sixth VAT Directive, which has effect in the UK through domestic legislation.

Classification of supplies

A supply (of goods or services) can be either:

1.   Standard rated – at 20%

2.   Reduced rated – 5%

3.   Zero-rated – 0%

4.   Exempt – outside the charge to UK VAT

5.   Outside the scope of UK VAT

A supply of goods involves a transfer of legal title.

The value of the supply is the value of the consideration given, whether monetary or in kind. Gifts of goods are usually treated as supplied at cost, unless the total cost of gifts to the customer in a 12 month period does not exceed £50 in which case there is no supply. Samples are not treated as supplies, except that this exception only applies to one sample if more than one identical sample is given to the same customer.

A supply of services is any supply, carried out for consideration, which is not a supply of goods. Consideration can be monetary or in kind. If there is no consideration, there is no supply.

The value of the supply is the VAT exclusive amount to which VAT must be added at the appropriate rate.

Taxable persons

A taxable person includes a sole trader, partnership, limited companies, charities and clubs/associations. Where a person is registered for VAT as a sole trader, he is the taxable person, and whatever business he conducts, will be liable to VAT, even where it is distinct from the original registered business.

A person becomes a taxable person upon exceeding the registration limits for VAT.

Learning example 22.1

Identify the amount of VAT that has been charged on the following standard rated supplies and purchases:

*   Sale of goods for £500 plus VAT

*   Purchase of goods for £325 (VAT inclusive)

*   Purchase of fixed asset for £650 (VAT inclusive)

*   Sale of goods for £1,000 plus VAT

Types of supply

Here is a list of different types of supplies and how they are classified for VAT purposes. You are NOT expected to remember this list for your exam.

Zero rated (0%)

- Food, although pet food and certain luxury items, such as confectionery and alcohol are standard rated.
- Sewerage services and water.
- Books and other printed material.
- New construction work or the sale of new buildings by builders, where the building is to be used for residential or charitable purposes (not repairs or enlargements to existing buildings or alterations).
- Transport, but pleasure transport and transport in vehicles seating fewer than 12 passengers is standard rated.
- Drugs and medicines.
- Exports of goods.
- Clothing and footwear for children.

Standard rated (20%)

- Stationery
- Furniture
- Computers
- Cars
- Petrol and diesel
- Accountancy fees
- Legal fees
- Advertising costs
- Adult clothes
- Confectionery
- Vans
- Lorries

Exempt supplies

- Land.
- Insurance.
- Postal services.
- Financial services – bank charges, credit card services.
- Education
- Health services.
- Burial and cremation services.
- Subscriptions to professional bodies.
- Rent of commercial property, however, the landlord can elect to treat the rent as standard rated if preferred.

London School of Business & Finance
shaping success in business and finance

Imports, Exports and Trading within the European Union

Imports

When a UK VAT registered business imports goods into the UK from outside the European Union, then VAT has to be paid at the time of importation. This VAT can then be reclaimed as input VAT on the VAT return for the period during which the goods were imported.

Therefore goods imported into the UK from outside the European Union are effectively treated the same as goods that are purchased within the UK. For example, if a UK VAT registered business purchases goods for £1,000 during March 2012 from a UK supplier, then it will pay the supplier £1,200 (1,000 plus VAT of 200 (1,000 x 20%)), and then reclaim the input VAT of £200. If the goods are instead purchased from a supplier situated outside the European Union, then the business will pay £1,000 to the supplier, £200 to HM Revenue & Customs, and then again reclaim the input VAT of £200.

In each case the business has paid £1,200 and reclaimed £200. Regular importers can defer the payment of VAT on importation by setting up an account with HM Revenue & Customs. It is necessary to provide a bank guarantee, but VAT is then accounted for on a monthly basis.

The same treatment generally applies when a UK VAT registered business is supplied with services from outside the European Union.

Exports

When a UK VAT registered business exports goods outside of the European Union then the supply is zero-rated. Supplies of services outside of the European Union are outside the scope of VAT.

Trading within the European Union

When a UK VAT registered business acquires goods from within the European Union, then VAT has to be accounted for according to the date of acquisition. The date of acquisition is the earlier of the date that a VAT invoice is issued or the 15th day of the month following the month in which the goods come into the UK.

This VAT charge is declared on the VAT return as output VAT, but can be reclaimed as input VAT on the same VAT return. Therefore for most businesses there is no VAT cost as the VAT charge and the corresponding input VAT contra out. The only time that there is a VAT cost is if a business makes exempt supplies, since an exempt business cannot reclaim any input VAT.

Although the end result is the same as with an import from outside the European Union, with a European Union acquisition there is no need to actually pay the VAT subsequent to its recovery as input VAT.

For example, if a UK VAT registered business purchases goods for £1,000 during March 2012 from a supplier situated in the European Union, then the business will pay £1,000 to the supplier. Then on its

VAT return the business will show output VAT of £200 and input VAT of £200.

When a UK VAT registered business supplies goods to another VAT registered business within the European Union then the supply is zero-rated. The same treatment generally applies where a UK VAT registered business is supplied with services from within the European Union, and where a UK VAT registered business supplies services to another VAT registered European Union business.

When a UK registered business supplies goods to a customer within the European Union who is not VAT registered then VAT must be charged on the supply in the normal way.

VAT registration

If a person's taxable supplies (sales) exceed the registration limits, then registration for VAT is compulsory. There are two separate tests for compulsory registration to determine whether the registration limits have been passed. The registration threshold is currently £73,000. You will be given this figure in the exam.

Historic test

- This test is done at the end of every month, to determine whether taxable supplies in the last 12 months have exceeded £73,000.

- If taxable supplies exceed the threshold of £73,000, must notify HMRC within 30 days of the end of the month in which the turnover limit is exceeded.

- Registration is effective from the end of the month following the month in which turnover exceeded the limit, or an earlier agreed date.

- Cumulative 12-monthly turnover totals should be kept to check when registration becomes necessary.

Learning example 22.2

Colin has started a sole trader business on 1 June 2011 and has not yet registered for VAT. His sales for the first 10 months were £6,250 per month. After that, his sales increased to £14,000 per month.

Required

When should Colin notify HMRC and register for VAT?

Future test

- This test is done at any time.

- If taxable supplies in the next 30-days are expected to exceed £73,000, HMRC must be notified within 30 days, and registration will be effective from the beginning of the 30 day period.

- There are penalties for late registration and there is a need to collect VAT retrospectively.

Learning example 22.3

Finance Ltd is a new company that started trading on 1 January 2011. For the first six months, it has sales of £7,750. On 1 July 2011, Finance Ltd signed a large contract with its main customer. This contract is worth £67,000 a month and would be in addition to the normal sales made by Finance Ltd.

Required

When should Finance Ltd notify HMRC and register for VAT?

London
School of Business
& Finance

shaping success in business and finance

Voluntary registration

Even if not required to register, a person may register voluntarily provided they are making taxable supplies. The key advantages of a voluntary registration are avoidance of penalties for late registration and the ability to recover input tax on their supplies. Voluntary registration is said to disguise the 'small' size of a business.

On the other hand, persons selling to final consumers (who cannot recover VAT) may find voluntary registration disadvantageous since by adding VAT to their selling price, the business loses some competitive advantage.

Other disadvantages are the administrative burden of preparing VAT returns, updating stationery (to quote the VAT number) and a greater complexity to the accounting records.

If the trader is making wholly exempt supplies, they will not be allowed to register for VAT. However, traders making zero rated supplies can register for VAT voluntarily, which means they can reclaim any input VAT suffered.

Intending trader registration

Where a business is newly incorporated, and the intention is to make taxable supplies, a trader can apply to HMRC for registration. In these cases, proof of intention to trade (contracts etc) will be required by HMRC before they will register the trader.

Exemption from registration

A person making only zero-rated supplies can request to be exempt from registration if they so choose.

Deregistration

Deregistration is a process whereby the trader ceases to require a VAT number. As with registration, there is a compulsory requirement and a voluntary option.

Compulsory deregistration

When a business ceases trading, the business must apply for deregistration from VAT within 30 days from the date of cessation. HMRC will treat the business as no longer VAT registered from the date of cessation. Failure to inform HMRC within 30 days of the cessation of trade can result in penalties being levied.

HMRC can deregister a business where the business appears to have ceased to be making taxable supplies. For this action to be taken, HMRC will usually write to the trader and seek confirmation that no further taxable supplies are expected in the near future.

Compulsory deregistration also occurs upon a company joining a VAT group, a sole trader becoming a partnership, a sole trader becoming incorporated, and an incorporated business becoming unincorporated.

Voluntary deregistration

If the trader expects his taxable supplies to fall below £71,000 in the next 12 months, they can apply to HMRC for voluntary deregistration. If HMRC are satisfied that the expected fall in taxable supplies will occur, they will deregister the trader from the date the request is made, or an agreed later date.

Voluntary deregistration is not allowed where there is a cessation of business or the trader will stop making taxable supplies for a period greater than 30 days. For these cases, compulsory deregistration is required.

After deregistration

After a trader has applied for deregistration, they will no longer have to charge VAT on their taxable supplies. Any input VAT claims post deregistration are restricted.

On the final VAT return the business must repay the input VAT reclaimed based on the value of goods on hand at the date of deregistration. However, by concession if the total of the input VAT owed is < £1,000 it can be ignored.

Transfer of a business as a going concern (TOGC)

Compulsory deregistration applies where a business is sold or otherwise transferred as a going concern to new owners.

Such transfers inevitably involve assets falling within the scope of VAT. If the following conditions are satisfied, then the sale/transfer will not be treated as a taxable supply (i.e. no output tax applies to the assets transferred by the seller which in turn means no input tax is recoverable by the purchaser).

The conditions are:

* the business is transferred as a going concern; and

* there is no significant break in the trading; and

* the same type of trade is carried on after the transfer; and

* the new owner is or will be registered for VAT immediately after the transfer.

Consequences of VAT registration

VAT numbers and returns

HMRC will issue the business with a VAT registration number and from the date of registration, output VAT must be charged on taxable supplies, with input VAT, subject to some restrictions, being recoverable on business purchases and expenses.

VAT returns are to be completed, normally once a quarter, and filed within 30 days of the end of the taxable period to which they relate. From 1 April 2010, electronic filing of VAT returns was made compulsory to all existing VAT registered businesses with an annual turnover, excluding VAT, of £100,000 or more. The electronic filing regime also applied immediately to all newly VAT registered businesses irrespective of their turnover levels.

Where a VAT return is filed electronically, the taxpayer now has an additional seven days to file and pay any VAT liability i.e. for a June 30 quarter end, the return and payment are due no later than 7 August.

For businesses still filing paper VAT returns, the return is still to be filed and VAT liability settled within 30 days of the end of the quarter.

Learning example 22.4

Pink Ltd has made the following sales and purchases in the VAT quarter to 31 December 2011. All sales and purchases are standard rated for VAT purposes. The VAT exclusive figures are as follows:

Standard rated sales	£150,000
Standard rated purchases	£80,000

Required

How much is the VAT payable/repayable for the quarter ended 31 December 2011?

London
School of Business
& Finance
shaping success in business and finance

Pre-registration input VAT

On the first return it is possible to reclaim input VAT suffered before the date the business became VAT registered - pre-registration input VAT.

Where the claim relates to goods purchased, the following conditions are to be satisfied:

* The goods were acquired for business use (in the business which is now VAT registered)

* The goods are still held in stock and have not been sold or consumed

* The goods must have been purchased within 4 years of the date of registration

Where the claim relates to services, the following conditions must be satisfied:

* The services were acquired for business purposes (in the business which is now VAT registered)

* The services were incurred within six months of registration.

Irrecoverable input VAT

In certain cases, input VAT on a purchase is irrecoverable and is to be included in the purchase price for direct tax purposes. Examples include:

* Input VAT on entertaining of UK based customers and suppliers. (Input VAT can be recovered on the expense of entertaining overseas customers and suppliers.)

* Input VAT on the cost of cars, unless the car is used 100% for business use.

* Input VAT suffered on the supply of personal expenses.

Input VAT on motoring expenses

The main input VAT issues regarding motoring expenses are in respect of the capital cost and the fuel costs.

As noted above, any input VAT arising on the purchase of the car, is not recoverable unless the car is used wholly for business purposes. Generally, this restricts the claim to cars used in self-drive hire companies, driving schools or taxi businesses.

If a car is leased and is not used wholly for business purposes only 50% of the VAT charged on the leasing costs may be recovered as input tax.

Input VAT on fuel costs can be reclaimed by a trader. However, where the fuel has a private use element, the trader must apply a fuel scale charge, based on the CO_2 emissions of the car, rounded down to the nearest 5g/km. The scale charge will always be provided in the exam. The output VAT must be increased by 1/6 of the scale charge.

Learning example 22.5

A business owns a petrol engine car. The car has CO_2 emissions of 185g/km. Petrol costs the business £2,000 (including VAT) per quarter and the fuel is used for 80% business purpose and 20% private purpose.

The VAT scale rate for a 3 month period is £345

Required

Calculate the input and output VAT for the quarter ended 31 December 2011 relating to the fuel.

Group VAT registration

Where companies are under common control (at least 50% of each company is owned by a common owner), they may apply for group registration. Each of the companies has to be established in the UK, or have a fixed place of business in the UK. For control purposes, partnerships are included.

A company can be added to or removed from a VAT group at any time. There is no requirement for the company which is to be added, to be VAT registered. An exempt company can join a VAT group but this will have the effect of making the VAT group partially exempt, which in turn restricts the input VAT recovery of the VAT group as a whole.

An application to join a VAT group is made through the VAT Group's representative member. This is a company which is responsible for the completion of the VAT return, and payment of any VAT liability arising. All members of the VAT group remain joint and severally liable for any VAT due from any of the group members.

Once a group registration is made, or a company added or removed from a VAT group, this is deemed to have taken place from the date the application is received by HMRC. Although notification by HMRC that the changes are effective can take up to 90 days, it is the responsibility of the representative member to ensure that VAT is correctly accounted for from the date of application.

Practical considerations of being a member of a VAT group include no longer raising sales invoices with the old VAT number (for companies being added), quoting the group VAT number, and not charging VAT on intra-group supplies.

A VAT group is often advantageous from an administrative point of view, as a single return is required, which may cover many companies. In practice, there is a requirement for stricter administrative controls to be implemented in order to collate all the data from various companies for inclusion in the single return within the VAT return filing deadline

Taxable supplies made between members of the same VAT group are deemed to be outside the scope of VAT and therefore, no VAT is charged. This can simplify VAT accounting for a group member where they conduct a lot of intergroup trading. It would also smooth cash flows on settled invoices between group members.

Tax point

The tax point is the date used to identify the VAT period which should be used to include the output or input VAT.

Basic tax point

For goods the basic tax point is: The date the goods are made available or delivered to the customer

For services the basic tax point is: The date the service is performed

Actual tax point

Often the date used as the tax point is not the basic tax point. The rule to determine the tax point is:

The actual tax point is the earlier of:

1. The date the cash is received

2. The basic tax point

If the basic tax point is earlier then replace the basic tax point with the invoice date if the invoice is issued within 14 days after the basic tax point.

Learning example 22.6

Jason is a sole trader and is in business selling machines. Jason made a sale of an excavator for £60,000 (inclusive of VAT) to Earch Movers Ltd. Details of the contract:

		£
28.2.12	Deposit received	6,000
30.4.12	Excavator was delivered	
11.5.12	Invoice was issued for the excavator	
31.5.12	Balance was paid for the excavator	54,000

Jason's quarters for VAT are 31 January, 30 April, 31 July and 31 October.

Required

Identify the tax point and state which VAT return(s) the sale of the excavator should be included on.

Treatment of discounts

VAT is always accounted for on the price after discounts, i.e. 'NET' amount when discounts of any type are offered. For example, where a 'prompt payment' discount is offered, VAT is calculated on the 'net' amount, assuming the discount is taken, irrespective of whether the discount is actually taken.

Learning example 22.7

Trevor is a sole trader and offers a discount to his customers who pay within 21 days. The discount offered is 8%.

Required

Compute the output VAT on a sale of £2,000 if:

(a) The customer pays within 21 days, and

(b) The customer does not pay within 21 days.

Relief for impairment losses on trade debts

Normally, output VAT is accounted for when an invoice is issued. If the sale becomes a bad debt, the seller has paid output VAT to HMRC and never recovers this from the customer. The trader may claim a refund for this output VAT if:

* the VAT has been accounted for and paid over;

* at least 6 months has elapsed since payment from the debtor was due;

* the debt has been written off in the seller's books.

Relief is obtained by adding the VAT element of the bad debt to the input tax and it can be reclaimed. If the debt is subsequently recovered, the corresponding amount of VAT must be paid back to HMRC.

There is a 3 year limit on making this claim.

Learning example 22.8

You are provided with the following information for the quarter ended 31 October 2011 relating to your client Valerie Vat who is registered for VAT

	£
Supplies (all VAT-exclusive):	
Standard-rated supplies	270,000
Sales invoices issued by Valerie who also offers a 3% discount for prompt payment	
Zero-rated supplies	30,000
Standard-rated purchases (excluding VAT)	125,000
Standard-rated expenses(excluding VAT).The total of £27,000 includes £3,000 for entertaining customers	27,000
Exempt purchases	12,500
Cars (excluding VAT and bought on 1.10.11)	15,250

Irrecoverable debts of £4,500 (exclusive of VAT) were written off in October 2011 in respect of three separate invoices, each of £1,500, for goods supplied on 11 January 2011, 12 February 2011 and 13 July 2011, payment for which was due on 1 February 2011, 1 March 2011 and 1 August 2011 respectively.

The car bought on 1 October 2011 was used 75% for business and has a CO_2 emission of 205g/km. Petrol for both private and business mileage was paid for by the business. The quarterly scale charge figure is £400 (inclusive of VAT).

Required

Calculate the VAT payable for the quarter to 31 October 2011.

Information included on the sales invoice

VAT invoices are the link in the VAT chain. Copies must be retained. Full VAT invoices must show:

- supplier's name, address and VAT registration number

- name and address of customer

- tax point

- invoice date and number

- description of goods, quantity of goods/type of services and rate of VAT

- VAT exclusive amount of each supply (unit price)

- total amount payable, before discounts, excluding VAT

- total amount of VAT chargeable

- rate of any cash or settlement discount offered.

Note: Rates of discount are shown on full VAT invoices because (normally) VAT is calculated on the net of discount value of supplies.

Schemes available to small business

Cash accounting scheme

Operation
The tax point is the date the cash is received and the date the cash is paid rather than using the normal tax point

Conditions
* Taxable turnover must be < £1,350,000
* VAT returns must be up to date
* Business must leave the scheme if taxable turnover > £1,600,000

Advantages
* Do not pay output VAT until receive it from the customer
* Provides automatic bad debt relief

Annual accounting scheme

Operation
* One VAT return prepared per year
* VAT return due 2 months after end of annual VAT period
* 9 payments due by direct debit on months 4-12.
* Calculated as: 10% x VAT paid last year

Conditions
* Taxable turnover must be < £1,350,000
* VAT returns and payments must be up to date
* Business must leave the scheme if taxable turnover > £1,600,000

Advantages
* Reduces administration
* Regular payments can help cash flow

Flat rate scheme

Operation
VAT liability is computed using a flat rate % of total VAT inclusive turnover (includes the value of taxable and exempt turnover)

Conditions
* Taxable turnover must be < £150,000 and total turnover < £187,500
* Must leave if total turnover > £230,000 (from 4 January 2011).
* Before 4 Jnaury 2011, must leave if turnover > £225,000

No question will be set requiring knowledge of the old rate

Advantages
* Reduces administration as need to keep less detailed records of input and output VAT

Learning example 22.9

Beneficial Ltd has annual sales of £100,000, all of which are standard rated and are to the general public. The company's standard rated expenses are £12,500 pa. These figures are inclusive of VAT. The relevant flat rate percentage for Advantageous Ltd's trade is 13%.

Required

Advise Beneficial Ltd as to whether it should use the flat rate scheme available to small businesses for year ended 31 December 2012.

Administration of VAT

Introduction

VAT is administered by HMRC, through a series of local offices in the UK. These local offices also provide advice to both registered traders and prospective registered traders.

VAT returns, once completed, are sent to a central office in Southend. If the trader fails to file a VAT return, HMRC may issue assessments for the VAT that they believe is due. HMRC may also issue assessments where they believe that the VAT returned by the trader is incorrect.

Errors on the VAT return

Where the error is below a certain limit, it may be adjusted on the trader's next return. The limits, which have changed with effect from 1 July 2008, are as follows:

*   £10,000 (overall over/understatement) or;

*   1% x net VAT turnover for return period (maximum £50,000)

whichever is greater.

If the error is outside of these limits, it must be adjusted using either a 'Voluntary Disclosure' form (VAT 652) or by a letter, to the local VAT office.

Where the error amounts to an underpayment of VAT, a penalty may be imposed and interest on the late payment of any under-declared, and hence, underpaid VAT, levied. Interest is only charged when there is a loss to the Exchequer, and not where an error led to an under declaration such that any VAT not charged would be recoverable by a VAT registered trader.

Interest is also levied on default assessments (returns not filed) and on the late payment of VAT.

Penalties

A single penalty regime has been introduced for incorrect returns.

The amount of penalty is based on the amount of tax understated, but the actual penalty payable is linked to the taxpayer's behaviour, as follows:

*   There will be no penalty where a taxpayer simply makes a mistake.

*   There will be a moderate penalty (up to 30% of the understated tax) where a taxpayer fails to take reasonable care.

*   There will be a higher penalty (up to 70% of the understated tax) if the error is deliberate, an even higher penalty (up to 100% of the understated tax) where there is also concealment of the error.

Where an error is made in a VAT return, a penalty may be incurred, unless the trader can show a reasonable excuse for the error. There is no statutory definition of reasonable excuse but there are statutory examples of what is not a reasonable excuse. These include:

*   Reliance on third party (accountant) to complete the return

*   Insufficient funds

Case law has also highlighted other reasons not held up to be reasonable excuse. These include:

*   Ignorance of VAT law

*   Time pressure

*   Work pressures

Penalties for late filing of VAT returns and late payments of VAT

New penalties of late filings of returns and for late payment of tax are being introduced over a number of years.

Although legislation has been introduced regarding the late filing of VAT returns and the late payment of VAT, HMRC has yet to introduce the changes. The changes will not be examined for the June 2012 and December 2012 sittings, however the existing rules may be examined as follows:

The default surcharge

Where a trader fails to complete a return on time, or pays the VAT late, they enter the default surcharge regime. This regime does not financially penalise the trader for a first offence. Upon a late filing or payment, the trader is issued a surcharge liability notice, which runs from the date of issuance to the anniversary of the end of the period to which it was raised.

Where the trader defaults again in the surcharge liability notice period, they will be issued with a new surcharge liability notice, and the original liability period extended to the anniversary of the end of the period to which the new default relates.

Where the default is in respect of a late payment, a surcharge is levied on the trader as follows:

Default number	Surcharge (% of VAT outstanding)	De-minimis limits
First	2%	£400
Second	5%	£400
Third	10%	£30
Fourth etc	15%	£30

The de-minimis limits, although not noted in VAT law, are the minimum amounts of surcharges levied that would be chased by HMRC. For example, if the surcharge levied is under £400 for a first offence, by concession, HMRC would not raise a demand notice. However, for surcharges calculated using the 10% or 15% rates, there is a minimum amount of £30 payable.

Appeals

VAT Tribunals are in place to hear appeals of taxpayers in relation to VAT. They are independent of HMRC.

To have an appeal heard by the Tribunal, the taxpayer must be up-to-date with all VAT returns and payments.

Any appeal must be lodged within 30 days of the date of any decision by HMRC, although where the taxpayer appeals to its local office first (it has 30 days to do this), the limits are extended depending on the outcome of the local appeal.

Learning example 22.10

Amelia is a sole trader and has been registered for VAT for many years. She accounts for VAT quarterly. Unfortunately, Amelia had an argument with her accountant and decided not to replace him. As a result, since then she has submitted a number of her VAT returns late. The history of her returns since then has been as follows:

	VAT payable	Timing
Quarter to 31 March 2011	£12,500	Late
Quarter to 30 June 2011	£18,000	Late
Quarter to 30 September 2011	£8,800	Late
Quarter to 31 December 2011	£9,100	on time
Quarter to 31 March 2012	£9,000	on time
Quarter to 30 June 2012	£800	Late

Required

Explain to Amelia:

(a) how the default surcharge regime operates;

(b) what liabilities she has incurred under it.

Learning summary

- VAT is charged by taxable traders on taxable transactions undertaken in their business.

- VAT supplies can either be taxable (zero rated, standard rated, reduced rate) or exempt.

- The reduced rate of VAT is 5% and standard rate is 20%.

- A trader is required to register for VAT where his taxable turnover exceeds £73,000 in any 12 month period or where the trader believes his taxable turnover for the next 30 days will exceed £71,000.

- Where the taxable turnover is made up of zero-rated supplies, the trader does not have to register for VAT.

- A trader can register for VAT on a voluntary basis irrespective their taxable turnover.

- Where a trader is making wholly exempt supplies, they are not permitted to register for VAT. Any VAT inclusive purchases made by exempt traders will therefore have a VAT cost.

- Once registered, the trader is entitled to reclaim input VAT incurred prior to registration, subject to certain conditions.

- VAT returns are required to be filed every 3 months, with VAT administered by HMRC. VAT payments are due 30 days after the end of the return period.

- From 1 April 2010, electronic filing of VAT returns is compulsory for all existing VAT registered companies with an annual turnover of £100,000 and for any company, regardless of annual turnover, which becomes VAT registered after this date.

- Where VAT returns are submitted late or VAT is paid late, the trader enters into the default surcharge period. If during the default surcharge period the trader defaults again, a default surcharge will be applied.

- A number of special schemes exist to assist smaller businesses manage VAT compliance and accounting. These include Cash Accounting, Annual Accounting and Flat Rate Scheme.

Learning solution 22.1

The VAT charged is:

		£
•	£500 × 20%=	100.00
•	325 × 20/120 =	54.17
•	650 × 20/120 =	108.33
•	1,000 × 20% =	200.00

Learning solution 22.2

	£
Sales to 31 March 2012 (10 × 6,250)	62,500
Sales to 30 April	76,500

Colin has failed the test on 30 April 2012 and must notify HMRC by 30 May 2012. He must start charging VAT on 1 June 2012.

Learning solution 22.3

Historic test:

	£
6 months to 30 June 2011 (6 × 7,750)	46,500
7 months to 31 July 2011 (7 × 7,750) + 67,000)	121,250

Finance Ltd would fail the historic test at the end of July 2011

Future test

On 1 July 2011, Finance Ltd signs a contract which will lead to taxable supplies in the next 30 days being over £74,750 (7,750 + 67,000).

Finance Ltd would fail the future test on 1 July 2011. This test is failed before the historic test and HMRC will deem you to fail the test which gives the earlier registration date.

Finance Ltd has 30 days to notify HMRC, so by 30 July 2011. Finance Ltd must register and start charging VAT from 1 July 2011.

Learning solution 22.4

VAT return quarter ended 31 December 2011

	£
Output VAT (150,000 × 20%)	30,000
Input VAT (80,000 × 20%)	(16,000)
VAT payable	14,000

Learning solution 22.5

	£
Output VAT (scale charge) × 1/6	57.50
Input VAT (2,000 × 1/6)	(333.33)
VAT reclaimed	275.83

Learning solution 22.6

Amount	Output VAT	Time of Supply (Tax Point)		VAT Quarter
£6,000	£1,000	Earlier of:		
	(20/120 x 6,000)	(1) Date the cash is received	28.2.12	Quarter to 30.4.12
		(2) The basic tax point	30.4.12	
£54,000	£9,000	Earlier of:		
	(20/120 x 54,000)	Date the cash is received	31.5.12	
		Basic tax point	30.4.12	

In this case the basic tax point is earlier but replace the basic tax point with the invoice date if the invoice is issued within 14 days after the basic tax point.

The invoice date is 11.5.12 which is within 14 days therefore the tax point is 11.5.12.   Quarter to 31.7.12

Learning solution 22.7

Customer pays within 21 days and gets the discount		Customer does not pay within 21 days and does not get the discount	
	£		£
Sale	2,000	Sale	2,000
Discount	(160)		2,000
	1,840	Output VAT	368 (still 20% x £1,840)
Output VAT	368	Cost to customer	2,368
(20% x £1,840)			
Cost to customer	2,208		

If a discount is offered the output VAT must be calculated based on the discounted amount irrespective of whether the customer gets the discount or not.

London
School of Business
& Finance

shaping success in business and finance

Learning solution 22.8

VAT return for the quarter ended 31 October 2011:

	£
Output tax	
Standard-rated supplies (270,000 - 3%) = £261,900	
20% x £261,900 (net of discount sales)	52,380
Zero rated sales (0% x £30,000 x (100 - 3)%)	-
Car fuel charge (1/3 x £400 x 20/120)	22
	52,402
Input tax	
Standard-rated purchases (£125,000 @ 20%)	(25,000)
Standard-rated expenses (£27,000 - £3,000) @ 20%	(4,800)
Bad debt relief (£1,500 + £1,500) x (100 - 3)% @ 20%	(582)
VAT payable	22,020

Due and payable date is 30 November 2011.

Tutorial notes:

* The car was bought on 1.10.11 – therefore, in this quarter = one month only!

* Relief for bad debts was available for the sales invoice issued on 11 January 2011 and 12 February 2011 as the payment for these invoices was due on 1 February 2011 and 1 March 2011 – debt written off and more than six months overdue. VAT would have been charged on the discounted amount on the original invoice.

* Relief for invoice issued on 13 July 2011, the payment for which was due on 1 August 2011 is not yet possible as the debt is not over six months old.

Learning solution 22.9

Beneficial Ltd has annual sales of £100,000, all of which are standard rated and are to the general public. The company's standard rated expenses are £12,500 pa. These figures are inclusive of VAT. The relevant flat rate percentage for Beneficial Ltd's trade is 13%. Using the normal basis of calculating its VAT liability, Beneficial Ltd will have to pay VAT as follows:

	£
Output VAT (100,000 x 20/120)	16,667
Input VAT (12,500 x 20/120)	2,083
VAT payable	14,584

If Beneficial Ltd uses the flat rate scheme then it will pay VAT of £13,000 (100,000 x 13%). There is a VAT saving of £1,584 (14,584 – 13,000) in addition to the simplified administration. As none of Beneficial Ltd's customers are VAT registered, there will be no need to issue VAT invoices.

Learning solution 22.10

Quarter 1.1.11 – 31.3.11	Late. A surcharge liability notice is served. Applicable for 12 months from 1.4.11 - 31.3.12.
Quarter 1.4.11 – 30.6.11	Late. Surcharge liability notice extended. Applicable from 1.7.11 - 30.6.12. PENALTY (1) Surcharge → £18,000 x 2% = £360 No surcharge is due as it is less than £400.
Quarter 1.7.11 – 30.9.11	Late. Surcharge liability notice extended. Applicable from 1.10.11 – 30.9.12. PENALTY (2) Surcharge → £8,800 x 5% = £440
Quarter 1.10.11 – 31.12.11	On time – no penalty.
Quarter 1.1.12 – 31.3.12	On time – no penalty.
Quarter 1.4.12 – 30.6.12	Late. Surcharge liability notice extended to 1.7.12 – 30.6.13 PENALTY (3) SURCHARGE → £800 x 10% → £80 → Persistent defaulter

Index

London
School of Business
& Finance

shaping success in business and finance

London
School of Business
& Finance

shaping success in business and finance